The Lean Practitioner's Handbook

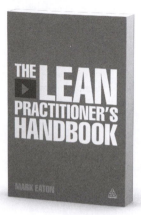

The Lean Practitioner's Handbook

Mark Eaton

KoganPage

LONDON PHILADELPHIA NEW DELHI

First published in Great Britain and the United States in 2013 by Kogan Page Limited

120 Pentonville Road
London N1 9JN
United Kingdom
www.koganpage.com

1518 Walnut Street, Suite 1100
Philadelphia PA 19102
USA

4737/23 Ansari Road
Daryaganj
New Delhi 110002
India

© Mark Eaton, 2013

The right of Mark Eaton to be identified as the author of this work has been asserted by him in accordance with the Copyright, Designs and Patents Act 1988.

ISBN   978 0 7494 6773 9
E-ISBN   978 0 7494 6774 6

British Library Cataloguing-in-Publication Data

A CIP record for this book is available from the British Library.

Library of Congress Cataloging-in-Publication Data

Eaton, Mark, 1968-
    The lean practitioner's handbook / Mark Eaton.
        p. cm.
    Summary: "The Lean Practitioner's Handbook bridges the gap between the tools and concepts of Lean and the practical use of the tools. It offers a practical, easily accessible resource for anyone preparing for, implementing or evaluating lean activities covering key areas such as: aspects of a Lean Programme; scoping a programme; value stream mapping; 2P and 3P events; Rapid Improvement Events; managing for daily improvement; engaging the team; spotting problems and communicating progress. In addition, it offers a quick snapshot summary of the key tool and concepts of Lean plus easily applicable templates"– Provided by publisher.
        ISBN 978-0-7494-6773-9 (pbk.) – ISBN 978-0-7494-6774-6 ()   1. Product management.
    2. Lean manufacturing.   3. Waste minimization.   I. Title.
        TS155.E23 2013
        658.5–dc23
                                                                                        2012039397

Typeset by Graphicraft Limited, Hong Kong
Printed and bound in India by Replika Press Pvt Ltd

CONTENTS

Lean checklists and templates are available online by registering at http://www.koganpage.com/Lean

Introduction

In writing this book I have attempted to create a practical reference guide that will be useful on a day-to-day basis for those who are looking to introduce Lean, or who want to get more from their existing Lean programme. I have also tried to make this book as applicable to someone working in a public sector organization as it will be to a manufacturer or anyone working in the private sector. In effect, I have tried to write the book I wish I had been able to access when I first started out as a practitioner.

I recognize that Lean has its own language and that, for those new to Lean, you may suddenly be presented with terms you have not encountered before. If you do happen across a term that has not been explained, you can rest easy that it is defined either in Chapter 13 (where I outline key tools and concepts in Lean that have not been covered elsewhere in the book) or in the Glossary. I aim to avoid using unnecessary jargon but also recognize that any book on Lean would be incomplete without some explanation of the key terms and an understanding of how and when to use them.

In terms of my experience, like many practitioners I came to Lean through an engineering route and then through running manufacturing plants. After my time in manufacturing I was lucky enough to get involved in consulting, and through this got to run publicly funded programmes aimed at transforming the manufacturing sector. In branching out from manufacturing I have also had the opportunity to deliver Lean programmes in the armed forces, health care, local government, logistics and retail. One of the key things that has struck me during my time working across all of these different sectors is that there are questions that come up time and again irrespective of the sector you are working with. In this respect, regardless of the sector, the challenges are surprisingly similar. In writing this book

I am trying to provide practitioners from across a wide range of sectors with answers to questions such as:

- How should I structure and plan a programme of improvement activities?
- What should I do first?
- How do I turn my knowledge of the tools into events and, ultimately, improvements?
- What are the things I need to do to ensure our Lean programme doesn't stall?
- How do I get all of my team involved in improving our organization every day?

Lean is something that is best learnt experimentally; whilst training provides an understanding of the skills, terminology and tools of Lean, it is only when you move from the classroom to the front line that you will realize that the theory of Lean is very different to what happens in practice. For example, understanding the theory behind how a *value stream mapping* (VSM) event (Chapter 4) is run is different to working with a group of people who put up barriers, aren't prepared effectively or believe that they are going to lose out in some way by doing it. Of course, this should never happen but the reality is that it does – and it is reality that I am trying to help practitioners with throughout this book.

Since first becoming involved in performance improvement many years ago, I have lost track of how many improvement projects and programmes I have been involved in, and amongst the successes I have also made many mistakes. Every project provides an opportunity to reflect on things, both good and bad, and experiment with different approaches. This has enabled me to develop a wide range of practical 'hints and tricks' to help ensure success, and I have peppered the sections of this book with practical advice gained through (sometimes) bitter experience – in the hope that you won't have to go through the extended apprenticeship in Lean that I have had.

As a pragmatist I do not believe that Lean is some form of new religion, only that it provides those prepared to invest the time with some structured common sense that enables them to move from the 'as is' process (termed the *current state* in Lean) to where they want 'to be' (called the *future state*). This pragmatic approach to Lean also means that I recognize that it is not always the 'whole solution' and that sometimes you will have to do things that might not be seen as 'true Lean'. At the same time, I also believe that this approach can be used in major strategic programmes as well as in tactical front-line activities, but that many organizations relegate it to dusty rooms rather than putting it centre stage in the strategic plans of the business.

In working with real people doing Lean projects, there are some common misconceptions about Lean that we must address. The first is that Lean is not an acronym and doesn't stand for anything. For example it doesn't mean 'less effort and nonsense' – although it makes for a fun exercise to get people to think about what Lean might stand for. Another misconception is that Lean is just about process mapping and tidy ups and, to be honest, there are a number of Lean practitioners who have helped reinforce this misconception. One major misconception is that just because the concepts of Lean are easily understood that it must be easy to implement; it is this simplicity of the basic message of Lean, a message we will explore in Chapter 2, that leads to management teams setting out with unrealistic expectations of the effort required, or relegating Lean to low-level improvement activities. One final misconception I want to discuss is that Lean is seen in some way as a 'fad' or that it was invented by Toyota in the 1950s. We will explore this misconception below.

A brief history of Lean

At its heart, Lean is structured common sense that is aimed at understanding what your customers want and redesigning the way you do things to ensure you deliver this in the most cost effective, timely and safe way possible.

Many people associate Lean with Toyota, and whilst it is fair to say that the Toyota team have done much to shape what we now consider Lean to be – through the development of the Toyota Production System – the concepts of standardization, flow and even understanding what the end customer would 'value' were well established long before they were picked up by Toyota in the late 1940s and early 1950s. Indeed, perhaps the only thing that is really 'new' about Lean is the name, which we will see was not adopted in popular culture until the mid-1990s.

In tracing the heritage of Lean we could go back as far as 1.6 million years ago to the period when archaeologists first start to find stone hand-axes in the fossil record. These tools were produced in hundreds of different places over many thousands of years to a remarkably consistent pattern that evolved solely from things that many people would struggle to recognize, from broken rocks through to the classic teardrop design of later periods. This implied that the process for creating them was in some way standardized and that the manufacturers of these tools improved the design slowly over many, many generations through a process of continuous improvement driven by experimentation and experience sharing.

There are many other examples through the ages, but to get to a commonly accepted 'start point' for Lean we need to jump forward in time to the Venetian Arsenal in the 16th century, where we find the most commonly quoted early example of Lean concepts such as standardized processes and interchangeable parts. The Venetians were supplying hundreds of galleys per year and established a narrow channel through their dockyards through which the hull of each galley could 'flow'. The channel was designed so that the hull floated past each assembly point enabling them to produce a galley from start to finish in as little as an hour.

War has always had a very dramatic effect on the development of new techniques and technologies and Lean concepts can be found in use throughout the 17th, 18th and 19th centuries. We see this in the adoption by the Royal Navy of rapid changeover and standardized processes that enabled them to deliver broadsides nearly twice as fast as their opponents and in the interchangeable parts used in the artillery of France during the Napoleonic Wars.

As we come to the end of the 19th century we see a systematic approach to organizing resources start to develop with the publication of the Italian sociologist and economist Vilfredo Pareto's findings about the distribution of land in Italy, which has entered everyday language as the '80/20 Rule'. Pareto found that 80 per cent of the land was owned by only 20 per cent of the people and that this applies to many other issues, for example 80 per cent of the problems you have to deal with will stem from only 20 per cent of the causes, and 80 per cent of the sales you get will come from only 20 per cent of the clients. This work, coupled with the work of Frederick Winslow Taylor who popularized the concepts of 'scientific management', Frank and Lillian Gilbreth who developed systematic ways of assessing efficiency that we have come to know as 'motion study', and others, created the basis of Lean that was taken up during the first decades of the 20th century in continuous flow processes in the factories of Henry Ford and others.

The great conflicts of the 20th century helped shape the development of Lean concepts through the introduction of the concept of *takt time* to control the flow of fuselages through German aircraft plants. The fuselages were 'moved' along the production line from station to station at a precise interval of time (the takt time). To enable this to occur, the work done at each station had to be lower than the takt time.

These early concepts of flow, takt time, the use of small batches and even employee involvement in problem solving were brought together by Toyota's Taiichi Ohno during the mid-1940s. Taiichi Ohno, who rose through the ranks of Toyota to become an executive, is now seen as the father of the Toyota Production System and the grandfather of Lean, and along with Shigeo Shingo and Eiji Toyoda was responsible for its development.

Further developments and challenges added numerous new concepts to the toolbox, including *mistake proofing (poka yoke)*, *total productive maintenance*, *value stream mapping* and many more before we had the ingredients that could be said to form the basis of what we now see as Lean.

The name Lean was first used in John Krafcik's 1988 article 'Triumph of the Lean Production System', although it did not enter general usage until the publication of the later books *The Machine that Changed the World* (Womack, Roos and Jones, 1990) and, most notably, *Lean Thinking* (Womack and Jones, 1996). The rest, as they say, is history.

Highlights in the history of Lean

From 1473 the Venetian Arsenal develop a 'continuous flow' process based on mass-produced and standardized items that ultimately enables them to produce an entire ship in less than an hour.

1776 Lieutenant General Jean-Baptiste de Gribeauval becomes Inspector of Artillery in France and starts to introduce reforms to reduce the diversity of artillery in use and replacing it with a more standardized range of weapons that also used a form of interchangeable parts and manufacture.

1799 Eli Whitney, inventor of the Cotton Gin, takes on the contract to produce 10,000 muskets for the US Army at a low cost of $13.40 each. To enable him to do this he had perfected the process of designing interchangeable parts between the muskets, which enabled the process to be divided up and standardized.

1894–1912 Frederick W Taylor publishes a series of articles on improving efficiency, with his key work *The Principles of Scientific Management* being published in 1911, with details of how to eliminate many of the inefficient practices existing in industry at the time and strongly advocating standardized work and the division of labour to improve efficiency. Collectively this approach is later termed 'Taylorism'.

1905–21 Frank and Lillian Gilbreth publish a series of articles and books on improving efficiency through time and motion study, culminating in 1921 with their book *Time and Motion Study As Fundamental Factors in Planning and Control.*

1910 Henry Ford and Charles E Sorensen create a comprehensive manufacturing strategy and move to the Highland Park Plant, Michigan, which was the world's first automobile plant that used an assembly line. In 1914 they create the first moving assembly line, thus reducing production times by a further 75 per cent.

1924–39 Walter Shewhart develops the concept of statistical control of processes and later his work is adapted by W Edwards Deming, with the work of Deming going on to form the basis of Six Sigma. Although a cousin of Lean, many of the concepts used by Six Sigma are also found in a Lean programme.

1943 Taiichi Ohno joins Toyota Motor Corporation and later (1947 onwards) builds on the work of Toyota's founder to create the Toyota Production System (TPS). This goes on to incorporate cellular working, waste reduction,

reduction of work-in-process (WIP), in-process inspection by workers and many of the other concepts that we will explore in this book, including the 'respect for people' principle.

1983 Robert Hall publishes *Zero Inventories*, which is seen as the first broad description of the Toyota Production System by an American author.

1988 John Krafcik publishes the article 'Triumph of the Lean Production System', the first use of the word Lean in association with the Toyota Production System.

1990–96 Jim Womack, Daniel Roos and Dan Jones produce *The Machine that Changed the World* (Simon & Schuster, 1990). Womack and Jones go on to write *Lean Thinking* (Simon & Schuster, 1996) bringing the term Lean into the public domain and defining the five principles.

Introduction to the rest of the book

Lean has expanded from its traditional origins in the manufacturing sector to now encompass almost every area of both the public and private sector. From central government to retail stores, elements of Lean can be found virtually everywhere. Equally, Lean can exist in the form of small-scale local improvement initiatives or enterprise-wide programmes, or anything in between. Whilst I would encourage you to make the most of your investment in Lean I have tried to make this book useful to anyone looking to 'go Lean', whether they are leading major transformation programmes based on Lean or are preparing to undertake a single Lean activity.

In structuring this book I have made the chapters fit the main steps that you might undertake in a single Lean event, a Lean project focused on one area, process or pathway or a Lean programme that spans entire organizations and involves many separate strands of activity. The book also includes a wide range of templates and checklists to help you prepare for and deliver Lean events and activities and embed the changes that arise. The aim of this book is to become one of the most read books in your Lean library, simply through its practicality and usefulness on a day-to-day basis.

I hope you enjoy the journey!

Planning for Lean

In this chapter I aim to answer the following questions:

1 How do I structure a Lean programme?

2 How should I use the other chapters in this book to help me?

3 What are the typical issues I will face on my journey?

4 What are the myths that we need to bust about Lean?

To answer these questions I have divided this chapter into three sections. The first section deals with the structure of typical Lean programmes of various sizes and directs you to the relevant parts of this book. The second section is concerned with discussing the typical issues that drive people to adopt Lean, as well as offering pointers to where you can find help within this book. The final section is concerned with the various myths that arise about Lean and, in addition to providing some comment, I will signpost you to further advice within this book.

Structuring a Lean programme

A Lean programme that spans an entire organization consists of a range of different activities. Some of the activities are concerned with managing the overall programme whilst others are focused on implementation of the changes. A structure for a typical Lean programme is shown in Figure 1.1.

FIGURE 1.1   Outline structure of a Lean programme

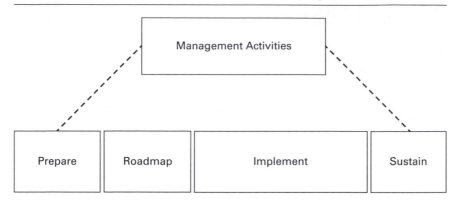

The five boxes shown in Figure 1.1 summarize all of the activities that you might ever need to undertake as part of any Lean activity and are described as:

- **Management activities** – the activities associated with the strategic planning of Lean and embedding a culture of Lean into an organization.

- **Prepare** – the processes associated with scoping individual Lean activities.

- **Roadmap** – creation of a high-level plan for major projects.

- **Implement** – planning and implementation of changes to processes, products and services.

- **Sustain** – this is concerned with implementing a concept of 'improvement every day' as well as embedding any changes made during the implementation phase.

The Lean activities that drop into each of the five sections, along with details of the relevant chapters in the book where you will find information about them, can be seen in Figure 1.2.

The aim of this book is to provide practical advice on how to implement Lean, whether you are looking to implement a single Lean event, a Lean project that involves a number of Lean events or a Lean programme that spans your whole organization. In addition to the chapters indicated in Figure 1.2 there are five further chapters that cover essential supporting information including:

FIGURE 1.2   A Lean programme

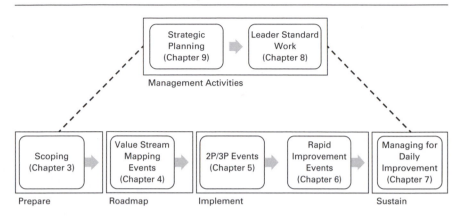

- Chapter 2 – Key Lean concepts: the background history and key principles of Lean and the Toyota Production System.

- Chapter 10 – Engaging the team: how to motivate the team involved in Lean.

- Chapter 11 – Ensuring success: warning signs and how to spot when your programme is going 'off the rails'.

- Chapter 12 – Communications and celebrations: how to communicate and celebrate activities.

- Chapter 13 – Guide to key tools and terminology: definitions and explanations of all of the key Lean tools and terminology that have not been covered elsewhere in the book.

The following section looks at the implementation of Lean at each of these three levels: a single Lean event, a Lean project involving multiple events and an entire Lean programme covering a whole organization. If I am making a point that applies equally to a Lean event, Lean project or a Lean programme I have used the term Lean 'activity'.

Planning a single Lean event

A definition of a single Lean event would be:

> A Lean event consists of the focused effort of a group of people for a finite period of time on a defined problem, at the end of which something has changed.

FIGURE 1.3   Activities associated with a Lean event

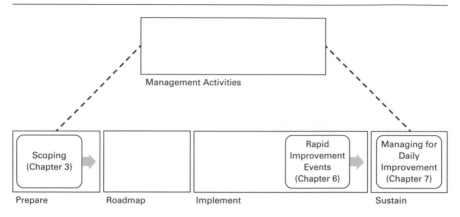

If all you have is a plan that needs to be implemented later on then you are dealing with a project (albeit maybe a very small project) and as such I will deal with that in the next section. For now, I want to consider the times when you are working with people to implement changes to a process. Lean events such as this have a variety of names including rapid improvement events, Lean blitzes, kaizen workshops and many similar terms. For consistency I will use the term rapid improvement event (RIE) to refer to any event where you are doing hands-on implementation work.

A single Lean event (Figure 1.3) will normally be preceded by *scoping* the activity, as covered in Chapter 3, whilst the complete process for undertaking a rapid improvement event is covered in Chapter 6 and the follow-up activities are covered in Chapter 7.

Planning a Lean project

A definition for a Lean project:

> A Lean project consists of all the scoping, planning and implementation events required to improve a process, however big that process is.

Lean projects can be large in scope, for example spanning multiple organizations by looking at an end-to-end clinical pathway in health care or looking at the end-to-end supply chain in the manufacturing sector. They can also be large in scale, for example the need to save 15 per cent from the corporate services budget of a local government organization or achieve large financial savings in the warehousing operation of a logistics business. Similarly, projects can also be small in either scope or scale. To differentiate between a Lean event and a Lean project I find the following definition helpful:

> If I can move straight from the scoping activity into implementation it is a Lean event. If I have to undertake any other activity prior to being able to move into implementation then it is a Lean project.

A typical Lean project (Figure 1.4) will consist of a number of different activities, the most important of which are described below.

Scoping

The process of seeking clarification about the project in terms of defining objectives, risks and issues, things you can't change and selecting the team who will be involved. The process of scoping is covered in Chapter 3.

Value stream mapping events

There are a number of approaches to value stream mapping. The most common format for a value stream mapping event consists of three phases. The first is concerned with understanding where you are today (called *current state* or 'as is') that brings everyone involved up to a common level of understanding. The second is a creative process that is designed to create a picture of what might be done if there were no limits (called *blue sky* or *ideal state*). The last phase consists of creating a realistic picture of where you are going and the plans to help you get there (called *future state* or 'to be'). Irrespective of the approach you take, the output of a value stream mapping event is normally a defined future state and corresponding implementation plan that will contain a mix of other types of Lean events, Lean projects and some 'do its'. All of the processes and terminology relevant to value stream mapping events are covered in Chapter 4.

2P events (process planning events)

A 2P event is used to 'de-risk' a process prior to implementation. It normally involves some work to understand how the process currently works, designing and testing solutions along with implementation planning. The easiest way to think of a 2P event is like a cut-down value stream mapping event that has a much narrower focus. For example, an end-to-end pathway in a health care environment that considers the process from initial referral into a hospital, through to the patient being back at home post-surgery, might benefit from value stream mapping, whereas looking in detail at the process involved in dealing with a patient's blood-test results or how the theatre/surgery processes work would be better suited to a 2P event. The 2P process is covered in Chapter 5.

3P events (product and process planning events)

There are a lot of similarities between a 2P and 3P event. The major difference is that a 3P event is focused on the redesign of both products and services, and the processes used to bring the product or service to market. Because of the similarity between the 2P and 3P events they are both covered in Chapter 5.

Rapid improvement events

As we have already seen earlier in this chapter, a rapid improvement event comes into play when we are considering the physical implementation of changes. Rapid improvement events are covered in Chapter 6.

Managing for daily improvement (MDI)

Managing for daily improvement (MDI) is concerned with two things. First, there is the aspect of MDI that aims to involve 'everybody every day' in reviewing issues and opportunities. This aspect of MDI is a key aspect of *leader standard work* that we will cover in Chapter 8. The second aspect of MDI is where it is used to embed changes that have occurred, helping teams to convert process changes into behavioural change. Both aspects of MDI are covered in Chapter 7.

Planning a Lean programme

A definition for a Lean programme would be:

> A Lean programme is where a senior management team commit to using Lean as a strategic way of improving their organization.

FIGURE 1.4   Activities associated with Lean projects

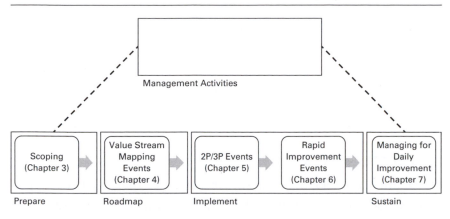

A key comment I want to make about this statement is that you do not need to put all your eggs into the Lean basket and that it is equally acceptable for Lean to be just part of your overall strategy. The structure of a Lean programme is shown again in Figure 1.5.

A Lean programme normally involves a whole organization, or certainly a large percentage of it, in a programme of improvement over an extended period of time. Lean programmes will consist of both the daily improvement activities that we will cover in Chapter 7, as well as a mix of Lean events and projects as needed. In addition, there are some very specific activities that need to be undertaken to ensure that a Lean programme is a success, the two most important

FIGURE 1.5   Structure of a Lean programme

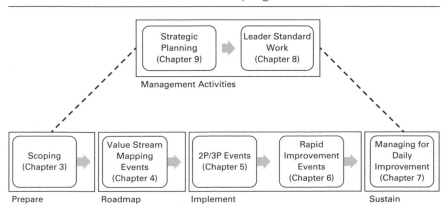

of which – *strategic planning* and *leader standard work* – are described below.

Strategic planning

There is a need to understand and link together multiple workstreams within any organization looking to organize a Lean programme. This can be achieved through *transformation map* or using *policy deployment* (*hoshin kanri*), both of which are covered in Chapter 9.

Leader standard work

There are a number of management activities that need to happen daily, weekly and monthly within organizations that are embarking on a Lean programme. From team meetings through to organizing a steering board for your Lean programme, we cover all of the relevant issues in Chapter 8.

Dealing with the issues that arise

In addition to planning events, projects and programmes, I suspect that many people will turn to this book when they encounter problems with their existing, or planned, Lean activities. In this section I want to explore the most important issues that arise and how you might deal with them, as well as offering advice on where to find help elsewhere in this book.

Issues with the implementation of Lean can occur from the very first time it is discussed at a management meeting. Not every issue proves fatal to the Lean programme, although as a rule of thumb the probability of success drops as the number of issues encountered goes up. Often the warning signs of problems are seen a long time before they manifest themselves, and I hope to be able to give you the foresight to spot when things are going awry and to be able to do something about it.

To facilitate this I have considered issues that arise in the following phases:

- just starting out;
- heading towards your first events and activities;

- following up and embedding the changes;
- keeping the momentum going.

I will consider the typical issues that arise in each of these areas in the following subsections.

Just starting out

It is not unusual for there to be teething problems with a Lean programme from the very outset. This often arises because Lean is a word that can generate the wrong reaction. For some it will mean, 'cut to the bone', and you will hear people immediately say, 'well, we're already Lean'. It also has an unfortunate association with the word 'mean'; people say, 'Lean is mean'. Other problems arise when people are worn out through the introduction of initiative after initiative. This occurs where the organization has failed to introduce previous initiatives well or where there is not enough work done to explain why there is a need for Lean. At senior management team level you will find that issues arise when there is a lack of understanding of what has been proposed or other initiatives that are competing for management time.

What you need to do	Where to find help
Create a clear message and communications strategy	Chapter 12
Work with people to engage them in the process of Lean	Chapter 10
Link together all the different initiatives within your organization	Chapter 9

Heading towards your first events and activities

The issues that arise here are normally about overcoming inertia. We have to remember that people who don't know what Lean is all about will often be reluctant to get actively involved. There is also the need to consider the disruption that taking people away from their day jobs can cause if not planned properly. There is a contrasting argument that says that you shouldn't proceed with an event that doesn't have the proper support – and I tend to say that if something is worth doing it is worth the disruption. If you can't justify the disruption you shouldn't go ahead with the activity.

What you need to do	Where to find help
Scope activities effectively	Chapter 3
Recognize when an event is in trouble and take effective action	Chapter 11
Plan activities ruthlessly and ensure you follow through on actions	Chapters 4, 5, 6 & 7

Following up and embedding the changes

Even when you have had a very successful rapid improvement event (RIE) you will still have things to do. The problem that most commonly arises is getting implementation activities closed off in a timely manner. In addition, when people encounter problems with a new way of doing things there is a natural tendency for people to return to the old way of doing things and this means you find that old practices start to creep back in. If you don't act to stop this you will find very quickly that all your good work has disappeared. Turning process changes into improved performance takes time and needs teams to follow up relentlessly.

What you need to do	Where to find help
Scope your Lean activity effectively and identify the plan	Chapter 3
Ensure you have a plan to follow up after every activity	Chapters 4, 5, 6 & 7
Make Lean on a daily, weekly and monthly routine	Chapters 7 & 8

Keeping the momentum going

After the flush of a few successful activities you may find that people stop engaging with the process. You will find that the focus goes into solving different problems and that senior managers can't be contacted as easily as they were before. You start to feel that the enthusiasm that everyone had at the start is slipping away. You will find growing reluctance to do things 'now' and increasing pressure to delay activities, not start new things and, basically, to scale down any activities you've already got planned. You will find that senior managers increasingly don't want to disrupt day-to-day operations irrespective of how badly organized they are and that front-line managers find increasingly inventive excuses not to participate.

What you need to do	Where to find help
Continuously engage the team and managers in Lean	Chapters 7, 8 and 10
Ensure your senior team know what the journey will really be like	Chapter 9
Recognize the warning signs early on and take effective action	Chapter 11

Myth buster

The final section of this chapter is concerned with the various myths that arise about Lean. This is not meant as a definitive list of myths that you will encounter, instead I have tried to capture the most frequently mentioned myths so that you are prepared for them when they arise.

Lean is just a fad

In the Introduction I presented a potted history of Lean. There is a very common misconception that Lean is 'something new' but actually it has existed in various forms for hundreds, if not thousands, of years. Lean is structured common sense, nothing more and nothing less.

Lean is just about 'tidy ups'

There is a generic misconception that Lean is only applicable to low-level, tactical improvement activities. This is perpetuated by people who choose to use Lean tools to do just small-scale activities and leave the 'big ticket' activities or use the red pen approach (where you simply put a red line through the activity and stop doing it). To help counter this misconception turn to Chapter 9.

Lean is mean

Sadly, this is less a misconception and more a reality in many organizations. There are people who have not been completely honest about why they are asking their staff to participate in Lean programmes and this has generated bad feeling. The key to this is in effectively planning your overall Lean programme, offering clear communications and scoping individual events and projects. You can find help on these in Chapters 3, 9 and 12.

Lean is just a bag of tools

There are many people who are obsessed by Lean tools. Indeed, there are internet forums full of discussions about the 'correct' way to apply the tools. It is true that there are many tools that you can draw on to help you with your Lean activities but unless you use the right tool, at the right time and in the right way, you are likely to encounter problems. All of the main Lean tools are described in Chapter 13 or in the Glossary, but you will also find useful tips to handling this popular misconception throughout the book.

Lean doesn't work here

This is an amazingly prevalent misconception and it doesn't matter whether you are working with a group of civil servants, assembly operators, warehouse staff, doctors or pilots. It often goes hand in hand with another misconception: now isn't the right time. The reality is that Lean is applicable wherever work is done. I know, it sounded strange to me when I started out many years ago, but it is true. There are short case studies scattered throughout this book that refer to examples from a range of sectors to help you with this misconception.

Now isn't the right time

The reality in the minds of many is that there never will be a 'right time' to look at the way you do things. I am amazed that people are prepared to waste thousands of hours on broken processes and yet will invest hardly any time at all on putting them right. Some of this is about engaging people in the process, giving them the skills to make the changes and explaining why things need to be done. You will find advice on all of these points in Chapter 10. It is also about setting a plan and sticking to it, which is really something that combines scoping, leader standard work and managing for daily improvement – topics you will find covered in Chapters 3, 7 and 8.

Rapid improvement events must be 'X' days long

The implementation of Lean needs to take only as long as it needs. You can run a successful Lean event in a couple of hours if the scope is very small. You might need longer for larger projects. The concept that every rapid improvement event (RIE) must last a certain number of days (most commonly stated as four or five days long) is just plain wrong and is promoted by management consultants. A related misconception is that you must run the days of an RIE 'back to back'. Sometimes this is true but often it can be beneficial to have a gap between the days (for RIE that last longer than one day) to enable you to answer questions that arise. It really does depend on each event and the key here is to act appropriately. More advice on this topic can be found in Chapter 6.

Lean is just something else I have to fit in

This is a clear sign that an organization has not integrated the various initiatives it is running. People are tasked with Lean without taking into account their day-to-day activities or current workload. It is a normal human act to focus your efforts on the areas in which you are most at risk of being put under pressure, and in organizations that have not integrated Lean into their strategic plans you can be assured that Lean will not be seen as strategically important. The effect can be quite dramatic because you will find it impossible to move forward. You can get help in this area from Chapter 9.

Closing thoughts

The aim of this chapter has been to provide you with a guide to how to use the rest of the book and to highlight how the different chapters link together to enable you to deliver a Lean event, Lean project or Lean programme.

However, before we get into the detail of exploring Lean activities, in Chapter 2 I provide details of the key concepts that underpin Lean. This introduces the principles of Lean and related details associated with the Toyota Production System, which is intended to provide useful background information.

Key Lean concepts

In this chapter I aim to answer the following questions:

1 What is Lean?

2 How does Lean relate to the Toyota Production System (TPS)?

3 What are the underpinning principles of Lean?

4 How does Lean relate to other improvement methodologies such as Six Sigma?

The aim of this chapter is to provide an understanding of the background concepts, philosophies and related information that underpin Lean. Many of the terms I introduce in this chapter will be referenced throughout the rest of the book. I also introduce many of the Japanese terms that are such a familiar part of Lean so that you can see how they fit into the overall picture (definitions for these terms can be found in the Glossary or in Chapter 13).

What is Lean?

In trying to define what Lean is I am going to start by exploring what it is not. For one thing it is not going to be a panacea for all business problems unless you have some years to invest in it. It is neither a new religion nor anything associated with something being 'lower in fat' and, in addition, it is neither an acronym nor is it a 'fad'.

In terms of defining what Lean is, there are numerous definitions to draw on and they all revolve around three key aspects:

1 Focusing on delivering better value to your customers.

2 Doing more with less.

3 Ensuring that when delivering 'more with less' you don't jeopardize quality, safety or the long-term stability of the organization.

Trying to bring these three elements together to create a '30-second pitch' for Lean – this being something you might say to someone when they pass you in a corridor and ask what Lean is – the following might be useful:

Lean is an approach to improving organizations that focuses on the needs of customers – and considers everything that is neither delivering value to customers nor ensuring the safety and security of the organization and its staff as waste and therefore a target for elimination.

It is quite easy to spot organizations that are on the Lean journey and doing it well because they will behave in some key defining ways that are consistent between sectors, namely:

- Everyone in the organization will have a deep understanding of what their customers really want.
- There will be a focus on continuously improving the way things are done in the organization.
- People will respect each other for their contribution to the organization.
- There will be a strategic and long-term view to improving the organization, backed up by short-term targets and actions.
- Lean will be seen as 'the way things are done round here' and will be part of everyone's job.

You may remember from the Introduction that Lean is not a new concept but that the name is relatively new. As I showed in the

Introduction, Lean has a long history of development and evolution. However, much of the thinking behind Lean was developed significantly in the post-war years by the Toyota Motor Company in their Toyota Production System (TPS). In the sections below we will explore the key concepts from the TPS that are relevant to an overall understanding of Lean.

Overview of the Toyota Production System

The Toyota Production System (TPS) evolved over many years as part of the strategy within the Toyota Motor Company to reform and improve their operations in the post-war years. The TPS initially drew on existing concepts such as standardized working, interchangeable parts and flow-based production processes. However, through the initial work done by Toyota's founder, Sakichi Toyoda, and the subsequent work by the engineer Taiichi Ohno and his colleagues Shigeo Shingo (a consultant to Toyota) and Eiji Toyoda, these initial concepts were developed into what is today the TPS.

The main objective of the TPS is to eliminate waste (termed *muda* in Japanese) from the process whilst designing out overburden (*muri*) and inconsistency or unevenness (*mura*). The focus is on developing processes that are capable of delivering the required outputs as smoothly, flexibly and free of stress as possible, utilizing the minimum amount of resource.

Many companies who decided to emulate Toyota's success latched on to the reduction in inventory (stock) that was causing major cash-flow problems for organizations and contributing to increases in cost. However, these very same organizations often failed to grasp that addressing just one aspect of the TPS does not generate the results they were looking for and many of them created additional problems for themselves by 'starving' their operations of resources and parts.

An often produced diagram that explains how the TPS works is called the 'TPS House' and a variant of this diagram is shown in Figure 2.1 below.

FIGURE 2.1   The TPS House

The roof of the house shows that the overall objective of the TPS is to enable Toyota to be the best provider of value to their customers (both internal and external) in the five areas of: quality, cost, delivery, safety and morale.

To enable the roof to stay in place it is supported by two main pillars, these being:

Just in time – the concept of producing only what is needed, when it is needed and in the amount needed.

Jidoka – the concept that quality should be built into the process.

Below the two pillars are four 'levels' or steps. The top 'step' is concerned with eliminating unevenness from all activities through the use of *heijunka* (a concept covered in Chapter 13). The second and third steps are concerned with two of the fundamental tools of the TPS (and Lean), namely *standard work* and *5S* and these are both described in Chapter 6. Underpinning the whole house is the Toyota philosophy, or the 'Toyota Way' that consists of a set of operating principles and practices. These were first summed up by

Toyota themselves in 2001 but were publicized by Dr Jeffrey Liker, professor of industrial engineering at the University of Michigan, in 2004 in his book *The Toyota Way*, where he described the 14 principles of the TPS.

The 14 principles of the 'Toyota Way'

The 14 principles of the Toyota Way are broken into four groups, which were defined by Jeffrey Liker as:

- Philosophy as the foundation.
- The right process will produce the right results.
- Add value to your organization by developing your people and partners.
- Continuously solving root problems drives organizational learning.

The 14 principles are unevenly spread across these four groups as we will see in the subsections below.

Philosophy as a foundation

1. Base your management decisions on a long-term philosophy, even at the expense of short-term financial goals

Whilst the need to cut costs is important (some would say vital) short-term cash-releasing activities should not be the main driver for the organization's strategy. The focus should be on creating a sense of purpose for the organization. This doesn't mean there won't ever be the need to make short-term decisions but means that there needs to be some explanation made to explain why things are being done and how they support the long-term strategy.

The right process will produce the right results

2. Create a continuous process flow to bring problems to the surface

The idea of *flow* is something that we will return to again and again in this book. It means reducing the time that any piece of work, person or project spends travelling between stages in the process, or waiting for the next stage in the process to start. The ultimate aim is to reduce this wait time and travel distance to zero.

3. Use 'pull' systems to avoid overproduction

Pull is the concept of triggering activity 'on demand' rather than doing work in advance of it being needed or ordered. Prior to the introduction of *pull*, organizations believed that the only way to serve customers was to hold warehouses full of stock 'just in case' they were needed. This frequently led to chaos, cash shortages and increased scrap and rework costs. Operations were planned based on forecasts in what could be termed a *push* process, leading to frequent examples where operational processes were tied up doing pointless work whilst customers were kept waiting. It was this that led to the development of pull thinking, where you provide small amounts of stock/raw materials and then you pull more materials to replenish your available stock as customers purchase goods and services from you. This thinking can be applied to non-manufacturing environments by considering how you would 'trigger activity only on demand'. For example, allowing customers to book an appointment online (pull) rather than having a letter sent to them with an appointment time that may be inconvenient (push), something that is as equally applicable to a GP practice as it is to booking a delivery from your local supermarket. We will return to the idea of pull later in this chapter.

4. Level out the workload (work like the tortoise, not the hare)

The aim here is to create stability in the workload, a term referred to as *heijunka*, as the only way to achieve flow in the long term. Large variations in activity trigger reactive behaviours. In factories you can achieve stability by planning production more effectively. But how do you achieve this in an 'on demand' service such as an emergency department in a hospital or a call centre? Well, in those scenarios it is often about looking at the pattern of demand (and there almost always are patterns that are reasonably predictable within limits) and ensuring that you deploy staff in the correct number to meet the demand as it varies, so that unacceptable delays don't occur for people waiting to enter the process or for those downstream of the entry point.

For example, if you have the right number of people staffing a call centre helpline for the volume of calls that arise during any period, then customers will not wait for long for their calls to be answered. By doing this you will prevent backlogs building up and in this way you will level out the activity for your organization.

5. Build a culture of stopping to fix problems, to get quality right the first time

The idea here is to selectively automate the detection of problems and empower people to stop and review the process when problems are detected. These two aspects underpin the idea of *jidoka*, also referred to (rather inelegantly) as *autonomation*. The focus should be on understanding why problems occur and spending time trying to prevent them occurring again. It is not only manufacturing companies that waste lots of time and money 'working around' problems rather than trying to deal with them. Of course, if you do empower your staff to stop the process when problems occur then you will want to know about it as quickly as possible. This led to the development of the *andon* signal, or visual and audible signal, by Sakichi Toyoda, the founder of Toyota. The idea of an *andon* is to alert people quickly that something has gone wrong and needs attention.

6. Standardized tasks and processes are the foundation for continuous improvement and employee empowerment

This is often confused either with flowcharts or with rigid processes where creativity is stifled. In the case of flowcharts, it is quite often the case that if 10 people are given a flowchart to follow they will find 11 different ways of following it. The idea of standardized tasks and processes is for teams of people to explore and implement the 'best practice' way of doing the things they need to do. During this process of exploring best practice they often find creative, effective and efficient ways of doing things, and this knocks out the second point about stifling creativity.

7. Use visual controls so no problems are hidden

As human beings we react well to visual signals. For example, most people react immediately to red traffic lights and obey signs telling them that there is 'no entry' to a certain area. The aim of this principle is to make the performance of teams visible so that people can see what is going on. This will enable them to see how the changes they make impact on the team's performance. There is reluctance in some organizations to making this information visible, especially when it might be seen by customers. My reaction to this concern is that you should not expect your front-line people to show much interest in helping to improve performance if they don't know what it is.

8. Use only reliable, thoroughly tested technology that services your people and processes

Technology shouldn't be used to drive processes and behaviours, it should support the work of teams and enable them to work effectively. This principle is concerned with selectively using technology to help you do what you need to do more effectively, responsibly and flexibly. It is this principle that is at the heart of the concept of Agile, which we will explore later in this chapter.

Add value to the organization by developing your people and your partners

9. Grow leaders who thoroughly understand the work, live the philosophy and teach it to others

The biggest impact on the day-to-day effectiveness of a team is the relationship between the team members. A good leader can bind a team together whilst bad leaders can create division, conflict and demoralized staff. In this context, the ninth principle is about having managers who support the TPS, can 'live and breathe' it and who work tirelessly to help others to work towards common goals.

10. Develop exceptional people and teams who follow your company's philosophy

This principle is concerned with developing teams not tribes. A tribe is a group of people who have their own rituals, beliefs and behaviours that may or may not be aligned with those of other tribes or the organization as a whole. Often different tribes will be in conflict as each tries to achieve their own local objectives at the expense of others. Teams, however, work together to achieve common goals that collectively benefit the organization.

11. Respect your extended network of partners and suppliers by challenging them and helping them to improve

Throughout the 1990s and into the early years of the 21st century there was a culture in many businesses of 'beating up' their suppliers to extract lower costs. This generated bad feeling in the relationships and led to a rigid 'compliance' or contract-based culture. Principle 11, in contrast, is concerned with respecting your partners and seeing them as vital to your overall success.

Continuously solving root problems drives organizational learning

12. Go and see for yourself to thoroughly understand the situation

Going and seeing what is actually going on and analyzing it deeply, referred to as *genchi genbutsu* (a term meaning 'go and see for yourself') is at the heart of this principle. This prevents people from guessing about what is really happening and as a result taking inappropriate actions. There is a wonderful term that is relevant here called 'mahogany mapping' in which groups of people sit in a mahogany-lined board-room guessing what is really going on at the front line. Principle 12 encourages people to go to where the action is (referred to as *gemba*, meaning the 'real place').

13. Make decisions slowly by consensus, thoroughly considering all options; implement decisions rapidly

This principle is concerned with getting to the 'root cause' of a problem and then exploring the options available to deal with it with a group of people. *Nemawashi*, a term that literally means 'going around the roots', is the phrase used to describe the process of gathering data and gaining a consensus view on problems. The idea is that once you have achieved a consensus you will rapidly be able to implement the changes required. For clarity, a consensus means there is a general agreement of what needs to be done, not that everyone necessarily agrees on how to do it.

14. Become a learning organization through relentless reflection and continuous improvement

Nothing is perfect and everything can be improved. This is about continuously reviewing how and what you do in order to find better ways of doing it. It means accepting that occasionally mistakes are made and having the courage to admit it, along with the strength of mind to find a better way of doing things in the future. This process of self-reflection is termed *hansei* in Japanese and can apply equally to parents asking their children to reflect on something they have done wrong as to a group of professionals reflecting on why something unexpected happened in their organization. The overall purpose of principle 14 is to encourage continuous improvement, for which the Japanese term *kaizen* is used.

The four headings used by Jeffrey Liker to group the 14 principles are directly related to another model used by Toyota to define the commitments they expect managers to make to the organization. These commitments are described as the 4Ps and are explored in more detail in the next section.

Toyota 4Ps – developing leadership commitment

Table 2.1 makes it obvious how the 4Ps relate directly to the four headings used in the previous section to group the 14 principles.

The 4Ps specifically define a number of commitments that apply to leaders at all levels within the organization, with these commitments being described in the following sections.

Philosophy

There are two main commitments needed to be made by leaders under this heading, namely:

- Commitment to the delivery of successful performance and growth of the organization.

- Commitment to the long-term contribution to society.

TABLE 2.1 Linking the 4Ps to the 14 principles

4P heading	Heading of the 4 groups for the 14 principles
Philosophy	Philosophy as a foundation
Process	The right process will produce the right results
People (and partners)	Add value to the organization by developing your people and your partners
Problem solving	Continuously solving root problems drives organizational learning

The first is a fairly obvious commitment; the second is a key part of Toyota's 'respect for people' policy.

Process

There are four mutual supporting commitments required of leaders under this heading, namely:

- Commitment to using Lean methods for waste elimination.
- Commitment to taking a 'value stream perspective'.
- Commitment to developing excellent processes.
- Commitment to using thoroughly tested technology.

We will explore most of these commitments later in this book, including a whole chapter on *value stream mapping* (Chapter 4).

People and partners

The two fairly self-explanatory commitments under this heading include:

- Commitment to developing leaders who live the philosophy.
- Commitment to the long-term development of people and partners.

Problem solving

The final three commitments are:

- Commitment to building a learning organization.
- Commitment to understanding our processes in detail.
- Commitment to undertaking a thorough consideration in decision making.

We will return to the commitment of managers in Chapters 8 and 9 when we consider both leader standard work and also the strategic planning of a Lean programme. However, before we can get to the underpinning principles there are two further, related concepts we need to cover that arise in the TPS and are relevant to Lean.

Muda, mura, muri

The team that developed the Toyota Production System identified three types of activity that were contributing to poor performance and gave them the names *muda*, *mura* and *muri*. A brief definition of each is given below:

- Muda: any activity that does not 'add value' to your customers is considered *muda*. Muda is alternatively called *waste* or *non-value-adding* (NVA) activity.
- Mura: variations in processes due to some form of imbalance are considered to be *mura*, also referred to as 'unevenness'.
- Muri: putting unreasonable stress on people, material or equipment is considered to be *muri*, another term for which would be 'overburden'.

We will look at each of these three issues below.

Muda (waste)

In any organization, activities are broken into two types: those that add value to customers and those that do not. We will explore the concept of *value* when we look at the five Lean principles later in this chapter, but for now assume that it is any task that a customer would be happy to pay for, if they had to. We will see that this is too simplistic an explanation for office, service and many public sector environments.

Muda describes any task that does not 'add value' to customers. Muda is used interchangeably with the terms *waste* and *non-value-adding* activity. All tasks that are muda increase organizational costs and lead times whilst also increasing the risk of errors arising. There are a number of different types of activities that organizations undertake that add no value and these are grouped together to form the *seven wastes* that I will cover later in this chapter.

There is a further subdivision of muda into type 1 and type 2. Type 1 muda is sometimes defined as 'necessary waste' or 'essential muda' and will include such things as essential training, servicing, testing, compliance and governance tasks. The focus should be on eliminating them where possible and streamlining what remains. Type 2 muda is anything that is genuine waste that adds no value to customers and that the organization does not need.

Both type 1 and type 2 muda are both types of waste: it is just that you are unlikely to rid yourself as easily of type 1 muda as you will of type 2.

Mura (unevenness)

Activities that create variability in a process, for example moving large batches of work through a manufacturing plant, large variations in calls to a call centre, or constantly running out of stock in any process, are considered as *mura*. These activities create problems that mean people have to stop one job and start another, rush what they are doing or simply just stop because they can't go forward, whilst knowing that they will have to work extremely hard to catch up. We will see that the fourth principle of Lean is designed to tackle mura in processes, and you may also find it useful to look at the descriptions for *kanban* and *heijunka* (found in Chapter 13).

Muri (overburden)

Muri, in addition to meaning 'overburden', may also be associated with the terms unreasonableness or even absurdity. In terms of the

Toyota Production System it is associated with activities where people, materials or equipment are put under unreasonable stress. For example, asking people to carry heavy burdens or undertake more work than they are capable of doing in a finite period, or requiring equipment to do more than it is designed to do.

Muri is overcome by reducing the amount of work people need to do by removing the muda, by looking at the working practices people are using through the concept of standard work and reducing the amount of time that machines, processes and equipment spend idle between jobs. We will see how aspects of the third principle of Lean is designed to tackle muri, but you will also find it useful to look at the descriptions given for *standard work* and *takt time* that can be found in Chapter 6 and for *Single Minute Exchange of Die* (SMED) and *Total Productive Maintenance* (TPM) that can be found in Chapter 13.

Considering muda, mura and muri

Of the three categories of activity described by muda, mura and muri, the one that has been most considered in Lean is that of muda. Indeed, the concept of muda (or waste) is essential to the understanding of the first principle of Lean, as we will see. However, whilst the other two areas (mura and muri) have not been forgotten, there are many Lean practitioners who have probably never heard of, and certainly not considered, either mura or muri.

Usually you will find aspects of muda, mura and muri in a process. For example, when work is unbalanced at one stage in a process (mura) you may end up with 'waves' of work arriving at the next stage creating (muri). In trying to deal with this, large amounts of time will be spent dealing with non-value-adding activities (muda). Therefore, to improve a process normally needs a Lean team to focus on all three.

I have already said that muda is perhaps the area that has the highest profile amongst Lean practitioners. In the next section we consider the various categories into which muda can be grouped.

The seven wastes (and eighth waste)

In terms of defining non-value-adding activities, I will quote from Shigeo Shingo, the co-developer of the Toyota Production System, who observed that 'it is the last turn of a bolt that tightens it'. The rest of the turns are simply wasted motion. Toyota's Taiichi Ohno is credited with categorizing seven different types of non-value-adding activity that were affecting the organization. Later, other people added another important waste, namely the waste of 'talent'. Table 2.2 summarizes the *seven wastes*, along with the eighth waste, and what they mean in both a manufacturing and non-manufacturing context.

TABLE 2.2   The seven (and eighth) wastes

Waste	Manufacturing	Non-manufacturing
1. Waiting	Waiting for parts to arrive at a process.	Waiting for information, people, materials or anything else to arrive.
2. Over-production	Producing more parts than can be sold or have already been requested by customers.	Doing more work than is absolutely required. In non-manufacturing contexts it is often better to refer to this waste as 'overprocessing' rather than overproduction.
3. Rework	Having to undertake a task more than once because it was done incorrectly the first time.	Having to undertake remedial work of any kind because not everything was done correctly the first time.
4. Motion	The movement of human beings.	The movement of human beings.
5. Transport	The movement of materials and equipment.	The movement of information, materials and equipment.

TABLE 2.2   *continued*

Waste	Manufacturing	Non-manufacturing
6. Processing	Undertaking any work that is not explicitly required by a customer. For example, producing an 'overengineered' product.	Undertaking any activity that is explicitly not required. For example, producing unnecessary reports, doing unwarranted testing, etc.
7. Inventory	The costs of holding, managing, storing and (often) disposing of stock.	Any unnecessary queuing of activity. For example, a stack of people brought in for an appointment, a stack of letters waiting to be typed, excess stock stored in operational areas, etc.
8. Talent	The waste of the expertise of human beings by asking them to do things that would be better undertaken by someone else or not done at all.	The waste of the expertise of human beings by asking them to do things that would be better undertaken by someone else or not done at all.

The first seven wastes listed in Table 2.2 are the original ones categorized by Taiichi Ohno, also referred to as the 'seven deadly sins'. The addition of the eighth waste changes this to create the *eight wastes*. A useful memory jogger to remember the eight wastes is the acronym *WORMPIT* that is summarized in Table 2.3.

There is also a further acronym used to remember the seven wastes – *TIM WOOD* – which is referred to in the Glossary and that uses slightly different but equally valid terminology.

We have now outlined all of the aspects of the Toyota Production System that we need to understand as part of a Lean programme. We can now explore how these elements relate to Lean. We will start by exploring the five principles of Lean.

TABLE 2.3 WORMPIT

WORMPIT	
W	Waiting
O	Overproduction or overprocessing
R	Rework
M	Motion and transport
P	Processing waste
I	Inventory
T	Talent

The five principles of Lean

As already mentioned, the tools and concepts of Lean have a pedigree measured in centuries but the name is relatively new. It was first popularized (not first published as many think) by Daniel Jones and James Womack in their book *Lean Thinking: Banish waste and create wealth in your corporation* (1996). In this ground-breaking book, Womack and Jones revisited the thought processes that led to improved performance at Toyota and other organizations and distilled this down to five Lean principles that now form a five-step thought process for improvement activities.

What will become obvious is that the five principles (Figure 2.2) that Womack and Jones defined were drawn from a mix of TPS concepts including elements of the 14 principles, the seven wastes and the ideas that surround the terms muda, mura and muri. In the following sections I will discuss each of the five principles and draw out some of the important concepts that are relevant to the rest of this book.

FIGURE 2.2   The 5 principles of Lean

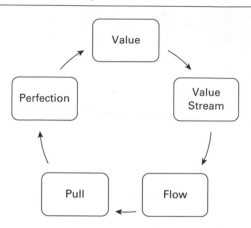

First principle: define 'value' from the customer's perspective

The first thing to say is that the term 'value' that we will use in this principle has little to do with the concept of the 'price paid' and, in much the same way, the term 'value adding' has little to do with the difference between the price of goods and the cost of the resources (time, materials, etc) used to provide them. Value in the context of the first principle of Lean is used to mean that you are doing something that the customer thinks has value, however that value is defined, and which is delivered 'right first time'. In effect, a value-adding step is one that transforms the product or service and increases the worth to the customer whilst being done 'right first time'. The last part of this statement is to avoid people claiming that any form of rework is value added. If a task cannot be defined as value adding then it is waste (muda) and we can use the categories of the seven wastes defined earlier to help us define which type of waste it might be.

The term waste is used interchangeably with the terms muda and non-value adding. As a personal preference I use non-value adding (NVA) as it seems to generate less negative feedback when you encounter some of the issues I will discuss later in this chapter.

Usually when you are talking about a task being value adding you are considering whether or not the customer would be willing to pay money for it, but they don't have to pay in monetary terms as it equally applies to tasks that they are happy to invest time and resources in.

In a commercial manufacturing context things that a customer is generally happy to pay for include machining, cutting, sawing, assembly and similar activities. But how do we define a value-adding task in a service or public sector environment where the customer is not directly paying for a product or service? Well, in the first instance we could still ask, 'Would the customer be prepared to pay for this activity if they had to?' But it is often better to use a slightly different definition that involves four distinct terms:

- Does the customer experience the activity?
- Does the customer want the activity to occur?
- Does it occur correctly the first time?
- Would the customer care if you significantly changed the activity?

A value-adding task will generate a 'yes' response to all four points. There are a number of examples given in Table 2.4.

What you may have begun to realize when looking at the list of examples given in Table 2.4 is that there is a little subjectivity to defining what is value adding and what is NVA and this is not un-usual. There are often multiple customers of a process. You could say that for any organization the staff, managers, shareholders, members of the public, local media and others are all 'customers' of a process in one way or another. Depending on the people or groups you choose as customers for a process will determine the steps that you ultim-ately identify as value adding. It is vital that you choose the correct customer for a process; in a commercial setting it is normally (but not always) the end customer (or consumer), but in an environment where the customer is less well-defined you normally have to choose the main beneficiaries of the process, whether that is a patient, service user, a regulatory body, management team or members of the public. It is best to identify only one customer per process, but sometimes this is impossible and you may need two or three. I rarely come across processes that need more than two customers and have never found

TABLE 2.4 Defining value-adding and non-value-adding tasks

Activity	Value adding or non-value adding (NVA)?
Visiting a doctor	I experience this and I probably want to see the doctor. If you changed it so that I saw the receptionist instead I wouldn't like it. Therefore this is a value-adding step.
Filing a complaint	I experience this and I probably want to submit a complaint but I shouldn't have needed to. Therefore this is NVA (in fact, it is specifically rework).
Searching for information or things	I experience this but I don't want it, therefore it is NVA in the form of 'motion'.
Waiting for an appointment	Again, I experience this but I don't want this and therefore it is NVA in the form of 'waiting'.
Having my blood taken	This is an interesting one. I experience my blood being taken and I probably want to have it taken but in reality it is not until I get the results back and some form of treatment plan produced that the value is actually added. Therefore, the step of actually taking my blood is NVA to the patient. We will see later how the choice of the process 'customer' changes the steps that you will perceive as value adding or not.
Producing a report that no one reads	I experience this and probably don't want to produce the report. Almost certainly if no one is going to read it we can do it a different way. This is definitely NVA in the form of 'processing waste'.
Calling a technical helpline when a problem arises	I experience this and probably want to talk to someone but again it could often have been avoided. This is therefore NVA in the form of 'rework'.

TABLE 2.4   *continued*

Activity	Value adding or non-value adding (NVA)?
Packing a parcel for a customer	This is another interesting example. Probably the customer wants the parcel to be packaged, but in reality the customer doesn't experience the step and, therefore, it should be NVA. In addition, using the commercial definition of value-adding step, would the customer be prepared to pay for the packing? Well, the answer is that in some organizations they would. Therefore, with the limited information available in this example, it is not possible for us to fully determine whether this is value adding or not.
Assembling a report for a customer	We can use the commercial definition for this and ask 'Is the customer prepared to pay for it?', which would normally be a yes, so the task is likely to be value adding.
Having to undertake a task twice because it was done incorrectly the first time	This is clearly an example of 'rework' but we can use either the commercial definition or the alternative definition given. In the first case, we would say that the customer would not be happy to pay for it; in the second, we would see that the customer does not want it to occur.
Carrying materials from one place to another	This is clearly an example of 'transportation'. Ask yourself whether you would be happy to pay for someone to move something from A to B and the answer would normally be no, but we will come back to this point later.
Issuing a parking fine to a driver who has parked inconsiderately and/or illegally	This is an emotive one. You might think that the driver of the car is the customer, but actually the customer in this case is 'the public'. The driver clearly doesn't want the ticket but members of the public who are inconvenienced by irresponsible parking would probably, I suspect, see the issuing of a ticket as value adding. I have included this example here to show that it can be a very interesting thought exercise working out whether something is value adding or not in certain circumstances.

one that has more than three true customers. As the number of customers increases the difficulty of redesigning the processes increases, so try to limit the customers of a process to one wherever possible.

A very important concept at this point is termed *VotC* (pronounced voit-ka) that stands for *voice of the customer*, because the only person who can define whether something is value adding or not is the customer. This means that you are likely to make mistakes if you try to guess what your customers really want.

Another issue that you will encounter is that people become very animated about tasks that they might have been doing for years that are classified as NVA (and this is one reason I use this term rather than waste, as it generates fewer negative reactions overall). Often the only reason organizations are successful is because people have been working very hard to keep the whole thing moving. Therefore, here are two useful things to consider: 1) just because something has to be done does not make it automatically value adding; 2) just because something is non-value adding does not automatically mean it is going to be got rid of but it does give us the right to challenge how and where it is done.

The first point addresses the issues where you will get people telling you, 'Well if I don't move it from A to B then it will not be there when you need it therefore it must be value adding.' The second point reduces the negativity you will get from participants in Lean activities. (We will return to the definition of value adding and non-value adding in some detail in Chapter 4 when we discuss value stream mapping.)

Second principle of Lean: understand the value stream used to deliver value currently

A value stream is simply all of the steps involved in delivering value in a process. It is clear that there are very few processes that are only involved in one type of activity and that does not vary very much at all: we need to consider three types of activities that virtually any process will experience: *runner*, *repeater* and *stranger*.

Runners

These form the bulk of activities undertaken within the process, making up 70 to 90 per cent of the total activity undertaken. Most commonly, a *runner* occurs daily but will certainly be very frequent.

Repeaters

These are still common activities making up 10 to 20 per cent of all activity within the process. A *repeater* occurs less frequently than a runner, perhaps arising every week (rather than every day).

Strangers

These typically make up a further 5 to 10 per cent of all activity within a process and generally there is no pattern to a *stranger* occurring, meaning that they often 'come out of left field'. In addition, there will tend to be many different types of stranger activities that could occur, thus making it difficult to plan for what will come up next.

When understanding a value stream you may need to look at a range of different scenarios, with each scenario being defined as a runner, repeater or stranger. I cannot think of a process where there are not multiple scenarios that could occur. To gain an understanding of typical value streams needs between 8 and 12 scenarios to be considered, as we will see in Chapter 4.

Third principle: creating processes that flow

Having understood the value stream, the focus moves on to understanding how to make the value *flow* by eliminating bottlenecks, delays, detours, waiting and rework. This means moving steps closer together both physically and in terms of the time taken from one step ending to the next starting. For example, moving two desks closer together and also reducing the delays between the receipt of a letter and the action in response to the letter. There are some important concepts involved in helping processes to flow, much of it concerned with balancing work between stages in the process and reducing the size of any 'batches' of work, both of which are considered in Figures 2.3 and 2.4.

FIGURE 2.3   Batch v flow

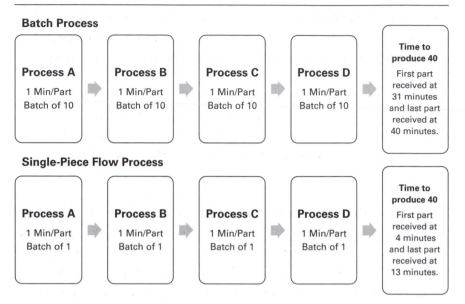

FIGURE 2.4   Unbalanced v balanced process

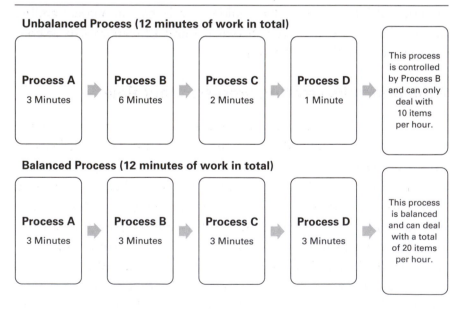

We will consider the process of flow in more detail when we consider rapid improvement events in Chapter 6.

Fourth principle: trigger activity when the customer 'pulls'

The fourth principle is concerned with doing things only when the customer 'pulls' (or demands) them to be done. The opposite to *pull* is a *push* system in which you try to predict what customers will want at some future point. Supermarkets feature heavily in the description of pull systems because they offer a readily recognizable example. I will use a modern example where the act of purchasing the item at the checkout records that the item has 'left the store' and places a demand for a replacement product. Effectively, the beep you hear at the till triggers a 'pull' to the supplier or warehouse to supply another product, albeit aggregated together over a complete day with other orders. If supermarkets operated a push system they would need teams of planners trying to guess what customers may want to purchase and then put that stock on to the shelves. Sometimes they would get it right and sometimes wrong, meaning that you would have lots of extra stock that you can't sell (increasing your wastage costs) and lots of lost opportunities where customers cannot purchase what they were looking for.

Two further examples of push and pull are described below:

A team were sending out letters to clients with appointment dates (push). They had a high cancellation rate because the times/dates were inconvenient to customers. They changed this to a system where they rang clients to ask what date would suit them (therefore 'pulling' the date from the client), which dramatically reduced the number of cancellations and changes.

A team working with a wide range of consumables were given new stock by a stores team on a weekly basis based on pre-set levels irrespective of what they had used (push). This meant the team were frequently running out of stock and having to place urgent orders to obtain replacement items. They switched to a system that used 'two bins', one green and one red that were placed one behind the other. As the green bin was emptied they moved it out of the way so you could see the red bin. The red bin acted as a visual trigger to 'pull' more stock from the stores team, who serviced the bins twice per week but only filled the bins that were needed. This reduced overall stock usage and the costs associated with couriers.

We will return to the issue of *pull* when we consider rapid improvement events in Chapter 6. Pull is also closely associated with the concept of *kanban* (described in Chapter 13).

Fifth principle: aim for perfection

The last of the five principles is concerned with treating Lean not as a one-off process but as a process of continuous improvement. In effect, it suggests you need to both return to the first principle and start again whilst at the same time continuously improving the things you have already put in place. We will return to this issue of continuous improvement in both Chapter 7 and Chapter 8.

Comparing the Toyota Production System with Lean

Whilst many would say that Lean is simply a more generic form of the Toyota Production System there are some fundamental differences that have emerged between the way that Toyota utilize the TPS and the way other organizations adopt Lean practically. The major differences are explored in Table 2.5.

Having said that there are differences I should also say that there are a large number of similarities between the TPS and Lean, for example the second and third principles of the TPS are identical to the third and fourth principles of Lean. The difference is that Lean is both easier to understand for the majority of organizations than the complexities of the TPS that have built up over an extended period. Also, Lean can be applied more readily to organizations that are setting out with processes and cultures that are far from being ideal.

In addition to being similar to the TPS, Lean is also related to, and draws on, other approaches to organizational improvement, as we will explore in the next section.

TABLE 2.5 Differences between the TPS and Lean

Toyota Production System (TPS)	Lean
Toyota is clearly focused on seeking profit as the driving force behind why things are done.	Many organizations looking to go Lean either don't have the same profit focus as Toyota or don't put it centre stage in their improvement activities, preferring instead to focus on different objectives such as customer satisfaction and patient safety.
Toyota has had a long time to develop the TPS and people are brought into this established system through rigorous training. They enter an environment that lives and breathes the principles.	Many organizations going Lean are starting with a culture that is not conducive to its success and need to use a different implementation approach. The focus is also often very much shorter term than Toyota.
The tools are there to help people make better, more informed decisions.	Often the introduction of a tool (commonly 5S) is seen as the basis of Lean.
Everyone is responsible for improvements at Toyota.	For organizations going Lean the problem is that they are starting with only a few people with the skills needed so it often gets delegated to a hardy band of change agents to lead changes. However, the long term objective should be to make Lean something that is practised 'everyday by everyone'.

Comparing Lean with other improvement methodologies

In this section we will explore a range of other approaches to organizational improvement in order to provide both a brief history of each approach and to show how many of the key concepts of these approaches are relevant to Lean.

Total Quality Management (TQM)

TQM can trace its origins back to the start of the 19th century when Carl Friedrich Gauss and others began to develop the theories that underpin the statistical analysis of processes. In the 1920s this thinking was applied to product quality and then in the 1940s was used by a range of statisticians to try to reduce the costs of production by reducing rework and wastage costs. One of the most famous advocates was Dr William Edwards Deming, who was instrumental in the transformation of post-war Japan. The term Total Quality Management (TQM) entered the language of improvement in the 1980s and consists of a range of concepts such as a focus on the customer, involving all employees in improvement and continuously improving, all of which are relevant to Lean.

Six Sigma

Six Sigma evolved from the drive to improve quality that gave us TQM. The term Six Sigma was first used by Motorola in 1986 and the term itself (often represented as 6σ using the Greek letter sigma) was drawn from statistics to mean developing a process where 99.99966 per cent of the products are statistically free of defects (3.4 defects per million). As a main focus, Six Sigma aims to reduce variation in a process and therefore is directly relevant to the elimination of mura (unevenness, as defined earlier in this chapter). Six Sigma uses a wide range of statistical and problem-solving tools that are based around the methodology of DMAIC:

- **Define** the problem and listen to the voice of the customer.
- **Measure** the process and collect relevant data.
- **Analyse** the data and seek out the root cause of problems.
- **Improve** the process.
- **Control** the process and ensure that deviations are corrected.

Elements common with Lean, such as voice of the customer, process analysis and continuous improvement, are clearly seen in the DMAIC approach of Six Sigma. Improvement tools such as *5S, standard work*, *poka yoke* (*mistake proofing*) and many of the other tools of Lean are shared with Six Sigma. This similarity between Lean and Six Sigma has led to the development of the concept of Lean Six Sigma or simply Lean Sigma.

Concurrent Engineering (CE)

CE is an approach to developing new products and services that has activities occurring in parallel rather than sequentially as a way of reducing the overall lead time and costs for development. The concepts of CE started to evolve at the end of the 19th century with the realization that new product development was very expensive, and with shortening product life-cycles there was less time available to recoup these costs. CE found its feet during the World Wars with the rapid evolution of technologies that wars tend to bring about and the need to quickly introduce new products into production. CE is based on two simple concepts: the first is that you need to consider the whole life-cycle of the product (or indeed the life-cycle of a service) during the design phase; the second is that activities should occur 'concurrently' to minimize the lead time. This requires multidisciplinary teams to work closely together and to focus on the whole product 'value stream', both of which are concepts relevant to Lean. The term 'concurrent design' is used interchangeably with 'concurrent engineering', often in non-production-related environments such as software development.

Theory of Constraints (TOC)

TOC takes as its premise 'a chain is no stronger than its weakest link'. It was first popularized in the book *The Goal* by Eliyahu M Goldratt (1984), although work on the concept was done earlier by people such as Wolfgang Mewes in the 1960s. TOC concerns itself with understanding and tackling the constraints within a process that are affecting the overall throughput, expense and inventory (or stock). A constraint is defined as anything that is preventing a system from achieving its goal, and a core consideration is that there are only a 'critical few' constraints that need to be tackled. It can also be thought of as a bottleneck. These aspects of understanding why a process is not capable (or is constrained) and putting in place corrective measures are also important in Lean activities.

Business Process Re-engineering (BPR)

BPR is concerned with the analysis and design of workflows and processes within organizations. It was first discussed by Michael Hammer, a former American professor of computer science, who stated that most of the work being done for customers added no value and should be removed rather than simply automated. Many BPR projects focused on the technological aspects of organizations and it was the disregard shown to the people aspects of change that led to it developing some very powerful critics. However, BPR is closely related to Lean in both the use of value stream mapping and its focus on radical change.

Agile

Agile is an approach to improving processes that stresses the use of cross-functional teams and the appropriate use of technology to reduce the time taken to develop products and services. Agile is concerned with enabling organizations to respond quickly to customer needs and market changes whilst at the same time managing costs and quality. In reality, Agile is an amalgam of all of the improvement approaches already discussed with elements such as the multidisciplinary teams of CE, a focus on re-engineering processes such as BPR and the use of appropriate use of statistics and information as you would find in TQM and Six Sigma. In practice, Agile is most easily thought of as the application of Lean to an entire supply chain along with the appropriate use of technology and partnering.

Continuous Improvement

Continuous Improvement, which is often associated with the Japanese term *kaizen*, is concerned with the introduction of small, incremental improvements to processes. It developed at the same time as TQM in post-war Japan and entered into the Toyota Production System, as you can see most clearly in the TPSs principles 5, 6 and 11. Continuous

Improvement is instrumental to Lean and is the basis of the fifth Lean principle and is also essential to the concept of *managing for daily improvement* that we will see in Chapter 7.

Closing thoughts

One of my other interests is palaeoanthropology, which is concerned with the evolution of human beings. You may have heard of hominids (human-like species) such as 'Homo Erectus' and Neanderthals but you may never have heard of Homo Rudolfensis and Homo Heidelbergensis or even earlier species such as Australopithecus Afarensis. In the world of palaeoanthropology it seems that every time a new bone is found there are people who want to identify it as a new species. The reason for this is that if you get to name a new species you generate a lot of kudos for yourself and your research colleagues. These are the 'splitters' who often see the small variations that exist within a species as a reason to allocate them to a new species. They are contrasted with the 'clumpers' who try to combine different species together. For example, they may argue that there is little difference between a Homo Habilis (also known as 'Handy Man') and a Homo Rudolfensis and that they are just variations within a single species along the same lines as you might see between a short, squat and square headed person and a tall, slender, round headed person found within our own species. In this area I am definitely in the 'clumper' camp and look for similarities rather than seeking out differences.

The same ideas apply to the various improvement approaches I have identified in this chapter. There are people who seek to identify fundamental differences in the methodologies with the aim of creating a new 'species' of improvement approach, and those who seek to say that they are all interwoven and are just different forms of the same aim: that being to improve the overall performance of an organization. One quite common example of splitting is for people to compare Agile and Lean and to say that Lean is represented by a thin, malnourished person only barely capable of walking and Agile is represented by an athlete, but I don't know of any Lean organization that would run itself into the ground in the way this implies and therefore believe this is an attempt to 'split' Lean and Agile into two distinct methodologies when they are much the same. As with palaeoanthropology, I am definitely in the 'clumper' camp when it comes to improvement methodologies. I believe that all of the approaches mentioned have something valuable to bring to improving organizations and, as a pragmatist, I have drawn the best of each to show how they can all be used to support an effective and successful Lean programme.

Scoping projects

03

In this chapter I aim to answer the following questions:

1 How do you scope Lean projects?
2 What is an A3 and how do you use them?
3 When is it appropriate to use an A3, project charter or project initiation document?
4 What are the practicalities of scoping projects?

Scoping is the process of answering key questions about your Lean project or Lean event such as:

- What do we want to achieve?
- How will we measure success?
- Who will be involved?
- What risks might we need to prepare for?
- What is the plan?
- What are the timescales?

Scoping is something you may be familiar with as it has been considered best practice in project management for a number of years and appears in the form of project charters and project initiation documents (PIDs). In the context of Lean events and projects, scoping provides clarity about the aims and objectives, as well as setting boundaries, considering the resources you will need and planning the timescales.

In this chapter I will consider the various ways that people scope projects. We will look at the Lean *A3* tool as well as considering both project charters and project initiation documents and how all of these can be used to provide the scoping for a Lean project. Throughout this chapter I will use the term Lean project (as defined in Chapter 1) although everything that is written could equally apply to a Lean event or even a Lean programme inside a smaller organization or department.

An overview of scoping

Having a document that clearly outlines the aims, objectives, roles, resources and risks for your Lean activity is one of the most important things you need to do to ensure the success of your project. The need for some form of scoping is even greater if you are working with suppliers/customers, service users or other people from outside your organization. However, even the smallest project involving only a single team will benefit from some scoping prior to the start of implementation. Many of the problems that Lean activities encounter can be traced back to something that either wasn't done, or wasn't done properly, during the scoping phase.

As we will see later in this section, there are a number of different ways of scoping projects, and a number of different ways of organizing the information in each of the document formats used. However, all scoping activities are concerned with answering the same questions and, in Table 3.1, I have summarized the questions that scoping, however it is done, needs to answer.

There are a number of different document formats used to help with scoping and an almost infinite way of filling them in but in the following sections I will outline the most common formats and how they can be used. Later in this chapter I will discuss how you might go about getting these documents completed and some of the practical problems that occur with scoping in real life.

TABLE 3.1   The questions that scoping aims to answer

Scoping question	Section title	Overview of section contents
What is the problem?	Problem background	A concise description of what is happening including any key statistics.
What are we going to do about it?	Problem statement or compelling need	Ideally something that clearly outlines why this is an important project, what is going to occur and a description of what the outcome of any work done will be.
What do we want to achieve at the end?	Measures of success or objectives	A series of objectives that will be used to focus the efforts of the team and also that will be used to measure the success of any work done.
Is this worth doing?	Business case	A summary of the return on investment of doing the project.
What are the boundaries of the project?	Project boundaries	A summary of the areas/people and teams that are 'in scope' for this project.
What things can't we do?	Constraints and assumptions or fixed points	The things that mustn't change during the project. Whilst there is an argument that it constrains creativity by having fixed points, it avoids teams developing solutions that can't be implemented.
What may go wrong?	Risks	What are the major risks that might be anticipated as occurring during the project, and what do you need to do to prevent them occurring or reduce the problems that arise if they do?

TABLE 3.1 *continued*

Scoping question	Section title	Overview of section contents
What else may affect this programme?	Business issues	What else is going on within your organization or the area affected that may impact on the success of this project?
Who will participate and what will they do?	Roles and organization	Who will be the sponsor? Who will lead the change? Who else will be involved in the project?
What will be done and when will it occur?	Project plan	This is an outline of the major things that will occur, along with the timescales.

Lean A3s

Not unsurprisingly *A3s* get their name from the size of paper they are normally printed on. A3s provide teams with a framework to help them identify, define, act on and review challenges and problems. A3s can be used to structure any type of Lean activity, whether it is for solving a simple front-line problem or looking at an end-to-end process within one or more organizations. The A3 is a 'living document' in that it is not meant to be fully completed prior to the start of a project but that it gradually gets more detail added as the process goes on.

Initially A3s were quite simple and were used to provide all the information that you would find in a *PDCA* (plan, do, check and act) cycle as shown in Figure 3.1. The PDCA cycle was popularized in the 1950s by Dr W Edwards Deming, a thought leader in quality control. Deming used the PDCA approach to provide a structure for solving problems and showed it as a cycle to emphasize that it is meant to be an iterative process. You may also sometimes read about a *PDSA* cycle, which is closely related to the PDCA cycle with 'check'

FIGURE 3.1 The PDCA popularized by Dr William Edwards Deming

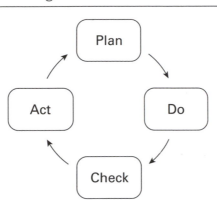

changed to 'study'. This modification was introduced by Deming himself when he realized that people associated the word 'check' with inspection, whereas he wanted them to analyse the process to determine whether or not changes had actually happened.

Subsequently, A3s have developed away from problem-solving templates to the point where they can be used to scope whole projects. In the following two sections I will outline how A3s are used in these two different scenarios, as well as providing a template for each approach.

A3 as a problem-solving tool (PDCA)

A Lean A3 can be used to provide a team with a structure for solving problems. The structure used, as mentioned earlier, is based on the PDCA cycle. An example A3 template that is suitable for use as a problem-solving tool is shown in Figure 3.2.

The sections of the A3 template shown in Figure 3.2 cover all of the four elements of the PDCA cycle as shown in Figure 3.3.

We can now 'go round' the A3 and start to understand what should go into each of the sections.

Problem background

This section provides essential information on the extent and importance of the issue under review and should also detail how, through tackling this project, the organization will benefit.

FIGURE 3.2 Example A3 template

PROJECT TITLE:	Project Owner:
A3 Problem Solving Template	Date First Created:
	Last Updated:

Problem Background

Future State

Current Condition

Confirmation of Future State

Measures of Success

Measure	Change Required	Notes & Issues

Root Cause Analysis

Follow Up Actions

Follow Up Action	Owner	Expected Completion Date	Status

FIGURE 3.3 A3 template showing how the sections align with the PDCA elements

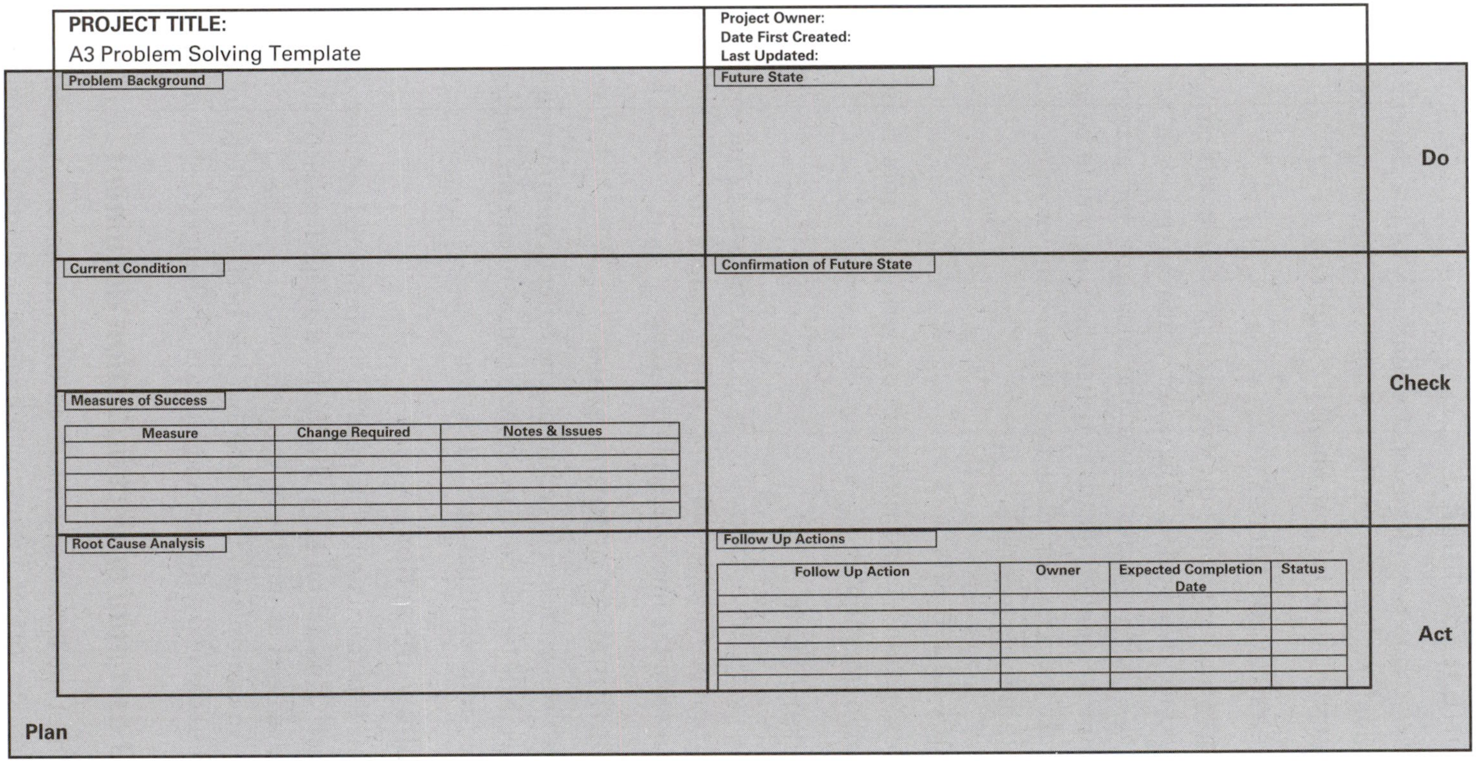

PROJECT TITLE:
A3 Problem Solving Template

Project Owner:
Date First Created:
Last Updated:

Do

Check

Act

Problem Background

Future State

Current Condition

Confirmation of Future State

Measures of Success

Measure	Change Required	Notes & Issues

Root Cause Analysis

Follow Up Actions

Follow Up Action	Owner	Expected Completion Date	Status

Plan

Current condition

This section provides a concise summary of the current situation and should include any charts, key statistics, drawings and anything else that will be useful in defining the problem.

Measures of success

This section specifies the expected improvements that will occur by tackling this project. The most common problem for this section is not being specific about the measure, for example what does 'improve quality' mean? A better measure would be 'reduce rework by 15 per cent' or 'eliminate 95 per cent or more of all packaging within three months'.

Root cause analysis

This section is concerned with exploring the root cause of the problem in question.

Future state

Also sometimes referred to as 'countermeasures' on some forms, this section provides a summary of the changes that will be implemented to enable the improvements to occur.

Confirmation of future state

Also sometimes referred to as the 'effect confirmation section', this covers the work done to study whether or not the implementation of the future state has been effective.

Follow-up actions

This lists the actions that need to be completed to 'close off' the future state. This action plan should be managed proactively to close off the actions as quickly as possible.

An example A3 template that has been completed up to the point of 30 days post the implementation of changes is shown in Figure 3.4.

A3 as a mini project initiation document

Whilst the Lean A3 template shown in the previous section is the most common format, I want to highlight a modern use for this established

FIGURE 3.4 Example A3 template completed to 30 days post implementation

---

PROJECT TITLE: Components Cell Improvement
A3 Problem Solving Template

Project Owner: Bob Smith
Date First Created: January XX
Last Updated: April XX

Problem Background

Lead times in the components cell (Line C) is currently averaging 6 weeks. Our customers are able to access like for like services from two local competitors on a four week turnaround time. Whilst our prices are comparable to our competitors and our quality is seen as industry best practice in terms of post-build failure rates the gap between us and our competitors is closing and we need to focus on reducing lead-times and reducing the stock held in the cell.

Future State

Exercise we have identified that Having undertaken a Value Stream Mapping the Components Cell is poorly laid out should be set-up as a flow cell as shown in the diagram opposite. We will also introduce operator self inspection and a visual performance measure located next to the integrated finished goods area. Finally, the cell will utilize the concept of Pull through the introduction of a Kanban system.

Finished Goods

Current Condition

The Components Cell is shown as 'Line C' in the following charts.

Average Lead Times
Line A Line B Line C Line D
→ Target
→ Actual

Average Stock Levels
Stock Value (£k)
£450
£400
£350
£300
£250
£200
£150
£100
Line A Line B Line C Line D
→ Target
→ Actual

Confirmation of Future State

Performance at 30 days post implementation:

- Lead-Time: Stable at 4.5 Weeks
- Stock Levels: Averaging £327k (down by nearly £60k)

Performance to be reviewed again at 45 days post implementation. Graphs to be inserted at 60 day review point.

Measures of Success

Measure	Change Required	Notes & Issues
Reduce Lead Times	6 wks to 4 wks	
Reduce Average Stock Levels	Reduce by at least £150k	
Improve customer communication	TBD	Determine with sales team

Root Cause Analysis

The root cause was identified as being the layout of the cell is encouraging the team to batch activity and delay the movement of stock between stages. Other problems identified include:

1. The distance from the cell to the Finished Goods area and the fact that the despatch team only pick up daily leads to up to 24 hours delay.
2. Operators should be empowered to inspect their own work to reduce the inspection time involved in the process. This will save up to 2 days overall.
3. Gathering data on progress is very difficult with the current layout and when the new layout is implemented we need to install a better performance measurement system.

Follow Up Actions

Follow Up Action	Owner	Expected Completion Date	Status

concept by showing how A3s can be used as mini project initiation documents (PIDs). A PID, as we will see later in this chapter, is a formal document that is commonly used in project management to provide all of the information required for a project. PIDs tend to be used for larger, more complex projects where the amount of information required is significantly greater than could be displayed on a single A3. However, there is a half-way house where projects are the right size of use with an A3 as a mini PID. It is also possible to use the type of A3 that I will show you in this section as a 'front cover' for a full PID if needed: if the project is too large to be usefully served by a single A3. Figure 3.5 shows a blank A3 template for use as a mini project initiation document.

The sections of the A3 in this format has additional information to that shown in the A3 PDCA template shown earlier in this chapter. In the following sections I will go through the information that you might expect to find in each of the sections.

Compelling need

The 'compelling need' should serve three purposes: inspiring people to get involved, informing them what will happen and protecting the reputation of the organization. Compare the three sentences below:

- We continue to knowingly deliver poor quality products to customers.

- We must improve quality so that our overall cost base reduces.

- We have the opportunity to transform our relationship with customers and at the same time create a more financially sustainable business that is better for everyone.

Whilst none of these three statements is perfect, I would argue that the first one does not protect the reputation of the organization; the second is bland and does not provide a truly compelling need for someone to participate in the project. The third statement is the only one that would seem to be suitable as the opening sentence in a compelling need statement.

Depending on the size of the project, a compelling need will consist of anything between one paragraph and several pages of text. It will

FIGURE 3.5 Blank A3 template for use as a mini PID

A3 Title:

Start Date:
A3 Last Updated:

Target Completion Date:

Compelling Need For Action | Go | No Go

Current or Initial State | Go | No Go

Implementation Plan: | Go | No Go

Action	Owner	Status	Notes

Measures of Success | Go | No Go

Measure	Change Required	Notes & Issues

Expected Future State | Go | No Go

Confirmed State | Go | No Go

New Performance Level	Confirmation State (RAG)	Notes & Actions

---

Fixed Points, Risks & Issues | Go | No Go

Issues	Controlling Action Required

Team Roles | Go | No Go

Senior Sponsors
Process Owners
Team Leaders
Change Agents
Core Team Members

Reflections & Lessons Learnt | Go | No Go

People	Process
Quality	Innovation
Productivity	Prevention

normally commence with an outline of what you are trying to achieve (sometimes called the 'noble goal'), followed by a statement about what you are going to do and ending with what I like to call the 'so-what?' statement. This last statement summarizes what the expected benefits will be after the project is implemented.

Sometimes a compelling need is referred to as *true north*, meaning the direction that you want your organization to be moving in. Two real life compelling needs are given below (with the organizational information removed):

Health care compelling need

We want to provide a seamless, high-quality service for vulnerable older people (over 75) offering appropriate care in the appropriate setting meeting the needs of individuals.

We will achieve this by avoiding duplication, simplifying the access to services and improving everyone's understanding of the roles and responsibilities required. We will facilitate this by giving patients all of the information about their condition and the appropriate services available to them.

Through this project we will improve the patient's experience, reduce their reliance on hospital services and needless admissions, promoting self care and self management.

Manufacturing compelling need

We live in changing times. Customers expect us to deliver our products faster with more demanding quality standards than we have done in the past. Our ability to respond to this challenge will determine our success in the future. Rising to this challenge will secure our existing customers and open up opportunities with new customers and markets.

We have already embarked on a wide-ranging Lean programme within our operational processes that has been extremely successful and will now be rolling this out across the group over the next 12 months.

Through creating this picture of where the business is going we hope to be able to create a better business; better for customers (so we retain them and find new ones), better for staff (more opportunities for development and better working conditions) and better for our local community.

Measures of success

This is identical to that found in the A3 PDCA template and should contain targets that the team should aim to achieve in each of the key measurement areas relevant to the project.

Fixed points, risks and issues

This section contains information on three important aspects that traditionally affect the success of projects.

The first is a definition of the 'fixed points', sometimes referred to as 'constraints'. These are the things that cannot or must not change during the process. For example, fixed points from real projects include:

- We cannot increase costs except where there is a corresponding and realistic pay-back that can be realized within six months.

- We must use the existing IT systems.

- We cannot change the contractual terms for our staff.

- We must not increase the risk or workload unfairly for any individual.

- We cannot impose changes on departments that are outside the scope of the project and are therefore not involved in the process.

There is an argument that I sometimes get presented with in that the existence of fixed points limits the creativity of a team, but my counter to that is based on the fact that teams without these fixed points are in danger of identifying solutions that are unaffordable, unsafe or simply unrealistic.

The second part of this section lists the risks that could be anticipated and also details what needs to be done to minimize the risk of them occurring or the problems caused if they do arise. The final part of this section is to identify the other issues that are going on that might affect the success of the project. This includes things such as the introduction of new technology, new products or new services, or the removal of them. It will also include changes to operating practices, new policies and expected acquisitions or disposals within the business. The aim of this is to minimize the risk of being half-way through a project and then realizing that a major issue has happened that means you either have to stop or even abandon the work done to date.

Current or initial state

This is the same as the A3 PDCA *current state* section above and contains statistics, measures, charts and key data about the current process.

Expected future state

This is the same as the A3 PDCA *future state* section and outlines the major improvements and changes you are going to introduce.

Team roles

This section outlines the key roles needed in the project and also outlines who else will be 'in scope', meaning whether or not they will participate. The groups listed in this section are:

- *Senior sponsors* – the senior managers or directors who will champion the project, who will sign off the A3 and will be the board level supporter for what you are trying to achieve.

- *Change agents* – these are the Lean team or other change agents who will lead/facilitate the project.

- *Core team members* – this is a list of everyone else involved along with the roles they will undertake (for example, being the day-to-day project manager) if they have a specific role.

Implementation plan

A self-explanatory section that contains the details of the main actions needed to implement the future state for the process.

Confirmed state

This is identical to the A3 PDCA 'confirmation of future state' section and is about confirming that the future state you have implemented has delivered what you had expected without introducing anything unexpected.

Reflections and lessons learnt

This final section is used to capture information about what you have learnt, enjoyed, disliked and would do differently next time related to the process you have been through, so that you improve on it each time you do a project. A part-completed A3 template is shown in Figure 3.6.

What Figure 3.6 highlights is that A3s are not just done and then forgotten but are living documents that grow and evolve over time, with sections that are not yet complete flagged as 'No Go'.

Project charters and project initiation documents

In project management terminology, the terms 'project charter' and 'project initiation document' normally refer to the same document. This document is issued by the project team and formally authorizes the project manager and project team to use organizational resources to tackle the project. Although both the terms project charter and project initiation document are traditionally interchangeable terms, I will use the term *project initiation document* (PID) throughout.

The PID bundles together information that might previously have existed in separate documents with titles such as 'business case', 'Terms of reference' and the organization's 'risk register'. The PID exists in a number of different formats and this reflects the needs of different organizations so I would treat this section as a framework that you can adapt to meet your own requirements. In Lean projects I would always aim to use A3s first, and only for the largest projects would consider using a PID, where either of the two A3 formats don't fit the bill because of the amount of information required for the project.

Structuring a PID

The most commonly found section headings within a PID are shown below.

FIGURE 3.6 A part-completed A3 template

A3 Title: Single Point of Access & Rapid Response Services | Start Date: Jan XX — A3 Last Updated: April XX | Target Completion Date: Dec XX

Compelling Need For Action [Go | No Go]

Our aim is to provide effective care to patients and to our partner organizations. To enable us to achieve this effectively we are establishing a Single Point of Access (SPA) for new referrals for Adults & Older People that will reduce duplication of effort, improve accessibility and enable us to support the delivery of the Out of Hospital Strategy. The SPA will operate 9-5 M-F and allied to this will be a 24/7 Rapid Response Service that will ensure patients can access the right clinician within 2 hours of a need being reported. Through this programme we aim to deliver a service that reduces risk to patients, improves the productivity of staff and enables us to achieve our commissioned targets. The first phase of the programme will be complete by Dec XX.

Current or Initial State [Go | No Go]

- <25% of services currently achieve 2 hour response target
- 0% of patients receive clinical triage within 20 minutes
- Approx 35% of referrals arrive in the wrong setting
- Approx 450 hrs/wk wasted in dealing with referral related issues
- Approx 1,100 patients are admitted into our two local hospitals who could have been treated in a community setting, costing (£TBD) to the local health economy

Finalize at Value Stream Mapping Event.

Implementation Plan: [Go | No Go]

Action	Owner	Status	Notes
Gather baseline data	XX	Complete	
Value Stream Mapping	XX	Date Set	Occurring 7th July
Identify team & skills gap needs	XX	TBD	
Finalize implementation plan	XX	TBD	After VSE

Measures of Success [Go | No Go]

Measure	Change Required	Notes & Issues
80% of call clinically triaged within 20 minutes	+80%	Sampling identified that this was achieved 0% of the time
100% of referrals to reach the appropriate service 1st time	+65%	A sample of 165 referrals found that 35% are duplicated or did not reach the right service first time
90% of patients with an identified clinical need to be responded to within 2 hours	Currently <25%	
Improve our goal attainment score	From 60% to 85%	

Expected Future State [Go | No Go]

This project consists of two main phases:

Phase 1 – Establish interim SPA/RRS service to cover CQUIN requirements. This service will run from Dec XX – Aug YY.

Phase 2 – Establish formal referral pathways and identify sustainable funding for the service running from Aug YY onwards.

This section to be finalized at Value Stream Mapping Event.

Confirmed State [Go | No Go]

New Performance Level	Confirmation State (RAG)	Notes & Actions

Fixed Points, Risks & Issues [Go | No Go]

Issues	Controlling Action Required
Budgets are fixed	N/a
We need to address skill mix	Skills plan to be created
Sustainability after Year 1	Plan for how cash can be released to support SPA/RRS for Year 2 and beyond
Need for consistency and an understanding of current service profile	We need to understand what the current pathways are for referrals and to understand our directory of services

Team Roles [Go | No Go]

Senior Sponsors	Name
Change Agents	Name, Name
Core Team Members	Name
	Name
	Name
	Name

Reflections & Lessons Learnt [Go | No Go]

People	Process
Quality	Innovation
Productivity	Prevention

Problem statement

This is equivalent to the 'compelling need' and 'current state' sections found in A3s and is a concise description of the problem, along with key statistics, graphs and other essential information about the performance of the processes currently. The length of the 'problem background' will vary based on the size of the problem you are trying to tackle and can vary from about a paragraph to several pages or more in length. Three short examples of problem statements are provided below:

- We have been experiencing high levels of rework in Cell X. This has increased our expenditure on overtime and is causing us problems with the ability to deliver 'on time and in full'. We must bring the rework rates back down to the acceptable level within the next four weeks.

- Over the last 12 months we have admitted 5,200 older people (defined as people over 75) through our emergency department (ED) and assessment units. Initial analysis of the reasons for these admissions shows that nearly 1,400 of these admissions could have been avoided had action been taken prior to admission.

- Complaints are currently tying up our customer services team. Last month we had 25 complaints and investigating these involved nearly 220 hours of time. Of the 25 complaints only two of them required any further action beyond the options available to the customer services team. We believe that we can save over 100 hours per month by redesigning the way that complaints are dealt with.

Measures of success

This is identical to the 'measures of success' section found in A3s. It is also sometimes referred to in PIDs as 'goals'.

Scope

This defines what areas/departments/functions are 'in scope' and which are 'out of scope' with regards to the project.

Business case

This section contains details of the expected return on investment for the project or details of the rationale for the project if the return is not purely financial.

Risk analysis

This identifies all of the risks associated with the project and what you might need to do to reduce the risk of them arising or reduce the impact of them if they do arise.

Constraints and assumptions

This is equivalent to the 'fixed points' and 'issues' sections of A3s and covers the boundaries of the things that cannot be done or must not change along with any assumptions that are made about the project.

Stakeholders

This section lists all major stakeholder groups (these being groups of people with an interest in the project or who will be affected by it) and outlines how they will be involved, communicated with or otherwise interacted with through the project.

Organization

This covers the names and roles of key individuals in the project such as the project sponsor, Lean team, project manager, etc.

Project plan

This final section of PIDs is identical to the 'implementation plan' seen in A3s and contains the expected project activities and completion dates.

There are three major differences between PIDs and A3s and these are:

1 PIDs are typically used for larger projects, where having an A3 would not provide sufficient space for all of the information.

2 PIDs are normally produced by one or two people and sent round to a wider audience for comment, unlike an A3 that is normally populated at a scoping session involving a wide range of people with an interest in the project.

3 PIDs often become more static documents, in that they are produced once and then not updated frequently, whereas the A3 is much easier to update.

The 'problem statement' part of scoping typically consists of two distinct parts. The first is concerned with providing a concise and factual description to the background to the project/problem. The second provides a statement of the compelling need for change.

The practicalities of scoping

There are two main ways that scoping might occur. The first is to hold a scoping session where a group of people work together to create a first pass scoping paper (whether that is an A3 or PID). The second approach is to have the document created by one or two people and then send around to a group on a 'round robin' where everyone comments on the document before it is finally signed off as ready to go. The time required to prepare the scoping paper is significantly less in the case of a scoping session (even if the session is followed up by sending round the draft scoping paper to everyone interested after the event) than the second approach. However, scoping sessions are difficult to organize, given that they need representation from people with an input into the project, making it logistically easier to organize the second approach of having the document created by a few people and sent round.

I will outline how each of these two approaches might occur in practice.

Running scoping sessions

A scoping session typically lasts two or three hours and is a structured way of planning a Lean project. The outcome of the session is normally a part-completed A3, although less commonly you will find PIDs being used instead. The purpose of a scoping session is to ensure that the project has clear objectives, an identified team and an action plan. Scoping involves a cross-functional group that ideally includes representatives from across the organization, process or value stream that is the focus of the improvement process.

The success of the scoping session will depend on things done before and after it, as well as how effectively the actual scoping occurs. The three phases of a scoping session are therefore defined as:

- before the session;
- during the session;
- after the session.

The actions that need to occur in each of these phases are described below.

Before the scoping session

The activities that occur prior to a scoping session are predominantly logistical, for example identifying the participants, finding a venue, setting dates/times, gathering background data about the project, etc. There are two specific activities that should occur that will affect the success of the scoping session, namely: 1) identify the senior sponsor who will attend the session; 2) help the senior sponsor to prepare a short opening statement that will ideally be given by the sponsor and that outlines the importance of the project, what the sponsor wants from the project and the key areas they want people to focus on during the project.

During the scoping session

On a practical level I have found that scoping sessions need a good two to three (or more) hours to get the best from them. You might therefore need to break the sessions into two or more 'chunks' if the team cannot participate for the whole period.

The agenda for a scoping session designed to complete an A3 as outlined earlier in this chapter is shown in Table 3.2, along with some comments about duration and issues to be aware of during each part.

Another area to consider is to identify different 'scenarios' that need to be considered. We will discuss this in more detail when we discuss value stream mapping, but scenarios are different conditions/events that could happen through the process that you are looking at. In Chapter 2 when we were discussing the Lean principles I mentioned the terms runners, repeaters and strangers. Nearly all processes will have a mix of different things that will happen every day (runners);

TABLE 3.2   Overview of a scoping session agenda

Agenda item	Description	Points to watch out for
Opening statement	This is a short (5–10 minute) overview of the issue/project and is given by the sponsor or given on their behalf.	
Open discussion	I have found it useful to allow time for an open discussion so that people can highlight their concerns about the project, the things they'd like to change and anything else relevant.	Don't allow the team to go off track moaning about things they cannot change. Also, keep them focused on what can be done in the project rather than focus on what won't be possible.
Develop the compelling need	Create an inspiring statement that details why this project must happen.	It is unlikely you will get a statement that everyone agrees on. If so, it is better to get down the points that people want included in it and then to draft it later based on their feedback.
Identify the measures of success	Outline 3–7 critical measures of success and try to put down targets for improvement against each measure.	You will find that for many measures of success that you won't know what the current performance is. Don't let this stop you putting targets for improvement against each measure as you can always find out what the baseline is later. For example, a 30% improvement target gives you something to aim at even if you don't know what the baseline is during the session.

TABLE 3.2   *continued*

Agenda item	Description	Points to watch out for
Outline who is 'in scope'	Detail which areas (and individuals) are going to be involved in the project and try to identify how much time they will need to contribute.	
Identify the 'fixed points'	Identify the things that cannot change or must not change in order to provide your team with some boundaries of what they can and cannot do.	A lot of these will be fairly obvious. For example, 'We must not increase costs', but it is worth ensuring you have them all captured.
Identify the risks	Identify any risks to the programme and the corresponding controls.	Ensure you identify the tasks that need to be done to control each risk.
Identify the 'issues'	Identify other activities that might affect this programme.	Often people skip this bit and then suffer later on.
Identify 'key roles'	Identify those who will lead and facilitate the programme.	
Set out your 'implementation plan'	Set out the plan for activities associated with the project.	It is likely your initial implementation plan will be quite sparsely populated.
Fix your communications strategy	Identify how the scoping paper will be communicated.	Agree what will happen after the session and how it will be communicated to everyone with an interest.

TABLE 3.3   Example runners, repeaters and strangers for three different environments

	Health care emergency department (ED)	Manufacturing flow line (food production)	Call centre helpline
Example runner	Minor fracture	Production line runs normally	Minor enquiry taking 5 minutes
Example repeater	Myocardial infarction	Minor equipment stoppage (<5 mins)	Extended enquiry requiring >10 minutes
Example stranger	Puerperal psychosis	Foreign object found in raw materials	Complaint

frequently but not necessarily every day (repeaters); things that occur at more random intervals (strangers).

Some example runners, repeaters and strangers for different settings are shown in Table 3.3.

To fully understand most processes you normally need to identify between 8 and 12 scenarios. We will discuss this more in the next chapter, but you may want to start thinking about scenarios at this point.

After the scoping session

Soon after you have completed the scoping session there are some tasks that need to be undertaken to get the ball rolling. These tasks include tidying up the scoping paper, distributing it for comment and then incorporating the comments that you get back, gathering any data, getting the document signed off as correct by the sponsor and, finally, planning for the first implementation activities.

Scoping on a 'round robin'

The alternative approach to holding a scoping session involves a very small group (often just one person) producing a paper to send to others for them to consider. Sometimes this is sent to one person who then sends it to a second and so on, until it returns to the sender, and this is called a 'round robin'. There are four phases to this approach to scoping:

- gathering background data;
- preparing the document;
- sending for comment;
- finalizing and signing off the document.

Each of these phases is described below.

Gathering background data

This is where the team preparing the scoping paper seek evidence and data related to the project. Sometimes this involves gathering feedback from stakeholders (those with an interest in the project) and it might help to send short questionnaires that tells them about the proposed project and asks four questions:

- What do you feel works well currently?
- What do you feel doesn't work well?
- What things would you like to see changed?
- What other things would you like to tell us?

Having gathered the data you will then be ready to prepare the document.

Preparing the document

As this approach to scoping is normally appropriate for PIDs you should prepare a document that follows the PID format described earlier in this chapter.

Sending for comment

This is where the timescales and effort for this section really start to diverge from a scoping session. Sending the document out for comments will normally result in an iterative process that will see you continuously chasing people for responses, editing the document to incorporate changes and then sending the document out again. I would recommend that you give people deadlines to respond to you by with their comments.

Finalizing and signing off the document

Once you feel the document is complete, you will need to finalize it and send it to the sponsor to get it signed off. Once signed off you will need to finally communicate it to the team and get on with planning the implementation actions.

Scoping case study

Towards the end of each of Chapters 3, 4, 5 and 6 I have provided at least one short 'warts and all' case study. These are provided to help you see how these different types of Lean activities are structured and to provide an overview of the types of issues that arise in practice. In this chapter I provide an example of a scoping session, starting with a snapshot of the session in Table 3.4.

TABLE 3.4   Scoping session snapshot

Scoping session snapshot

The organization: manufacturing plant (investment casting) located in Italy. Part of a larger group spread around the world.

Duration of session: 2.5 hours.

Present at session: Group Chief Operating Officer, site MD, Lean Manager, Plant Director, Head of Quality, two Production Supervisors, Procurement Manager, Auditor, Financial Manager.

Focus of scoping session: preparation prior to value stream mapping event covering the whole of production from order receipt, through the manufacturing and assembly stages, quality and testing and finishing at the despatch of goods.

Prior to the scoping session

The client had already created a *transformation map* (something you will come across in Chapter 9) for the group and a number of the manufacturing plants had also created a site-level transformation map. The Italian site was the first to progress beyond the planning stage with their Lean activities, with the aim being to undertake a value stream mapping exercise. The decision was taken to look at the end-to-end process from order receipt to despatch, something that was made significantly easier by the fact that all products passed through the same sequence of process steps. Some further work was done to clarify the objectives for the plant and also to gather together information on expected changes in the market within which the organization operated. The team also calculated the *takt time* for the plant, something we will discuss further in Chapters 3 and 6.

During the scoping session

The Group Chief Operating Officer gave a short opening brief that outlined the importance of making changes within the plant and his expectations from the value stream mapping exercises. We then spent the first 20 minutes outlining the problems that the people in the room wanted to tackle with the aim of creating a 'Top 10 Hurts' list that summarized the major issues/opportunities for improvement.

Having done this, we then started to identify what everyone wanted to see in the 'compelling need' statement. The draft was created in the session and then ultimately refined after the event with the resulting summary being:

> Our competitors are able to deliver products 33 per cent faster than we are currently able to achieve. They also achieve this with lower operating costs. Historically this hasn't been a problem but with changing customer expectations in terms of lower costs and shorter lead times there is a pressing need for us to close this performance gap. Rising to this challenge will secure our existing customers and open up opportunities with new customers and markets.
>
> As part of the group's Lean programme we are embarking on a site-level programme to understand, plan and improve our operational

performance with the aim of both shortening lead times and reducing the costs, particularly the costs of rework. Our immediate aim is to create a future state for the business that will see us undergo radical changes over the next 12 months.

Through creating this picture of where the business is going we hope to be able to create a better business: better for customers (so we retain them and find new ones), better for staff (more opportunities for development and better working conditions) and better for our local community.

Having spent some time on the compelling need we then worked through the measure of success for the project. It is normal for people not to know what their current performance is against some of the measures. For example, we identified that there was a need to improve 'on-time delivery' to greater than 90 per cent but were unsure in the meeting of the actual performance 'today'. Overall, the team came up with five main objectives:

- Create a business capable of delivering 30 per cent EBITDA (earnings before interest, taxes, depreciation and amortization) on a turnover of $62 million (the group worked in US dollars hence the use by an Italian plant of a US currency).

- Improve on-time delivery from ? to >90 per cent.

- Reduce lead times by at least 30 per cent from ? to ?

- Reduce scrap rates from 4.5 per cent to 3 per cent.

- Exceed our health and safety obligations (measure to be improved).

The question marks in the measures above highlight where the team did not have the data to hand. We went on to discuss the fixed points (things that cannot change), risks (things that could go wrong) and issues (other things in the organization that affect this project). There is always some discussion about fixed points constraining creativity, but what they do is provide boundaries that prevent people developing solutions that cannot be implemented. In this case, there were only two fixed points that the team wanted, namely: 1) no additional expenditure without a corresponding (and very short-term) business case; 2) no increase in risk to staff, products or customers. The second fixed point might seem a bit strange, but by having it there you can test whether your *value stream map* (VSM) future state is safer than your current state.

Two further activities were undertaken in the session. The first was to identify the team (including the sponsor who was the site MD); the second involved identifying different scenarios for the actual value stream map. In total, we identified 12 scenarios for products that covered all of the major product groups, different clients, the development of new products and rework. These scenarios can be summarized as:

- Four runners (commonly occurring) products where we did not anticipate experiencing rework.

- Two runners where there was frequently rework involved.

- Two repeater scenarios concerning the development of two different products.

- Two repeaters for complex products that arose in medium to low volume.

- Two strangers in terms of complex, low volume products.

It was felt that these 12 scenarios would give us the best understanding of the organizational processes.

After the scoping session

Afterwards, we had to write up the A3 and confirm the baseline for the measures of success where the data was not available at the time of the scoping session. We also sent this to all managers and supervisors for them to comment on and discuss with their teams.

Key learning points

We could have done with better customer input into the session. The marketing team had done some research on the market and had spoken to customers but all the team had was the data and not the comments from customers (both existing customers and ones that had been lost). We also spent a lot of time discussing scenarios, and that put a time pressure on the whole session. We could have (in this organization) identified the scenarios either before or after the event.

Tactics for making scoping easier

In the last part of this chapter I offer four tactics that I have found useful in managing a wide variety of Lean programmes.

Screen projects

This is a problem that often affects larger organizations in that they start to identify more projects than their Lean team can tackle. The problem is that the limited resources normally available find themselves stretched too thinly to support any of the projects effectively. It is therefore useful to consider screening projects before you even start scoping them. You might measure each project against five criteria to help you with this such as:

- Does the project align with the organization's objectives?
- Is the project going to deliver benefits that are worth the time investment?
- Has the project got the active support of senior managers?
- Are the team who proposed this project committed to supporting/delivering it?
- Is the project free of financial and operational limitations that would prevent successful delivery?

Only if you have answered 'yes' to at least four out of these five questions would you then go on to scope the project.

Put deadlines on communications

A more tactical action than the one above is to ensure that whenever you send information to people you make it very clear when you are expecting to receive a response from them.

Don't let the fact you can't do everything stop you doing anything

It will sometimes feel like you won't be able to achieve anything because of the wide range of constraints, issues, risks and problems that affect most projects. Always look for the things that you can do rather than becoming stressed by the things that you are genuinely unable to do.

Invite comment (but don't expect much)

It is always a good idea to seek input to your scoping paper and I would urge you to seek comment from as many stakeholders as reasonably possible. However, I wouldn't hold out for too many responses but at least you cannot be blamed with not having communicated with people.

Closing thoughts

For some reason, inappropriate amounts of effort are often put into scoping projects. Sometimes people move from discussion into action without being clear about the objectives and risks, and at other times the amount of effort put into scoping is disproportionate to the expected benefit. However, I would say that it is more likely that scoping will be underdone rather than overcooked. If you scope a project badly then don't expect the resulting project to be the success you are looking for.

In the next chapter I explore the concepts of value stream mapping (VSM). If you have scoped a large-scale project then VSM will often be the next logical step. However, for smaller projects you might be more interested in 2P/3P events (covered in Chapter 5) or even a rapid improvement event (Chapter 6).

Value stream mapping events

04

In this chapter I aim to answer the following questions:

1 What is a value stream mapping (VSM) event?

2 How do you go about undertaking a VSM event?

3 How do you turn a VSM into an implementation plan?

4 What are the alternatives to traditional VSM?

Value stream mapping (VSM) is one of the most useful tools for understanding and improving larger processes such as end-to-end processes that cover one or more organizations. For example, an orthopaedic pathway from the point of an initial GP referral through surgery until the point that the patient is back home, or a manufacturing process from initial order receipt through to despatch of goods, or any similar sized pathway in any other sector. VSM can be used for smaller processes that span only one or two departments within an organization, but as the size of the process under investigation reduces the cost/benefit of VSM drops as well.

There are a number of different ways of undertaking a VSM event (this being where people come together for the purposes of creating a *value stream map*) and the three most common approaches are outlined in this chapter. These are: three-stage value stream mapping with process analysis, two-stage value stream mapping with symbols, and value stream mapping with swimlanes. Of the three, my preference is the first of these. I have also outlined an approach called vertical value streams, which is used to help plan out a project or to map the implementation of a new process when no process currently exists. It is not therefore a VSM approach in the traditional sense but is very similar, hence why it makes an appearance in this chapter. One further variation of VSM, *enterprise-level value stream mapping* (ELVSM), which is used to get a very high-level picture of an entire organization, will make a brief appearance in Chapter 9.

Key concepts in value stream mapping

VSM is a technique that is used to map out, understand and redesign information, people and product flows. When done correctly it is very powerful and is a great way of getting groups of people to understand why processes are not as effective as they could be and to work together to improve them. A VSM event typically aims to achieve three things:

1 To understand how current processes work (called *current state* analysis or 'as is').

2 To create an improved plan of how the process will work (called *future state* or 'to be').

3 To develop the implementation plan that will take you from the current state to the future state.

A full VSM event is not applicable to every situation, being more suited to larger processes, although you will often find that even the smallest of processes could use some of the tools we will discover when we look at current state mapping. To understand a process fully you often cannot just map the most commonly occurring activities and this introduces an important aspect of scenarios that I will cover in the next section.

Scenarios

Very few processes in organizations are involved in just doing one repeatable activity without variation, and indeed no process anywhere is exempt from variations to a 'norm'. For example, even in a bottling plant where the only job is to fill milk bottles, the plant will experience episodes of stock shortages, equipment breakdown, mispours and other scenarios that mean that very few days are completely alike. Without understanding these variations in activity within a process we will not be able to create a realistic future state. Each of these variations provide us with a different scenario and, as a rule of thumb, you need to identify somewhere between 8 and 12 scenarios for most processes to give you a good understanding of how a process really works.

Scenarios come in three flavours, as we discussed in Chapter 2 when looking at the second principle of Lean. These are:

- Runners – everyday or very common activities that form the bulk of activities within a process.

- Repeaters – frequent but not necessarily everyday activities that form the second largest group of activities.

- Strangers – things that come up or happen on odd occasions and form only a minority of activity.

There is a tendency for people to believe that strangers form a bigger part of the workload than they do in reality. This is because they re-member stranger activities more easily than 'normal' activities. For example, very few of us remember the many journeys to work that were uneventful but we will remember the one day when the road was blocked because an unoccupied car was crushed by a falling tree. Another common problem is for people to say that there is no repeat-ability in their process, something very common in environments such as law, health care, call centres, project planning departments or even bespoke manufacturing companies where the response is normally given as, 'Every client/patient/call/project/order is different.' Even here you will find that there is a lot of commonality between events, with the bulk of calls (for example) being ones that take be-tween 5 and 10 minutes to resolve without any further action being required (runners); a smaller number that require some investigation (repeaters); a small number that cannot be resolved without a call back (strangers). We are not looking for exactly similar scenarios just groups of like events. Some example runners, repeaters and strangers for different sectors are shown in Table 3.3 (page 77).

Understanding process symbols

Irrespective of the route you take in your VSM event you will encounter the need for symbols at some point. Symbols are not meant to be stressful to use but to provide a shorthand way of representing lots of steps. Once you have learnt the symbols you will find that you should be able to read anyone's value stream maps, irrespective of the sector or even the language. Of course, you might not understand the fine detail but you will be able to see what is going on. The use of symbols can be stressful for some people who are used to using words to describe activities and I will return to this point later in this chapter. For now, I want to introduce you to the most commonly used symbols, as shown in Figure 4.1. This is not meant to be a definitive list but consists of the 18 most common symbols. Later in this chapter you will see some examples of the symbols being used in maps.

Kaizen burst

This is a way of showing the presence of a great idea. The idea is written inside the kaizen burst.

Input or output

This symbol is used to indicate the start (inputs) or end (outputs) of a process. It is meant to represent a factory building but could apply

FIGURE 4.1   Common VSM symbols

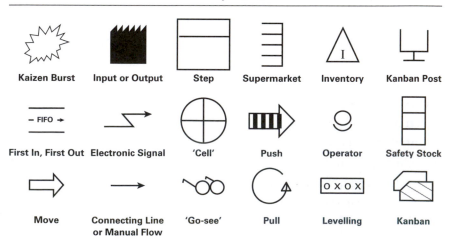

to a patient located at home, the receipt of an e-mail, a referral letter, materials being delivered, or anything else that triggers either the start of the process you are looking at or the end.

Step

This is used for details of a specific step in a process. The top half of the box should be labelled with the name of the step and the bottom part used to put in any additional details such as number of operators (or staff), and stock held, etc.

Supermarket

Used to indicate a stack of parts, people or information that is controlled in some way. For example, a queue of people waiting to be seen by a GP, raw materials arriving at a plant and being held in stores, or people waiting in a managed telephone-queuing system.

Inventory

This is similar to a *supermarket* but normally means stock that is held without being controlled or managed. For example, excess production held between stages, referral letters pending action or passport applications received but not processed.

First in, first out (FIFO)

This indicates that the first person or part arriving at this step will be the first person seen or dealt with. We see this in queues at cinemas and amusement parks but also in areas such as triage in health care or in dealing with customers at the till in a retail environment.

Electronic signal

This indicates, via a lightning flash, that information has been sent from one device to another, for example an e-mail sent from one person to another or data entered into a computer that then backs it on to a remote server.

Cell

A *cell* is simply a group of workplaces that are designed to deliver a product or service. For example, you could say that a reception desk is a cell as it is designed to deliver a service, or a pathology team are a cell because they are designed to deliver a pathology service, etc. It originated in manufacturing, where cells consisted of all of the elements required to build one or a range of related products, including all manufacturing, machining, inspection, assembly and test activities.

Controversially I have shown this with a non-standard symbol. The traditional symbols for cells are U-shaped, T-shaped or L-shaped (because the traditional manufacturing cells would be shaped this way). However, for office-based, virtual or service sector cells these symbols do not mean anything because the cell will rarely be formed into this shape. Hence I have proposed this non-standard symbol, which I have found useful in my work.

Not all cells are Lean cells because a Lean cell will have the elements of *flow*, *pull*, *standard work* and *visual management* (5S). The first two of these were discussed in Chapter 2 and the last two will be discussed in more detail in Chapter 6.

One way to help you think about the relationship between 'steps' and 'cells' is that a cell combines together a range of different steps. For example, the steps 'receive, process, log, confirm and despatch' could be combined into a cell called 'admin team'. Cells are a shorthand way of showing lots of steps.

Push

This indicates when parts, information or people are moved forward to the next stage before the next stage is ready to deal with them.

Pull

The counterbalance to push is pull. The pull is also sometimes referred to as 'withdrawal' or as a *kanban* although an actual physical kanban that is normally a signal, ticket or other visual trigger has its own symbol. Pull indicates that material, people or information is drawn when required.

To emphasize the difference between push and pull consider the following: a person arrives at desk A and is told to go to desk B – this is push; a person arrives at desk A and is told to wait until they are called by desk B – this is pull.

Operator

This is the symbol for someone doing any type of work. This is commonly found in manufacturing environments where it is used to show how many operators are working in a process and how they might be arranged in a working pattern. It is rarely found outside of manufacturing, except where depiction of the physical location of individuals helps, such as a servicing group, theatre team, pit teams in motor racing, etc.

Move

An arrow used to show when something has been moved. Sometimes this is accompanied by a picture of a lorry, trolley, foot, plane, etc, in order to show how the item was moved.

Connecting line/manual flow

Sometimes you need to connect different points on a map without wanting to show whether it was by push or pull: for this you would use a simple connecting line. You can also use this in conjunction with a push/pull symbol where the two points being joined are a long way apart. You would first connect the points with a connecting line and then draw above or below it the relevant push/pull symbol to show how information/items are exchanged between the points.

Go-see

Go-see is concerned with a physical inspection activity where someone 'goes to see' a person or product to determine its state. For example, a GP home visit to see a patient, an inspector going to see a part in production, or even a random visit by a mystery shopper to 'go see' how a team are doing would all use this symbol.

Levelling

This symbol is closely associated with the concept of *heijunka* and indicates that the activity undertaken by that part of the process has been levelled to avoid large variations in demand or activity (more information on heijunka can be found in Chapter 13).

Safety stock

This indicates material of any kind that is held as a 'buffer' to prevent a process running out of stock.

Kanban

More details about *kanban*, which is synonymous with the ideas of pull, can be found in Chapter 13. There are two different kanban symbols used here. The plain version indicates a 'production kanban', this being a card or device that tells someone to 'produce' something, for example producing a defined amount of stock, or ordering a defined amount of replacement consumables. The second image, with the hatched lines, shows a 'withdrawal kanban' that instructs someone to move something from one place to another, for example instructing someone to 'go to stores shelf A and return with five parts'.

Kanban post

This final symbol indicates the location or place where *kanban* cards are stored.

Key terminology

Before we get into understanding how to run a VSM event there is some additional terminology that we need to explore.

Takt time

A key measure used to assess activity is the *takt time*, which originates from Germany in the work done by a conductor to regulate the speed, beat or timing of an orchestra. Takt time determines the 'pace' of a process in terms of how frequently you are asked to do work. It is calculated by taking the available time and dividing it by the number of 'demands' that arise in this period as I will illustrate:

- In a call centre there are 30 calls between 8am and 10am, therefore the takt time is calculated as available time/demand = 120 minutes/30 calls = 4 minutes.
- In an emergency department there are eight patients who attend between 11am and 12pm and the takt time is therefore 60 minutes/8 patients = 7.5 minutes.

- In a manufacturing plant a production cell receives 240 orders over a typical 40-hour week (2,400 minutes) and the takt time is therefore 2,400 minutes/240 orders = 10 minutes.

Takt time can also be used as the basis for working out how many people you might need for a process, as you will find when we look at standard work in Chapter 6.

Data tickets

There is also a need in VSM events to add data to steps in the process. This is often achieved using data tickets. These can be designed to include any relevant information; in Figure 4.2 I have included an example you might use in manufacturing (a) and another for a service sector organization (b).

FIGURE 4.2 Example manufacturing data ticket (a) and the same for a service environment (b)

a

STEP/s	
Cycle Time	
Manual Cycle Time	
Machine Cycle Time	
Changeover Time	
Up-Time	
% Right 1st Time	
Problems/Notes	

b

STEP/s	
Lead Time	
Manual Cycle Time	
Waiting Time	
% Right 1st Time	
Problems/Notes	

Cycle time

Cycle time is the length of time that it takes an average item or product to complete a step or number of steps. Taking two steps of a process as an example: 1) cut out item (30 minutes); 2) assemble item (60 minutes), then the cycle time for cutting out is 30 minutes from the start to the end of the process (including all set-up activities and any in-process delays) and the cycle time of assembly is 60 minutes. The cycle time for the total cutting out and assembly process is 90 minutes.

That is an easy example but imagine that there were 10 different machines available for assembling the item (and assuming each can only do one part at a time) then the average time taken to complete the assembly stage would drop to 6 minutes (time/number of machines), meaning that the cycle time for the two steps would drop from 90 minutes to 36 minutes (30 minutes for cut out and an average of 6 minutes for assembly).

Cycle time is directly related to the output rate of a process and defines the average time between successive items being completed. So if I complete 4 items per hour then the cycle time is 15 minutes. Cycle time is measured in 'time per activity' using measures such as minutes/customer or hours/part and it is therefore not the same as *lead time*, which is measured using 'elapsed time'.

Lead time

This is the total elapsed time (including all delays, set-up times and waiting) from the start to the end of a process for an individual item. For example, the total elapsed time from the receipt of an order until the item is despatched, or the time taken from receipt of a request for a new licence to when the licence is issued.

Returning to my example used to describe cycle time, and the two steps of cut out and assemble, we can now imagine the whole process consists of the following: wait to start, 45 minutes; cut out item, 30 minutes; assemble item, 60 minutes; wait to end, 45 minutes. The lead time is therefore 180 minutes (45 + 30 + 60 + 45), this being the total elapsed time from the start of the process to the end of it. It doesn't matter how many machines there are at the 'assemble item' stage as the lead time for an individual item would still be 180 minutes.

Lead time is also sometimes referred to as 'throughput time' but is clearly not the same as cycle time.

Manual cycle time

This defines how much work is required to be undertaken by people during one cycle of an activity. For example, the amount of time required to process one blood test result, deal with one call or build one product. Sometimes this is referred to as either 'touch time' or 'processing time', although technically processing time also includes all 'machine cycle time' as well.

Machine cycle time

This defines the amount of time needed by machines to process parts.

Waiting time

The amount of time spent by a product, person or information waiting for something to happen.

Up-time

The amount of time spent by machines working as opposed to being stopped due to breakdowns, maintenance or changeovers. This is normally stated as a percentage of the total time available.

Changeover time

Time lost due to a changeover from one job to the next. This is something related to *SMED* (Single Minute Exchange of Die) that we will discuss in Chapter 13.

Per cent right first time (%RFT)

This details the rework rate for a process or part of a process. For example, if I receive 100 items and 5 of them have problems then my *%RFT* is 95 per cent. This is not the same as how many come out of the process correct 'in the end' but how many experience problems. The reason this is an important distinction is that it often has a big impact on the manual cycle time where a five-minute job on something that occurs 'right first time' could increase to several hours if a problem occurs.

Problem/notes section

The last part of the data ticket is used to record details of the major problems that occur with that process.

Armed with this background knowledge we are now ready to review the different approaches to running VSM events.

Three-stage value stream mapping

As I briefly mentioned earlier this is my preferred method of under-taking a VSM event as I have found it easier to incorporate different scenarios into the *current state*. It is less daunting when working with a group of individuals who are unfamiliar with mapping as it provides a very logical format for mapping processes. The introduction of a *blue sky* or *ideal state*, the key differentiator between the two-step and three-step approach to VSM, enables the team to develop creative solutions to complex problems before getting bogged down in the reality and limitations of a realistic *future state*.

The three steps of this approach to VSM are:

- understand the *current state*;
- create a *blue sky diagram*;
- develop a realistic *future state*.

However, before exploring each of these three steps I will first outline the actions that need to occur prior to undertaking a VSM event.

Prior to the VSM event

In the weeks leading up to a VSM event there are a number of things that should be done to ensure the success of the event. One of the most important tasks is to complete an A3 or similar planning document, as outlined in Chapter 3. This will also require you to collect the data that will support the baseline measures and ensure that the right team are available to participate in the VSM event and that they have the right skills.

In addition, it is useful for the person leading the VSM event to have walked the process that is being looked at prior to the session and to obtain examples of all of the different types of paperwork and records used so that they are available during the VSM event.

Understanding the current state (current state analysis)

Analysis of the current state (or 'as is' process) is concerned with getting teams to understand what is really going on in a process. What I have discovered is that everyone knows their own job well and they 'guess' or believe they know what other people do. Current state analysis is concerned with ensuring everyone has a clear understanding of what really is going on, and can take anything up to two days to do properly, depending on the size of the process you are working on.

When we look at the two-stage approach to VSM I will show how you can go straight into using the symbols introduced earlier for current state, but for now I want to show how you would use the tools of process analysis to understand what is going on currently.

There are a couple of rules of thumb that you will find useful when doing any form of VSM. The first is to always aim to work in groups of no more than four to six when doing current state analysis (and for creating the future state that we will see later). That means if you have 20 people you break them into four groups of five and you organize it so they are mapping different scenarios or different parts of the process. The reason for this is that larger groups result in people standing around not feeling involved and also get bogged down in (often pointless) discussion. The second rule of thumb is that you should aim to map every process, irrespective of length, using between 50 and 100 steps. Less than 50 steps and you will find that you are struggling to see what the problems are and with more than 100 you will be overwhelmed with data. This means that the size of the steps will vary depending on the length of the process. For a process lasting a year each step would represent one to four days of activity, whilst for one lasting a minute each step would represent one to two seconds of activity.

Obviously, before you get to the VSM event stage you will have already scoped the process (Chapter 2) and you should have available copies of the A3 or the project documentation you have created, along with the data to support the measures of success and other related paperwork. Having got this together we can go through the relevant steps of current state analysis.

Opening brief

It is always beneficial to get a senior sponsor, director or manager to open a session and remind people of why they are there and what the aims are. I would be careful about allowing lots of questions for the sponsor here if you expect the group to be negative or difficult (I am a pragmatist, remember) as it can cause problems with the morale of the group.

Refresher training

It is advisable to have done some training with participants before the event so that they understand the difference between value and waste and some of the tools. Irrespective of any pre-event training you should do a refresher session and use this to explain the process you are going to go through and outline how teams will work together.

Current state mapping

The teams should map the process aiming to get between 50 to 100 steps. At this stage they just need to write the description rather than worry about the symbols (hence why teams new to this find it easier). They should map one scenario at a time starting with the most common runner. It is common that you will reach a step and people will say, 'Well, depending on the scenario either this or that could happen,' hence my advice to only map one scenario at a time. Even then you will still encounter situations where it could go one way or another and at this point I say that you should always map the most likely route.

One thing you will encounter frequently in mapping the current state is what I call 'psychic jumps' where people skip over a large number of steps, for example:

- Step 1 – order received;
- Step 2 – production starts.

This may look correct until you realize that the actual process is really:

- Step 1 – order received;
  - step 1a – order picked up by sales team;
  - step 1b – order entered into planning system;
  - step 1c – confirmation sent back to customer;
  - step 1d – order sent to planning team;
  - step 1e – planner schedules production;
  - step 1f – planner launches order;
  - step 1g – order received in production;

   – step 1h – order kitted by supervisor;

   – step 1i – kit of parts taken to production team;

- Step 2 – production starts.

Therefore, in the first example, the team have had a psychic jump that has missed nine intervening steps and made it more likely that they will not see where the problems really are. It is fair to say that it is impossible to avoid psychic jumps without thousands of steps, for example we can see that between steps 1h and 1i we could add a further set of steps involved in the actual kitting, movement of the supervisor, etc, that would pad it out even further. The art of this is being sensible and I have found that teams generally find the right level of detail, although at the end of this chapter I will give you some hints about how to spot when they have got it wrong.

   Having completed one scenario, you can then add the steps that are different for a second and all subsequent scenarios. It is better if you differentiate each scenario, perhaps by using different coloured pens or different coloured sticky notes, but by adding scenarios to your runner means you do not have to repeat many of the steps over and over.

Identify the value-adding and non-value-adding steps

It is useful to identify the *value-adding* (VA) and *non-value-adding* (NVA) steps in your current state map by putting a green dot on VA steps and a red dot on NVA steps, or simply by writing VA and NVA on the steps.

Add data tickets

I have found it useful to find a group 'blocks' of steps and add a data ticket (as described earlier) to the process as shown in Figure 4.3.

   When you have done this completely you will be able to add up the total lead time for the process and see whether or not it makes sense. Where you have different scenarios on the same current state map you will need to ensure you don't get mixed up and count things twice.

Create a spaghetti diagram

A *spaghetti diagram* (also called a *string diagram*) shows how a person or product moves around a process. It is created by making (or

FIGURE 4.3   Data tickets in action

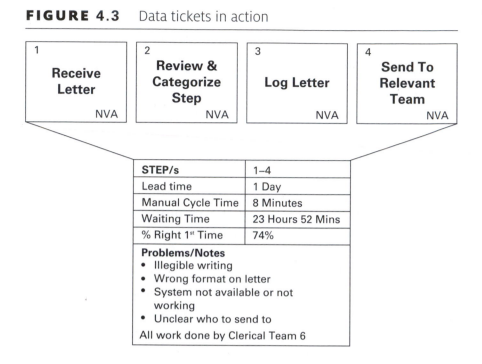

STEP/s	1–4
Lead time	1 Day
Manual Cycle Time	8 Minutes
Waiting Time	23 Hours 52 Mins
% Right 1st Time	74%

Problems/Notes
- Illegible writing
- Wrong format on letter
- System not available or not working
- Unclear who to send to

All work done by Clerical Team 6

obtaining) a plan of an area and then drawing a continuous line showing how people move around the process, as shown in Figure 4.4.

FIGURE 4.4   Example spaghetti diagram

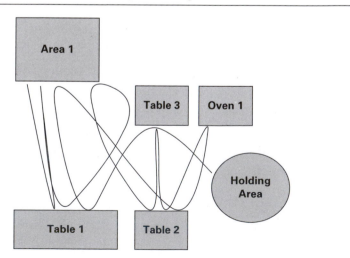

Not all processes are suitable for this type of diagram, for example processes spread across multiple sites, ones where all the people remain 'still' and just send information electronically or where there is no permanent physical layout to work from (for example, district nurses visiting patients at home, highways inspectors investigating pot holes in roads, etc). However, where appropriate to use this diagram, it is a useful, quick and easily understood tool.

Create a handoff diagram

A *handoff diagram* (also referred to as a *circle diagram*) is an extremely useful diagram for identifying bottlenecks in your process when you have more than four or five people involved, spotting when you have missed steps and also for creating a bit of a visual 'shock factor'. To create them simply draw a large circle on a sheet of flipchart or A3 paper and then list around the edges all of the people involved in the process. Taking one scenario at a time you simply follow the journey around the circle, showing how information, people and products are 'handed off' from one person to another, as shown in Figure 4.5.

An example of a process with four handoffs is shown below:

- Person A does work and takes it to person B (first handoff).

- Person B does a series of tasks.

FIGURE 4.5   Example handoff diagram

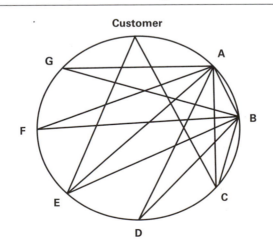

- Person B contacts person C to request them to come to see the item (second handoff).

- Person C comes to see person B and checks the item (third handoff).

- Person C then takes the item back to person A (fourth handoff)

As a rule of thumb I have noticed that when you are looking at a process that spans more than one organization then each handoff represents an average of around a half-day delay in the process. Some handoffs will be quicker and some slower but it often averages out to around a half-day delay per handoff. This means that if you have 50 handoffs in a process involving more than one organization it means the fastest that process could be completed in is around 25 days. When you are looking inside one team, or two very closely related teams, this delay per handoff drops to a half hour or less. Often the focus of a VSM event is on reducing the number of handoffs as each represents a delay, cost and possible risk.

Car park

A key part of current state analysis is to capture ideas, questions and comments for later work. You want to avoid teams getting bogged down in dealing with unnecessary detail at this stage but at the same time you don't want to lose any ideas. This is where a *car park* of ideas is useful. Normally this is just a space on a wall containing stick-notes with thoughts written on them. When a team has mapped the current state you might want to ask them to spend some time coming up with further improvements for the process before you introduce them to the *blue sky* stage we will see next.

Blue sky or ideal state

The *blue sky* or *ideal state* is a creative process that aims to create a diagram that generates additional ideas that can be used in the future state. In this approach to VSM it also introduces participants to the symbols so they can be used in the future state. Blue sky diagrams are best completed by people working in pairs, or at most a group of three. Again, my experience shows that any group larger than three will, at this stage, find it very difficult to come up with a successful blue sky diagram.

The briefing for the team is:

1 Anything is possible.

2 The solution must answer the question.

3 Don't try to re-create the current state.

The first point is to emphasize that this is a creative process. The second avoids problems that I have encountered where people put answers such as 'peace breaks out in the world' (in the defence industry) and 'people don't fall ill' (in health care), which, whilst being admirable aims, don't really help you to answer the problem you are trying to solve. The third point is aimed at preventing people spending the first 20 minutes re-creating the current state using the symbols – just trust me, lots of people do it.

Creating a blue sky diagram can take 30 to 60 minutes and you also need to allow time beforehand for people to be briefed and afterwards for them to present their solutions. In reality this means that *blue sky state* can take around half a day to complete. If you haven't got half a day then you might benefit from doing a brainstorm instead, rather than trying to rush it.

When people present their blue sky diagrams you are looking to extract ideas that are feasible and can be used in the future state. Sometimes this isn't easy and you might need to look at partial solutions. For example, the team may present the following blue sky idea: 'All customers will be required to send orders electronically.' This may not be possible for all customers but it might be possible to encourage a large number of customers to use electronic order placement. The aim here is to collect as many new ideas as you can to add to your future state diagram.

Creating a realistic future state

Future state (or 'to be') diagrams provide a picture of how a process or organization will work 'in the future' (normally 6 to 18 months ahead). The first step in creating a future state is to organize your team back into groups of four to six. This means that if you have 15 people you might organize them as follows:

- five people in your future state team;
- five people answering the questions that are in your *car park*;
- five people collecting any data that you need to identify to complete your current state analysis.

The next step will be to cluster all of your ideas from your *car park* and to assess how feasible each are going to be. The ones that are feasible and can be implemented within the timescales you have set for the future state should be used to help you create your future state diagram.

Two example future state diagrams using the symbols are shown in Figures 4.6 and 4.7.

Running along the bottom of Figure 4.6 you can see what is called a 'timeline' that shows the amount of processing time (the total manual cycle time and machine cycle time) versus the overall lead time of a process.

FIGURE 4.6   Example future state for a manufacturing environment

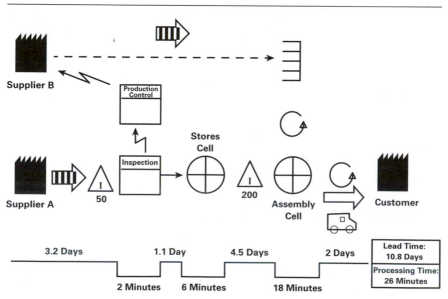

FIGURE 4.7   Simple health-care process

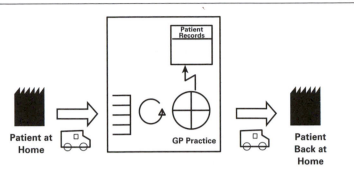

In Figure 4.7 I have shown a very simple health-care process that starts with a patient at home and sees the patient going to a GP practice by vehicle, where they wait to be 'pulled' in to see the GP before going home. The GP can also be seen entering information on to the patient's record in the diagram. In order to avoid extra clutter in the image I have not shown a timeline.

In addition to actually creating a future state there are some important stages in this phase that need to be undertaken.

Testing of the future state

Having created a draft future state I have found it extremely useful to undertake an exercise called 'Make it Fail' where you ask people to play the role of the most cynical person they can think of while looking at the future state and trying to identify the circumstances under which the future state will fail. You will then need to make changes to the future state in order to cope with any valid failure modes that are identified (it is better to find them now than later).

Add notes

The symbols don't just exist in isolation. You should add explanatory notes to the future state diagram to explain what is going on and to list the major changes you are proposing.

Revised layout

To accompany the future state, you may need to create a new layout for your office, factory, clinic or department if appropriate.

Implementation planning

Your future state should by this time have a range of actions that need to be implemented. There is a need to categorize these and put together a project plan or else all your effort in creating the future state will have been wasted.

There are three types of actions that you will identify in your future state:

- Projects – these are things requiring further authorization, such as buying large equipment, recruiting people, changing IT systems, etc.

- Events – these are things that suit being tackled by a 2P/3P event (Chapter 5) or rapid improvement event (Chapter 6). Fundamentally this means activities that can be fixed by a small group of people working together for a finite period of time.

- Do its – these are things that do not need further authorization or design and can just be implemented.

The next thing you will need to do is to prioritize actions. One quick way of doing this is to assess each task to determine how easy it is to do and the impact it will have, as shown in Figure 4.8.

FIGURE 4.8   A simple prioritization matrix

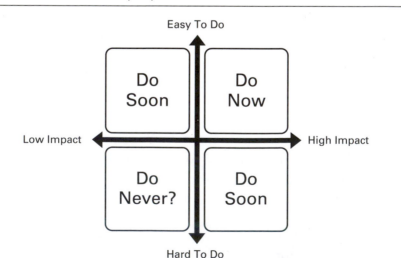

FIGURE 4.9 An example planning sheet

Title					PRIORITY		OWNER
					N/A L M H		
PROJECT ☐	EVENT ☐	DO IT ☐					

Specific Task Objectives	Questions/Issues To Answer
Expected Benefits	**People To Involve**

Lastly, there will be a need to provide some detail about the task using some form of planning sheet such as the one shown in Figure 4.9. This is because if you don't do this you will quickly forget what 'integrated team' actually means.

Even having done all this you will still have questions to answer that should be documented as part of your 'To Do' list following the event.

Closing brief

At the end of the future state you should arrange for the team to present back their solutions to the sponsor and other managers as well as colleagues. The format for a 20-minute closing brief could be:

- welcome (1 min);
- findings from the current state (4 mins);
- blue sky diagrams (3 mins);
- overview of future state (6 mins);
- benefits of the future state (2 mins);
- implementation plan (3 mins);
- thank you to the team (1 min).

After this you will probably have a variable amount of time available for questions to the team. You should brief the sponsor to be positive about the solution and not to try to rip it apart. If the team have missed anything obvious it can always be modified later on.

After the event

When the team have dispersed there will still be a need to document the process and communicate it to others for their input. Sometimes people draw the future state map in some software package, whilst others just tape it down and keep it. Whenever you implement anything on the future state, the idea is that you roll out the whole thing and show people how the task they are doing contributes to the overall future state.

Two-stage value stream mapping

Having explored the three-stage value stream mapping (VSM) process we can now look at a two-stage process that uses only symbols. The activities required prior to and after the event are identical to those I outlined for the three-stage VSM, so they are not repeated here.

Understanding the current state

The major difference in this approach is that the team use symbols to understand processes from the start. The advantage for this with an experienced team is speed, as it is very quick to do. The downside is that you will find it difficult to add multiple scenarios to your diagram. The principle of mapping the service or process using symbols is identical to that shown in Figures 4.6 and 4.7 and often the *car park* is replaced with *kaizen bursts* that appear on the current state diagram. You will also find it useful to still use data tickets. An example of current state using symbols is shown in Figure 4.10.

Again, in addition to showing a very simple example, in order to reduce clutter in the image I have also chosen not to show a timeline.

In the two-stage approach to value stream mapping you will definitely need to encourage people to be creative with the ideas they are

FIGURE 4.10   Example current state with symbols showing a kaizen burst

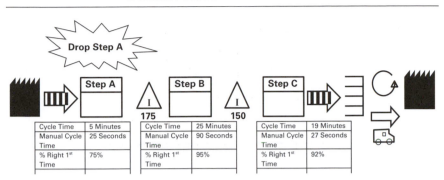

coming up with for the future state as there is no blue sky diagram for them to express their creative ideas in. You will also continue to identify questions and issues you can't answer so it may still be useful to have a car park to keep things in.

Creating a future state

The creation of a future state and the implementation plan for a two-stage VSM is exactly the same as that in the three-stage VSM, so I refer you back to that section.

Alternative approaches to value stream mapping

In this section I outline two further related ways of doing VSM. The first (*swimlanes*) is used in place of a current state map, either with or without symbols. The second (*vertical value streams*) is more of a planning tool that is useful when a process has no current state, such as during the development of new products and services, to help create a project plan.

Swimlanes

Swimlanes provide an alternative way of mapping a current state. They are useful when you have less than about eight different groups of

FIGURE 4.11   Example swimlanes diagram

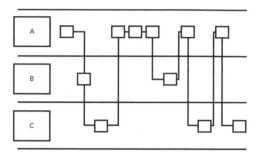

people (operators, planners, supervisors, machine operators, etc) involved; above that number it becomes too complex to use. In that way they are very useful for smaller processes than when you might use the two- and three-stage VSM described earlier. Swimlanes are difficult to use if you want to add further scenarios, hence why they only warrant a footnote in this chapter. The concept of swimlanes can be seen in Figure 4.11.

Down the left-hand side of the swimlanes diagram you can see a representation of three different 'groups' of people, such as a 'planner, engineer and operator' or 'doctor, nurse and pharmacist'. The tasks undertaken by each 'group' of person appears in the relevant swimlane so you can quickly see the tasks done by each group of person. To complete a current state using swimlanes it is clear you would still need to do the other tasks outlined in the three-stage current state such as spaghetti diagrams and handoff diagrams.

Vertical value streams maps (VVSM)

Vertical value stream maps (VVSM) are used to help plan out a project or the development of a new product or service. It consists of a number of steps that need to be undertaken to create the map and these are outlined below.

Identify the project 'stage gates'

You should identify somewhere between four to six *stage gates* through which your project may go between concept and implementation. In Table 4.1 I have shown three different projects from different sectors,

TABLE 4.1 Example project 'gates' for different projects

	Local government – new format case conferencing in children's social care	Manufacturing – new product development	Health care – move of eye clinic
Stage Gate 1	Sign off PID	Market research	Finalize budget
Stage Gate 2	Design new format	Conceptual design	Contract for services
Stage Gate 3	Partner feedback	Product development	Agree final design
Stage Gate 4	Implementation	1st prototype	Implementation
Stage Gate 5	Review and sign off	2nd prototype	
Stage Gate 6		Pre-production launch	

showing the gates that were identified for each. You will see that they have identified different numbers of project gates.

Obviously you will need to define how you know that you have reached the point of each stage gate, for example you might say that 'contract for services' is complete when both parties have signed the contract and it has been filed with the commercial team. You should also put an expected date for you to reach each stage gate.

Identify the people involved

The next step you will need to do is identify the people or the teams involved. You are now in a position to create the first pass of the VVSM, as you can see in Figure 4.12.

Figure 4.12 shows how the tasks that each team need to undertake to enable the project to pass through each of the four stage gates are lined up underneath them. The tasks for each team will have their own timescales but the VVSM shows that you will not meet the deadline

FIGURE 4.12   Example vertical value stream map

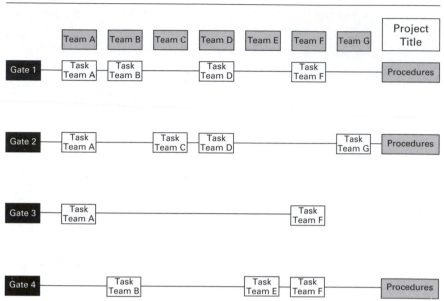

of the project gate unless all of the relevant tasks are completed. On the right-hand side you will see a list of procedures relevant to each gate (if there are any), for example contracting procedures, development procedures, clinical testing, etc.

The practicalities of value stream mapping

The theoretical approach to VSM is often very different to the reality of doing it with teams. I have already outlined some of the things I would encourage you to think about when working with teams, such as group size and car parks. In this section I discuss a few other practical things that affect the success of a VSM activity.

Involving a wider team

VSM is unnerving for people not directly involved in it. Having a group of their colleagues sitting in a room for a day or more working on redesigning how your team works can generate rumours very quickly. You should offer the opportunity for those who are interested to ask questions about what the VSM team are up to and/or consider offering a daily closing brief at the end of each day for people to come in and quiz the team on what is going on. You will also need to ensure you promptly communicate the future state to the wider team as quickly as possible after it has been created.

Feeling the squeeze

There will be a pressure in many organizations to cut the time spent doing a VSM event. It can be cut so radically that in the end you don't have enough time to do a good job. I would resist this and even be prepared to 'call it off' if insufficient time is allocated to a VSM event. That doesn't mean that you shouldn't always look to minimize the time impact of doing VSM, just not to try and fit too much in to too short a period.

Representing the whole value stream

The team should include a representative from every team that plays a part in the process you are looking at. If you can't get them in the room, ensure you have them available on the phone if needed and also get their input prior to the event.

Customer input

Having real-life customers providing an input into the process can be really valuable. The best time to have their input is right at the start, for example have some key feedback as part of the opening brief by the sponsor, and at the future state stage where they can comment on what has occurred. During *current state* and *blue sky state* customers can often get bored, or indeed you may not want to share openly the problems you have, so think carefully about when and how you involve customers.

Wild cards

Having people who do not work in the process you are looking at but are brought in to add a different perspective is very powerful and I would recommend doing it whenever you can. You need to brief the people concerned so that they know their role is to add in creative ideas and question what the main team see as 'immovable' otherwise they can end up sitting quietly listening to others.

'Drop-in' people

Sometimes people will want to participate but cannot stay for the whole time. Particularly for senior engineers, doctors, scientists, solicitors and the like, they will often want to drop in, tell you what they want in the future state and depart again without really contributing. You should be wary of operating this type of drop-in service because if people haven't been through the 'pain' of current state they will not be fully equipped to comment on the future state and could cause serious disruption.

Maintaining morale of the team

Be aware that people will go through an emotional cycle when participating in a VSM event. By the end of the current state many of them will feel de-energized and stressed. They will come out of it by the end of the process but it helps to let people know that they are going to go through an emotional swing during VSM.

Value stream mapping case study

As I provided at the end of Chapter 3, I have outlined another 'warts and all' case study here. This one covers value stream mapping of a project in the health care sector and is summarized in Table 4.2.

TABLE 4.2   Value stream mapping event snapshot

Value stream mapping event snapshot

The organization: Acute Trust (hospital) with input from partners from community health care, GPs and social care.

Duration of session: three days.

Present at session: a mix of clinical staff from the hospital including doctors, nurses, pharmacists, pathology and diagnostics as well as admin staff involved in booking appointments and managing theatres etc. In addition, we had input from two GPs, two social workers and various staff from community health care including a district nurse, community physio, etc.

Focus of value stream mapping event: the redesign of the end-to-end orthopaedic pathway from initial patient meeting with their GP through to the patient being back home post treatment.

Prior to the VSM event

We had prepared a scoping paper and communicated the dates with staff giving them eight weeks' notice to allow time for people to re-schedule their clinical commitments. Also, the hospital's Lean team had carried out some pre-emptive Lean training with nearly all of the participants. Data and examples of paperwork were also collected, although we were missing key information on the expected changes in demand for the service.

Running the VSM event

The Director of Human Resources and Organizational Development, who was the organization's lead for Lean, gave an opening brief. On reflection this would have been better done by the Head of Orthopaedics and one or two others from the participant organizations. I then did a 15 minute 'Lean Refresher' outlining the concepts of value/waste and discussing how we would go about value stream mapping.

We had around 20 people attending and had already worked out how to break them into groups of four and five for current state. We had two teams looking at the 'front end', one looking at the journey of the patient from initial GP appointment through to the outpatient appointment at the hospital, and the second group looking at diagnostics. The third team looked at the interaction between the theatres for elective care (planned activities) and emergency care and the last looked at the process from the point that the patient was listed for surgery until they were discharged and safely back at home.

Each grouped mapped their processes in 50 to 100 steps, identified value-adding and non-value-adding steps and handoff charts. We didn't produce spaghetti diagrams as the process was spread over multiple organizations and areas. They also all produced a long list of issues/questions/ideas for later use.

At the end of day one we had an 'open doors' event to allow people to attend to discuss what the team had found. In reality, only five people turned up to this and one of those was the Director of HR and OD. However, it was useful for the team to review what had been achieved.

Day two

Only 12 people were able to stay from day one into day two and we had three new people attending. The first part of the day was spent finishing off the current state maps and cross-presenting to each other. I then led a short presentation on blue sky diagrams, introducing participants to the symbols. They were then organized in groups of two to three to produce blue sky diagrams for either the whole process (if they felt comfortable doing it) or just the bit they had mapped during day one. This worked surprisingly well as a concept, as some people wanted to give their view for the whole process and would have been constrained looking at just part of it, whilst some others only wanted to focus on their part of the overall picture. The teams presented back their solutions and we pulled from them ideas for implementation in the future state, completing the whole exercise by about 1pm.

After lunch we organized them back into groups of five with one group focused on creating the future state, one focused on answering the questions that had been raised during current state mapping and the third acting to collect the missing data to support the current state (such things as confirming the lead times and manual cycle times).

We did not hold an end-of-day washup on day two.

Day three

At the start of day three the future state team discussed their draft map and the other two groups undertook a 'Make it Fail' exercise, pretending to be the most cynical person in the organization. As we had four new people turn up we also had to spend some time bringing them up to speed on what had gone on. The future state team then finalized the future state map and the other teams started working concurrently on producing the implementation plan. By 12 noon this was nearly complete so we did another run through just before lunch to confirm that the future state 'worked' and that it delivered everything in the scoping paper.

After lunch we finalized the implementation plan and then started preparing for a closing brief. At 3pm we did a dry run of the closing brief and at 3.45pm we did it for real. We had about 25 people turn up to hear the closing brief. At the end of the session, the Director of HR and OD thanked the team and the session ended, although the 'owner' of the future state (the Head of Orthopaedics) and I spent quite a while collecting together the materials afterwards and planning out the first implementation events from the implementation plan.

After the VSM event

Straight afterwards we drew the future state diagram and e-mailed it to a wide range of people to invite comment and also got on with planning the implementation activities. Over the following six months we implemented six rapid improvement events plus three 2P events. Collectively this work saved over £600k in costs, eliminated the waiting list, shortened length of stay by over three-quarters of a day and led to increased integration between the community health-care organization and the hospital team.

Key learning points

We should have better publicized the end-of-day washup sessions to increase attendance. Also, the dropping in and out of people caused us some delay, especially as we were on tight timescales. Lastly, the arrival of a very negative senior nurse on day three, who seemed only to want to prevent progress, could have been a disaster had I not been able to divert him away from the future state team.

Closing thoughts

VSM is an extremely powerful tool when used effectively. My example was for a three-day VSM that occurred on concurrent days (Monday to Wednesday) but it could just have easily been done over three individual days or even having a small group create a draft current state to take for comment to the larger group. The exact format for your VSM will vary depending on the size of the problem and the time available, but my advice is that 'sooner is better' rather than drawing it out over an extended period.

VSM works well for larger scale projects but sometimes you will want to focus in more detail at a smaller area or part of an overall process and that is where you will find the use of 2P and 3P events very useful, as I will cover in the next chapter.

2P/3P events

In this chapter I aim to answer the following questions:

1 What are 2P and 3P events and when should you consider them?

2 How do you go about undertaking a 2P and 3P event?

3 How do you turn a 2P/3P event into an action plan?

4 What is the relationship between a 2P/3P event and a rapid improvement event?

2P (*process planning*) and 3P (*product and process planning*) events are activities focused on designing, testing and planning the implementation of critical, but typically small-scale processes. The difference between them is that a 2P event focuses on how to design, organize, lay out and operate processes whilst a 3P event covers these issues plus considers the design of the product/service itself. This means that the work done to re-lay out an individual manufacturing cell, a theatre block or call centre to improve flow and introduce other Lean concepts would be covered by a 2P event, whilst adding in the re-engineering of a product to make it easier to build in the manufacturing cell or changing the range of services offered by the call centre team would be a 3P event. As you will guess, there is a lot of opportunity for things to overlap and blur the boundaries between a 2P and 3P event.

Forgetting the semantics of the definition, fundamentally both 2P and 3P events are designed to achieve three things:

1 Understand what is needed.

2 Develop and test creative solutions to answer this need.

3 Plan the implementation of the solution identified.

The three objectives of 2P and 3P events are similar to that of value stream mapping (VSM) and I often say that a 2P/3P event is like a mini VSM event combined with the testing of solutions. In this way 2P/3Ps are often used to de-risk a process prior to implementation. For example, you wouldn't want to go straight into making changes to the way that security is managed at an airport or changing the way that high-pressure testing is undertaken without having tested whether your new solution works or without having identified the safest, most effective way of making the transition from what you have to what you want – and that is where a 2P/3P event is invaluable.

Because the majority of events undertaken inside real organizations are primarily concerned with process planning rather than making substantial changes to the products or services, I will focus first on the 2P event format.

2P events

2P (process planning) events are also referred to as process preparation or production planning events. Whatever the name people use for them, they are designed to achieve the same thing, namely the design, test and implementation planning of a key organizational process. By virtue of the fact that they are not focused on changing products and services, 2P events tend to be less technical than 3P events and are easier to explain, another reason for discussing this first within this chapter. Like a VSM event that we covered in Chapter 3, there is a need to undertake some key tasks prior to the 2P event and this is covered next.

Prior to the 2P event

If the 2P is the main focus for the entire Lean project then you will have an A3 or similar document that outlines the requirements. However, for many 2P events they will be only part of a larger project,

TABLE 5.1 Example 2P events that arose from different value stream mapping events

	Health care	Manufacturing	Logistics (warehouse)
Value stream mapping process	Orthopaedics	Investment casting	Drop to ship
2P events	• Diagnostics • Outpatients • Pre-assessment • Theatre scheduling • Discharge planning	• Production planning • Foundry scheduling	• Unloading bay design • Picking layout • Rack planning

perhaps having been identified during the VSM. Table 5.1 shows the various 2P events that have arisen from a VSM event.

Where you are dealing with a 2P event that arises from a VSM event then you may still find it useful to create a checklist for the event that links back to the A3 for the overall project but allows you to do some detailed planning for this specific activity. A template for a planning sheet for such an event is shown in Figure 5.1.

The keys to successful preparation for a 2P event are similar to that required for VSM, namely getting the team identified, gathering data, carrying out some pre-event training and identifying the sponsor who will provide an opening brief to the group. Without a clear set of objectives for the 2P event you are likely to not achieve the expected outcomes.

Running the 2P event

Depending on the size of the problem you are looking at you will require anywhere between half a day and five days to undertake a 2P event, although the largest I ever had to undertake was with the Armed Forces and took 10 days spread over two weeks but that was very exceptional. More commonly the event duration is around one to three days.

The 2P event itself is broken into three stages: understanding the current state, designing and testing options and planning implementation.

FIGURE 5.1   Example event preparation form

Event Title								
Event Type	2P		3P		RIE		Other	
Event Objective/s								
Event Owner								
Start Date			Opening Brief Time					
End Date			Closing Brief Time					

Why is this event important to the organization?

Who will give the Opening Brief for the event?

Who are the team that will be involved?

Who will be the Lean Change Agent responsible for facilitating this event?

Where will the event be held?

What information needs to be gathered before the event?

The 2P event should kick off with an opening brief given by a sponsor and some refresher training for participants, in the same way you would do for a VSM event, so I will start by exploring each of the four main stages.

Understanding the current state

This phase for a 2P event will use the same tools as a VSM event such as current state mapping, data tickets, handoff diagrams and spaghetti diagrams. As the processes that you look at during a 2P event tend to be much smaller than those you would look at during a VSM event, you will find that my rule of mapping the processes in '50 to 100 steps' means you are looking at a process in more detail than maybe appeared in the VSM event and that is absolutely correct. Again, like a VSM event you will also need to look at a range of different scenarios for the process (runners, repeaters and strangers) and make use of a car park. You will need to ensure that the team are fully up to speed with the needs of the customer (remembering *VotC* – voice of the customer) and also with what are the expected outcomes of the 2P event.

Design and test options

The next step in a 2P event is to design options and this can use the same approach as the blue sky diagram that we came across in the VSM event, but it is more common to use other tools to get the team to come up with a range of options. One method is called '7 Ways' and, put simply, means that the team are tasked with finding seven unique ways of designing the new process. There is a danger here that people will come up with seven aspects of the same solution. For example, if I said, 'Design seven new ways of organizing the space you are in right now', you might answer with such things as new carpet, paint walls, better lighting, etc, but these are all part of one solution that is 'redecorate the space'. '7 Ways' means finding seven fundamentally different ways, which, continuing my example, might mean such things as redecorate, destroy, build extension, remove roof, etc. What I have found in practice is that trying to get seven distinctly different ways of doing things proves very difficult for most teams so I tend to ask them for three or five and call it accordingly 'Design 3' or 'Design 5'.

At this stage you will probably also need to create a 'paper layout' showing how you are proposing to lay out each process. A paper layout, which is also referred to sometimes as a 'paper doll', uses a scale plan of an area along with cutouts that are to scale of any equipment, storage, tables, etc, that you arrange to show how the area will operate for each solution. A conceptual paper layout is shown in Figure 5.2.

The testing of options can be done in a variety of ways. Sometimes this is as simple as cutting out a scale shape to represent a person, piece of equipment or product and moving them through your paper layout as they would do in reality and sometimes it may involve

FIGURE 5.2 Conceptual paper layout of an area

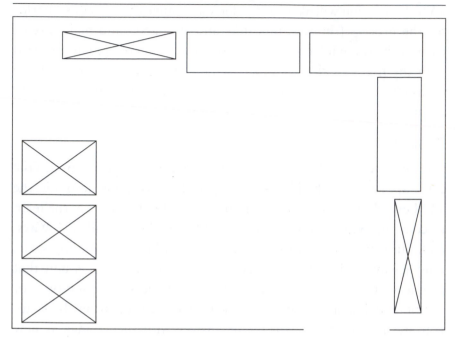

'walking' a real patient/person or product through a process. The most common approach though is to undertake an exercise called 'cardboard engineering', where you use cardboard, wood or other materials to create a 'quick and dirty' mock-up of how the process could be laid out. This might involve you in cutting out life-size pieces of cardboard to represent (for example) machines in a manufacturing plant, racks in a warehouse or beds in a hospital and then seeing whether or not they will fit in the space you have provided. The concept is to quickly and cheaply create something that people can touch/see and experience so that they are better informed when we come to selecting options. As I say, not every process needs cardboard engineering but it is an exciting exercise to undertake at least a few times in your Lean career.

Having designed and tested options, only one thing remains to be undertaken and that is to select the option you are going to go forward with. For this I have found the idea of a 'rational decision-making matrix' extremely useful.

FIGURE 5.3 Example rational decision-making matrix

Selection Criteria	Weight (1–10)	Option 1 Private Vehicle		Option 2 Public Transport		Option 3 Cycle	
Safety	9	8	72	7	63	5	45
Comfort	5	8	40	5	25	3	15
Cost	6	4	24	6	36	9	45
Speed	7	7	49	7	49	5	35
Reliability	4	8	32	7	28	10	40
TOTALS		217		201		180	

The purpose of the 'rational decision matrix' (also loosely referred to as a 'beauty competition' as you line options up and compare them) is to help you select the best option from a range of options. In Figure 5.3 I have chosen a subject that I hope everyone can relate to – transport – and it is being used to select the best option for getting to work which, for the purposes of this example, consists of three options: private vehicle, public transport and cycling. I have also shown five criteria for selecting the best of the three options and these are shown as safety, comfort, cost, speed and reliability. In reality you would normally have your criteria based on the needs of customers and also will have to define what you mean for each criteria. Even in my simple example shown in Figure 5.3 it is not exactly clear what I mean by 'reliability' so I would probably need to explain it in better terms to the team I was working with if I wanted us all to be working towards the same criteria. In the 'weighting' section of Figure 5.3 you can see that I have given safety the highest weighting (9 out of 10). You can give each criteria the same weighting if you want (although it would make the weighting process pointless and you should aim for as big a spread of weightings as possible).

Having got the criteria and the weighting we can now use them to help select the options. What we do is apply a score of 1 to 10 against each option using the mantra, '1 is bad, 10 is good'. So for my example in Figure 5.3 for 'cost' would be 1 = bad = very expensive and 10 = good = very cheap. For 'speed', 1 = bad = extremely slow and 10 = good = very quick and so on. We then multiply each score by the weighting factor to give us the value in the top right-hand corner of each of the boxes with a dividing line through them. When complete, we add the scores and can see that the best option (in this case) is to drive with a score of 217. Of course, we may have chosen different criteria, such as environmental impact, which would have changed the score – but this is just for illustration of the tool.

Plan for implementation

Having selected an option that works, the next step is to get on with planning its implementation. There are too many 2P events that result in a wonderful design but no action – thus warranting the statement that unless you plan the implementation, and then do it, you will have wasted your time. The only occasion when this isn't true is when you have identified through your 2P event that there is no safe/better/more cost effective way forward (although I have never come across this situation).

Some of the things that you will need to create include a paper layout for the final design (as we discussed earlier) and to undertake some form of risk assessment for the new solution, if you didn't do that as part of testing your options. However, the planning of the implementation can be achieved with a tool that I loosely call 'process backbone and ribs' but for which the proper name is '7 flows' as shown in Figure 5.4.

Running down the middle of the image in Figure 5.4 are the main steps of your new process, for example 'receive paperwork', 'check paperwork', etc. Coming off each step in the process are six other flows that come off to the side of each step, as you will see more clearly in Figure 5.5 that shows a cut-down version of the process in Figure 5.4. Each of the six other flows can be customized to the environment you operate in, with some examples shown in Table 5.2.

FIGURE 5.4 Example 7 flows conceptual layout

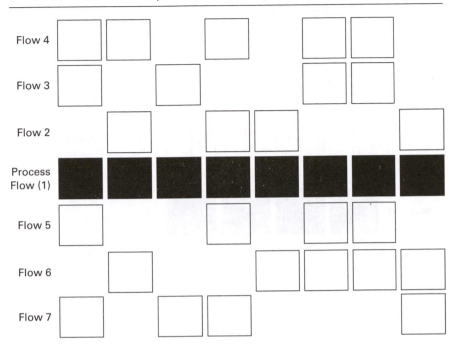

TABLE 5.2 Examples of the types of things that you might find in each of the 7 flow categories

	Manufacturing	Health care	Armed forces
Flow 1	Product flow	Patient flow	Servicing flow
Flow 2	Raw materials	Information	Machines and equipment
Flow 3	Tools and tooling	Clinical staff	Technical team
Flow 4	Consumables	Non-clinical staff	Planning team
Flow 5	Instructions	Drugs	Tooling and tools
Flow 6	Operators	Equipment	Instructions and documents
Flow 7	Machines	Consumables	Spare parts

FIGURE 5.5   Part of a 7 flows showing a 'blow out' example of
one of the notes

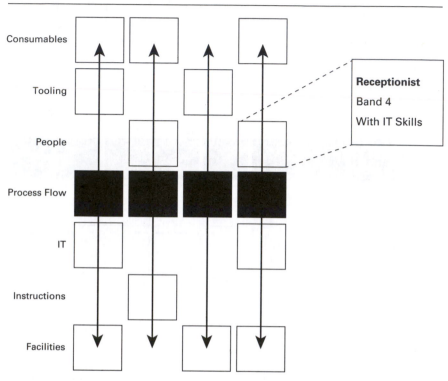

Where a step doesn't use tools (for example) you would see the gaps
in the sequence that you can see in Figure 5.4. You wouldn't of course
just put a sticky-note on to say that you needed tools but would write
down exactly what you needed. In Figure 5.5 I have shown a 'blow
out' of one of the 'people' notes to show what might be written on
it. Once you have completed your '7 flows' everything that appears
on the 'ribs' of the main process forms your implementation plan.

The last part of a 2P event, in terms of a closing brief, and the
actions that need to occur after the event are the same as detailed
for the VSM event in Chapter 4. The next step after a 2P event will
be a rapid improvement event (RIE), as covered in Chapter 6, but
between the end of the 2P event and the start of the RIE you will
probably have to get many actions from your implementation plan
completed and the effectiveness with which you manage that task
list will determine the success of the RIE.

3P events

The major difference between a 2P event and a 3P event is that we introduce the complexities of changing products and services at the same time as changing the process. 3P stands for 'product and process planning' although you will find variations in the definition of the 3Ps including such things as 'production preparation process' and 'product and process preparation'. Whatever the name used they are designed to do the same thing, which is to transform a product or service, and the underlying processes used to deliver the product/ service so that they better meet the needs of customers and can be delivered with the minimum of fuss, cost and risk.

A 3P event has the same three stages as the 2P event, namely: understand the current state, design and test options and plan for implementation. However, as you would expect, there are some differences in the tools and concepts you might use in a 3P event to that used in a 2P event. I outline these in the relevant sections but first will introduce the 16 catch phrases that apply to 3P events. These have developed from the work of Toyota and I have included them here for completeness.

16 catch phrases of 3P

The following are the 16 catch phrases that form the basis of 3P events. I have taken the liberty of changing the words in some of them to make them easier to understand.

1 Production preparation should be lightning fast – avoid overplanning and use what you have to hand to get the job done.

2 Ensure a smooth flow of materials in your build and layout – flow like a river don't act like a dam.

3 Use small equipment that can be added to – have lots of speedboats instead of one large tanker.

4 Ensure your equipment is easy to set up – design equipment using the principles of *SMED* (Single Minute Exchange of Die).

5 Ensure your equipment is easy to move – don't let them put down roots, put everything on wheels.

6 Avoid multipurpose equipment wherever possible – have simple 'one purpose' machines that perform one function well rather than multipurpose machines that do things badly.

7 Make workstations narrow and tall to reduce the waste of motion – have town houses rather than bungalows.

8 Make it easy for people to move around in their working area – remove obstructions and use *5S*.

9 Eliminate lost machine time – design out processes that increase machine movement and waste time.

10 Make equipment that enables you to have small, swift and flexible flow lines – design things to fit in the smallest space possible and utilize *standard work*.

11 Use short vertically integrated flow lines – establish multidisciplinary cells rather than working in functional groups.

12 Design processes that support one-piece *flow* (and one piece *pull*) – minimize batch sizes and adopt the principles of *pull*.

13 Design in quick changeover processes – another one that focuses on *SMED*.

14 Link machines so that they don't require excessive loading and unloading – reduce the motion of human beings and also stop the line when it is 'full'.

15 Use multiple lines and ensure that the flow is always in one direction – avoid rework loops and have options.

16 Strive to eliminate errors and make the detection of errors automatic – spiral upwards towards *jidoka*.

Having listed the 16 catch phrases, listed below are the key things you need to do prior to your 3P event.

Prior to the 3P event

Many of the things you need to do prior to a 3P event are identical to those you would do for a 2P event. However, because we are focusing on changing products and services there is a much greater need to ensure you understand what customers want. This means listening to the voice of the customer (*VotC*) and then taking appropriate steps to ensure that your product/service meets their need. Prior to the 3P event it is extremely valuable to gather feedback from customers and to identify what it means for your organization. Table 5.3 contains a simple interview/assessment template that helps teams to do this.

TABLE 5.3   Simple assessment template for understanding the voice of the customer

Product name: Name of product/service
Customer name: A. Customer
Interviewer/s: A. N. Other
Date of interview: XX/YY/ZZ

Question	VotC	Interpreted need	Importance
What do they use our product for?	List all of the uses that your client uses your product or service to achieve.	Write here anything that you need to consider in your 3P event.	Identify the importance of each issue.
Likes	List here what they like about your current service.	Identify what you could do to enhance the product/service to increase the perceived value to the customer.	
Dislikes	List here what they dislike about your current service.	Identify what you need to change to move this from a dislike to a like.	
Suggested improvements	List here anything they would like you to improve or change.	Identify if this means you have to make any further changes.	
Other information	List here anything that the customer tells you about future developments, changes or other things going on in their world that will affect your product or service offering to them.		

Another tool that does the same thing, but is significantly more complex to use, is *quality function deployment (QFD)*. However, I have always found the above format to be sufficient for the majority of 3P events.

Running the 3P event

Like a 2P event, a 3P can last anywhere between half a day and five days and consists of three stages. Also like a 2P, the focus of any 3P event is to ensure that products and services can be delivered as easily, safely and cost effectively as possible with the difference being the focus on changing the product/service as well as the processes. The differences between a 2P and a 3P during each of the three stages are explained in the following sections.

Understand the current state

Broadly you will use the same concepts to understand the current state that you used for a 2P event. One concept that you will need to consider during this phase that is different to a 2P event is *design for manufacture and assembly (DFMA)*. This consists of two separate strands of thought:

- Design for manufacture – how easy is it to make the parts for our product?
- Design for assembly – how easy do we make it for our people to assemble the product?

Obviously, DFMA has most relevance in a manufacturing context; an equivalent concept for a service environment might be called *design for access and delivery (DFAD)*:

- Design for access – how easy is it for people to access our service?
- Design for delivery – how easy do we make it for our people to deliver our service to customers?

The questions you are aiming to answer in this section are fundamentally technical. They cover aspects of how your product/service is defined, accessed, assembled, delivered, packaged, reported on and invoiced. The aim is to expose problems that need to be fixed.

Design and test options

Having assessed your current state, and reviewed the VotC, this stage of a 3P event is concerned with analysing the 16 catch phrases and seeing how many of them can be incorporated into the combined product/service and process. The process of testing options is the same as we discussed when considering 2P events.

Plan implementation

The concepts of planning implementation that you would use for a 3P event, including creating a paper layout, 7 flows, etc, are the same as I outlined for the 2P event.

2P case study (local government)

As I provided at the end of Chapters 3 and 4, I have outlined three further 'warts and all' case studies in the following sections. The one in this section covers a 2P event in local government whilst the next section covers a 2P event in health followed by a 3P event in manufacturing. The details of this first 2P event are summarized in Table 5.4.

TABLE 5.4 2P event snapshot

2P event snapshot

The organization: County Council.

Duration of session: 1.5 days.

Present at session: Head of Lean, six people from the different complaint-handling teams within the organization, plus two observers who had recently attended a Lean Green Belt course and were interested to see a 2P event in practice.

Focus of 2P event: to standardize the handling of complaints within three of the four teams handling complaints. Those in Children's Services were not included as they had a legally defined process to follow when dealing with complaints.

Prior to the 2P event

The aim was to integrate the complaints processes within the organization, except where there was a legal requirement to follow a set process. We had therefore undertaken a short scoping session and collected together examples of the complaints forms and data (in terms of numbers of complaints and the takt time) as well as the different scenarios (runners, repeaters and strangers). Some briefing about the event and what to expect had been e-mailed to participants prior to the event to give them some background to what was going on.

During the 2P event

The session was opened by the Head of Lean with some support from the two managers responsible for the various teams involved. There was a short (~10 minute) presentation from me and we then got into mapping the various complaints processes used in the different teams. This took about two hours to complete, including doing the handoff diagrams. It was not appropriate to do a spaghetti diagram as most of the complaints were transmitted electronically. We then cross-presented the different solutions and together produced a list of the things that were different and those that were the same.

After lunch we prioritized the things that we considered to be 'best practice' that could be shared between the teams and began working on creating a future state process for each of the three teams in the form of a 7 flows diagram. At the end of the day we cross-presented the solutions and also undertook a 'Make it Fail' exercise to check whether anything had been missed.

Day two

Day two was purely about planning the implementation of the changes to the working practices within the teams. It was decided to use three small rapid improvement events, one in each of the three areas affected, to change the paperwork and reporting structure. Prior to the implementation we also identified some of the other tasks that needed to be done, including changes to the IT system used by two of the teams. We then summarized the benefits of the changes and closed the session at 12pm.

This was a very low-key project with quite a simple set of aims. As there were many events going on within the organization at this time, we did not organize a specific closing brief for this simple 2P event. Instead, the Head of Lean did a presentation after the event as part of a briefing to the Transformation Board within the council.

The implementation of the changes happened over the following eight weeks and led to a reduction in the time taken to manage complaints (enabling two people to be transferred to other duties) as well as introducing consistency in the management processes.

Key learning points

The complaints team members felt a little threatened by the need for change and we should have spent more time addressing these issues before the event as it limited the creativity of the team.

2P case study (health care)

This second 2P event example comes from the health-care sector and is summarized in Table 5.5.

TABLE 5.5   2P event snapshot

2P event snapshot

The organization: hospital.

Duration of session: three days

Present at session: Lean team, pre-assessment Sister, four nurses, anaesthetist (two different ones over the three days), surgical registrar (part-time), pre-assessment clerk, phlebotomist, pharmacist (two different ones over the three days), Head of Orthopaedics (part-time), clinical lead for orthopaedics (a surgeon) (part-time).

Focus of 2P event: only 75% of patients were having a pre-assessment meeting prior to their surgery and this was leading to many patients being found not to be fit on 'day of surgery' or to have issues that would complicate their discharge, such as the unexpected need for a home care package. Also, there were problems being experienced with patients taking too long to go through their pre-assessment checks, thus leading to complaints.

Prior to the 2P event

This was part of a larger programme of work to redesign the end-to-end orthopaedic pathway that you were introduced to in Chapter 4. This event was one of the first 2P events that was identified during the VSM event and occurred only six weeks after the VSM event had finished. During this six-week period we had produced an event summary to clarify the specific objectives for this project, gathered data about demand and capacity and undertaken a study to look at room utilization.

During the 2P event

The session was opened by a short briefing given by the Head of Orthopaedic Services who then stayed on for the rest of the first day. The first objective was to map a number of patient journeys from arrival in the pre-assessment area through to leaving the hospital. For this we mapped each scenario in 50 to 100 steps, identified the value-adding steps, produced a spaghetti diagram and a handoff diagram. This highlighted that patients were having to get dressed and undressed on average three times and also had to travel for up to 1.5km to have their blood taken. Many of the patients were elderly and frail and this was causing much of the delay and complaints.

Towards the end of day one we undertook a 'Design 3' exercise to create three distinctly different solutions to the layout and processes in pre-assessment. For this, we didn't use value stream mapping symbols, instead we just created a paper layout and a simplified 'high level' pathway in words.

At the end of day one we reviewed the processes created and discussed the questions that had arisen during the day.

Day two

We started day two by cross-presenting the solutions developed on day one and identifying the things we would like to see in the new process. This highlighted over 40 changes, some quite substantial, and we therefore had to do some prioritization work to select the most valuable activities.

Having got an example pathway we then tested it by having two nurses pretend to be patients on a 'walk through' of the new process. The roles of the pharmacist and medical staff were played by the appropriate people from within the team. This highlighted issues such as the lack of privacy in several of the rooms; the space allocated to take blood from patients not being big enough; and the need to keep patients in one place and have staff 'go to the patient' in order to save the patient from having to keep getting dressed and undressed. Some fairly useful issues were identified as to how we would track patients in the area to ensure there was a good flow.

Towards the end of day two we started to produce our '7 flows' document and the paper layout for the new area. We finished the day with a quick washup session for all the pre-assessment team to get their feedback on our proposals.

Day three

We started the day with two teams: one focused on finalizing the '7 flows' and paper layout and the second focused on dealing with the remaining questions that had yet to be answered and assessing the impact of the changes we had proposed. At the mid-morning break, these two teams cross-presented to each other and we undertook a very quick 'Make it Fail' exercise to test whether the solution we had developed had any obvious flaws or not.

By midday on day three the process was nearly complete. After lunch the team tidied up their notes and prepared a closing brief. This was rehearsed at 2.30pm and given at 3pm to a larger than normal audience (approximately 45 people) who had turned up to find out what the outcome was. After questions, the event was closed formally by the Head of Orthopaedics. The last part of the day, after the crowd had left, was to go through the implementation plan and ensure that every task had an owner and that the timescales were realistic.

After the event

In the weeks following the event we held a rapid improvement event (see Chapter 6) and there were many smaller actions implemented.

Two months after the 2P event, when everything was in place, we confirmed the new performance of the team. All patients were now able to be seen in pre-assessment (up from just over 75 per cent) and there had been a corresponding reduction in 'day of surgery' cancellations caused by patients being unfit for surgery. Patients were spending less than 50 per cent of the time they had previously taken in pre-assessment and only had to get undressed once; blood was taken without requiring patients to go on a 1.5km round trip. More patients were being seen with the same number of nurses and a vacant post was no longer required to be filled.

Key learning points

Having doctors who 'dropped in and out' caused us a number of problems and it would have been better to have had consistency in personnel. Other than that, this was a textbook 2P event.

3P case study (manufacturing)

The 3P case study is from a manufacturing context and is summarized in Table 5.6.

TABLE 5.6   3P event snapshot

3P event snapshot
The organization: manufacturing business (electronics).
Duration of session: two days.
Present at session: Operations Director, Engineering Lead, Test Equipment Lead, Head of Design, manufacturing cell leaders (three off), manufacturing operators (two off) and Sales Lead. The purchasing team were involved on day two.
Focus of 3P event: during the development of a new product, when the first prototype was available, the team wanted to plan the layout and assembly sequence of the production cell and make any necessary changes to ensure the product could be assembled and tested without hindrance.

Prior to the 3P event

The product was being developed using a multidisciplinary team involving design engineers, manufacturing engineers, test engineers, sales and a production team representative. For the 3P we also had to engage some of the team who would be responsible for building the new product when launched. All of the participants were already familiar with Lean. We therefore didn't have much to do prior to the event other than produce an event preparation form and provide some details of the overall objectives, which were to design a process capable of building between 1,000 and 1,500 products per week (depending on demand) with a fixed unit cost and requiring less than £50,000 of equipment costs (including all additional test equipment).

During the 3P event

The Director of Engineering (who was responsible for both the design engineers and the manufacturing engineers) gave a quick opening brief. The Sales Director was also there to answer some questions about expected demand for the product and the market expectations about cost. After that the team confirmed the takt time and used the prototype to work through, and map out, the sequence of assembly and test steps required to produce the product. We then ran through a simulated process of building and testing the product and looked at how easy it was for the manufacturing team to build and test it. This identified a number of issues related to problems with the design that made the product harder to assemble than necessary.

After lunch we created a rough paper layout for the process before cutting out larger pieces of cardboard to represent benches and key equipment, as well as shuffling some real equipment into the area, used to help us finalize the design of the manufacturing cell. During this process we also noted there was going to be a problem with the storage of printed circuit boards (PCBs) with the existing racking and we produced two different examples of how the boards could be stored.

At the end of day one we did a presentation to a mixture of engineering, production and sales staff about the proposed cell layout and some of the changes that would occur with the product to make it easier to build.

Day two

Overnight, a number of people had identified some further ideas about how to make the product easier to manufacture, so we started the day by summarizing the major changes to the product that needed to occur prior to its introduction into production. We also had input on day two from the purchasing team about the cost implications of changing some of the components to make them easier to assemble, and also to get a view on possible savings from changes to the design of the test equipment that had to be purchased.

We then started the process of creating a 7 flows diagram for the assembly and test process and a final paper layout for the assembly cell, as well as producing a list of design changes for the product itself.

At the end of the day we organized an informal closing brief with the directors of operations, engineering and sales, plus anyone from assembly and engineering who were interested to get their comments on the new process and proposed product changes.

After the 3P event

The product changes required the team to do some feasibility assessments but most were incorporated. The product was released into production six weeks after the 3P event, and in this period many of the actions on the 7 flows diagram were implemented. The cell took two days to get up to speed (250 units per day) and overall the product beat its manufacturing cost targets by 12 per cent.

Key learning points

One minor learning point was to ensure we had enough cardboard; another was to ensure we had the area cleared before the 3P event, as there was a lot of equipment and racking 'dumped' in the area we were reviewing. Also, we should have made better use of the purchasing team as they had some really good ideas about reducing the product costs, which actually caused us to change the ultimate design of the product with a knock-on effect on how the product was assembled.

Closing thoughts

There are typically lots of actions that need to be undertaken after a 2P or 3P event. Like a VSM event you will be able to group these under the headings of project, event or 'do it'. In addition to planning your projects and events, you may find it useful to group some of the do its together to make a small event, meaning that you get a few people together for a short period to actually implement the 'do its'. However, whatever approach you take, if you do not implement the actions you have planned through your 2P/3P event then you will have wasted your time and the time of everyone else involved. One of the key events that arise from VSM events and 2P/3P events are rapid improvement events (RIE), which are the subject of the next chapter.

Closing thoughts

Rapid improvement events (RIE)

In this chapter I aim to answer the following questions:

1 What are rapid improvement events (RIE)?

2 How should you structure an RIE?

3 What are the key tools of an RIE?

Sooner rather than later in your Lean programme you will reach the point at which it is time to physically implement changes. You may have reached this point via a number of routes. For example, you may have undertaken a value stream mapping (VSM) event and through it identified the need for a 2P event and are now thinking about implementing the changes, or you may simply have done a quick scoping session and be moving straight into implementation. Whatever the route you have taken to reach this point, any change that needs to be implemented within a finite period of time is best done through using a rapid improvement event (RIE). Modifying the definition of a Lean event used in Chapter 1 to include the term rapid improvement event gives us:

A rapid improvement event focuses the effort of a group of people for a finite period of time on a defined problem, at the end of which something has changed.

Unlike other aspects of Lean, there is far less agreement on what to actually call these implementation events and you will find the use of various alternative names such as kaizen blitz, point kaizen event and Lean workshop. Whatever the name used, they all aim to achieve the same thing, which is the implementation of changes to a process.

RIEs are flexible in duration and can be used to tackle an enormous variety of issues, drawing on virtually any Lean tool or concept as needed. The aim of this chapter is to provide you with a structure for running RIEs along with a detailed overview of the three Lean concepts that are common to the majority of RIEs, namely *5S*, *standard work* and *cellular working*. All the other main Lean tools commonly used in an RIE are discussed in Chapter 13.

Key RIE concepts and tools

5S and standard work are such common concepts in Lean activities that they warrant a more in-depth review than many of the other tools and concepts of Lean that I will cover in Chapter 13. Cellular working is also very common, although admittedly less so than 5S and standard work, but it is so closely associated with RIEs as to also warrant its inclusion in this chapter.

5S – creating the visual workplace

5S is the tool used to create a *visual workplace*. You will be familiar with these whether you have been on a Lean training course or not because they are all around us. For example, when you are driving a car you are guided by lane markings, road signs, traffic lights and the physical design of the road, including the layout of junctions. All of these things are designed to achieve two things: to keep the traffic flowing and reduce the risk of things going wrong (ie accidents). Another familiar example is found in supermarkets where 'like things' are stored together, for example you find all of the pet food in the same (or very nearby) aisles. You are also able to find things very quickly even in unfamiliar supermarkets because of visual signals (normally overhead signs) telling you what is in each aisle. This is another example of a visual workplace that is designed to reduce your searching time for individual products (and also stop you needing to ask supermarket employees where items are located). Of course, there is a lot of psychology that goes into the design of a store to maximize your spend whilst you are in the store, but that is a different issue. Visual workplaces can also be seen in the way that cars are designed so that the driver's hand and foot has access to all the controls they need when driving. Similarly, airports are designed to keep passengers flowing with only the occasional interaction with airport staff, and so on.

The aims of visual workplaces is to reduce the time taken for people to find what they are looking for, keep them doing the right thing and reduce the risk to everyone. 5S is the Lean tool used to create the visual workplace and its introduction should reduce the amount of time lost by staff looking for information, people and products and reduce the risk to staff, customers, the public and products. Given that it is not uncommon for people to spend up to 30 per cent of their time looking for things (activities that can be called 'hunting and gathering') 5S can also have a big impact on productivity as well. In addition to the hard benefits of improved productivity, better flow and safer processes, a visual workplace is also nicer to work in and more aesthetically pleasing, something both employees and customers often value.

There are, unsurprisingly, five steps to a 5S programme. Each of the steps is defined by a word beginning with, of course, S. There are the original Japanese words (for which I have used English letters to represent the sound of the Japanese word) and then English equivalent words that are all summarized in Table 6.1. Note that there are sometimes different English words used and I have given the most common alternatives where appropriate.

Below are each of the 5S steps – sort, set, shine, standardize, sustain – itemized in more detail.

Sort

The first S is concerned with removing rubbish and ensuring that only the necessary items are located in a work area. It also has the purpose of highlighting faulty equipment. The way 'sort' is often carried out

TABLE 6.1   5S overview

Japanese word	English equivalent	Description
Seiri	Sort	Removing unwanted or unused items, highlighting faulty equipment and eliminating sources of clutter.
Seiton	Set (simplify)	Arranging items into logical 'home' locations, marking the home locations if needed and establishing guidelines for use.
Seiso	Shine (sweep)	Both the visual and physical cleaning of an area and work undertaken to reduce the accumulation of rubbish and mess such as stopping oil leaking from machines or improving the disposal of packaging and other waste materials.
Seiketsu	Standardize	Making an area more recognizable by using common colouring and also putting in place easy to understand procedures about how and where things are stored, replaced and highlighted as faulty.
Shitsuke	Sustain (stick to it, or self-discipline)	The regular review, auditing and improvement of the 5S process to ensure standards are being maintained.

is via a 'red tag attack' that involves touching (yes, physically touching) each item and asking the questions:

- Is this rubbish? If yes, dispose of it.
- Is this item used regularly? If no, and if not safety related, remove it to your 'red tag' holding area.
- Is this item broken? If yes, flag it for repair with a 'red tag'.

The reason for touching items is that people stop noticing items very quickly. If someone leaves a box in a corner it will effectively become 'invisible' within a few weeks. Touching things brings them back into conscious thought.

Anything other than rubbish should not be thrown out immediately. Instead, move it away from the area into a holding location in case people realize that they need it. This 'red tag holding area' should be regularly reviewed and any items that have not been claimed within a reasonable period should be scheduled for disposal or sale.

A key point to note is the reluctance of people to remove some items from their workplace 'just in case' it is needed. Except for safety related items, unless something has been used in the last three months and/or will definitely be used in the next month move it to your red tag holding area.

You also need to avoid demeaning staff during this exercise. During one exercise at the UK's HM Revenue and Customs in Scotland in 2007, a team of external consultants were doing a 5S exercise on the content of people's desks. On one desk there was a banana and the Lean consultants asked the owner of the banana whether it was 'active or inactive' (meaning, was it in use or not). I don't know what your reply would have been but mine would have been something like, 'Well, it is inactive now and will become active around lunchtime.' This was demeaning to the staff involved, resulted in a complaint to the trade union and the story ended up being reported in the national press. Don't fall into the same trap!

Set

This is about giving a logical home to items that remain after your 'red tag attack'. You should think like a builder, meaning the more frequently you use an item the closer you keep it to the individual. For example:

- If a builder uses a hammer every few minutes they will keep it on their tool-belt.
- If they use a drill once an hour they will keep it in a toolbox.
- If they use a set of spanners once a day they will keep it in their van.
- If they use a stepladder once a month they will keep it back at their yard.

Set is also concerned with setting the limits of how much stock, or how many items, can be stored in an area. This means preventing excessive amounts of items at any one time.

Set involves giving key items a logical and clearly marked home. Again, you can go too far with this: I have seen examples of people putting bits of tape around the staplers and pens on their desks. You know you have gone too far when people start painting outlines of their feet on the floor with the words 'left' and 'right'. Keep focused on key equipment only is my suggestion.

Shine

This involves two things. First practising a start and end of shift '5-minute shine' in which the team ensure that all the items are returned to their home location and any rubbish is disposed of. Second, seeking to eliminate any sources of mess or rubbish. For example, machines that throw waste materials and oil on to the floor should have guards installed to guide this material into waste bins, or where items are delivered with multiple layers of packaging then the supplier should be asked to reduce the excess packaging.

Standardize

This is concerned with creating standard processes that explain how the area works, for example the daily '5-minute shine' and how to highlight when equipment is faulty. It is also concerned with creating a standardized map of the area, providing instructions for visitors and team members about how the area functions and highlighting any safety hazards, as shown in Figure 6.1 in what is termed a 'standard work layout sheet'.

Sustain

The last of the 5Ss is a management discipline aimed at ensuring that 5S is not just used as a surrogate word for a tidy up. 5S should ideally be something that is practised every day through the '5-minute shine' and something that should be improved regularly. To sustain 5S it is common to undertake a regular 5S audit. An example 5S audit form is shown in Table 6.2 and a scoring matrix for 5S is shown in Table 6.3. A description of how to score each question is provided in Table 6.3.

FIGURE 6.1 Example standard work layout sheet

Storage Area A	**Storage Area B**	**Warning** Sharp Blade	

Storage of items with a shelf life of less than 4 weeks.

Storage of items with a shelf life of longer than 4 weeks.

Machine

Information Desk

Any notes being provided should be logged into the area via the information desk.

Standing Instructions
• 5S Audits twice weekly

Safety Hazard	Area: Out patients	Name: A N Other

TABLE 6.2 Example 5S audit form

5S audit form						
Check question		**1**	**2**	**3**	**4**	**5**
Sort	Are there unneeded items in the area?					
	Is there any unused equipment or other materials being held in the area?					
	Is there any unused paperwork or documents in the area?					
	Is it obvious which items are current and in use?					

TABLE 6.2   *continued*

	5S audit form					
	Check question	**1**	**2**	**3**	**4**	**5**
Set	Is it obvious what is supposed to happen in the area?					
	Are there signposted storage places for documents and equipment in place?					
	Are all shelved and stored items labelled and located correctly?					
	Are the purposes of different areas clearly marked and are they correct?					
Shine	Are the work areas and floors tidy and free of clutter?					
	Are items returned to their 'home' locations at the end of the day/shift?					
	Are the required equipment and materials available?					
	Are staff putting things back in the right place at the end of every day/shift?					
Standardize	Does everyone understand the purpose of their 5S activities?					
	Is there a maintenance process for each key piece of equipment?					
	Is there a clear improvement plan for the work area?					
	Are there clear instructions visible for how to operate the area's 5S process?					

TABLE 6.2 *continued*

5S audit form						
	Check question	**1**	**2**	**3**	**4**	**5**
Sustain	Do employees implement the 5S process consistently?					
	Is there a regular audit schedule to monitor 5S performance?					
	Does the area leader take an active interest in 5S and the actions arising?					
	Do employees and managers take action to correct low scores on the 5S audit?					

TABLE 6.3 Scoring matrix for the 5S audit

Score	Summary	Description
5	Exceptional	No room for improvement at all.
4	Very good	Could be used as 'best practice example'.
3	Good	Requirements exceeded in some areas.
2	Acceptable	Requirements met.
1	Poor/no evidence	No evidence or need for substantial improvement.

The minimum you can score during a 5S audit using the form in Table 6.2 is 20 and the maximum is 100. A realistic score for an area starting out on their 5S journey is between 30 and 50 and you should be aiming to exceed 80 within a reasonable period.

One final aspect of a visual workplace, namely the use of information centres to display performance data, instructions, audit results and provide an area for people to put ideas and comments on to, will be covered in Chapter 7.

The sixth 'S'?

Sometimes you will read about a sixth S (normally referred to as 6S) where the additional S is used to indicate 'safety'. You may choose to use this, but my own view is that 'safety' is not something you 'add on' to a 5S programme but something that is integral to every step. For example, you may only rarely use an eye-wash to remove grit and chemicals from people's eyes and therefore doing a 'sort' exercise you might decide to move it away from the work area, but the problem is that when you need it, you need it quickly. Similarly, you want to ensure that you can find fire extinguishers, defibrillators and similar equipment very quickly so you may give them dedicated homes during the 'set' part of 5S. We could go on, but the reality is that the safety cuts through all of the 5Ss and I would recommend not implying it is an addendum to 5S.

Standard work

We are all familiar with the concepts of standard operating instructions because they exist all around us. For example, the cooking instructions on food packets, rulebooks covering how to play different sports, and information from our banks telling us how to access information online. However, in a Lean context, standard work is concerned with more than just the provision of SOPs (standard operating procedures). For one thing, most SOPs are in the form of a flowchart or simple process instructions and if you give these to 10 people to follow they will normally find 11 different ways of doing it. Lean standard work aims to introduce consistency into working practices as well as defining the 'least waste' way of doing any work.

Takt time

As we have already seen in Chapter 4, takt time defines the average time between the arrival of individual pieces of 'work', whether that is the average time between the arrival of complaints, the arrival of patients or the arrival of orders. The aim of any process is to get the balance right between the arrival of 'work' and the process used to consume the work. Putting this into different words, calculating the takt time, is the first step in ensuring that you have the right number of people, the right equipment and the right capacity to process the work you need to do.

We can work through a simple example to show the calculation of takt time and how it might be used. I want you to imagine there is a process (doesn't matter what it is) where over a period of eight hours, 240 pieces of 'work' arrive at the start of the process. We would calculate the takt time using the following equation:

Available time/demand: in this case, the available time is 8 hours (480 minutes) and the demand is 240. Therefore we have 480/240 = 2 minutes

The takt time of this process is two minutes. This means that, on average, over the eight-hour period a piece of 'work' (which could be people, products, services, vehicles or anything similar) arrives every two minutes. In reality, work will often arrive much less linearly than this but stick with it for now.

If the person working at this stage can do any work required in under two minutes then they can keep up (on average) so that at the end of the day there is no backlog. This process is therefore said to be 'balanced' because the incoming work and the outgoing work are balanced. However, if the person at this stage needs three minutes to do their job then it means that they will fall behind, because the work is coming in every two minutes and they will be one minute behind after the first product, two minutes behind after the second. Therefore the process is not balanced.

In the example above, we calculated the takt time for an eight-hour period. Depending on the process under review you may have to calculate takt time for shorter or longer periods. For example, an emergency department in a hospital will often have very busy periods (say Friday nights) that have a very different takt time (ie the arrival of patients) than, say, a Sunday between 12pm and 2pm. Alternatively, an FMCG (fast-moving consumer goods) plant bottling products on a 24/7 basis may be able to calculate a takt time that remains constant for weeks on end. There may also be variations over a year (think of the difference in sales of ice cream in summer and winter), quarterly, monthly, weekly or daily.

To enable us to calculate the takt time for a process we need to do the following:

- Identify patterns in how the demand for your services/products vary over a day, week, month or year as appropriate to your organization.
- Identify periods with similar demands for work (ie Mon–Fri, 2–4pm, the month of August, etc).
- Calculate the takt time for each period.

Whilst it is possible in some organizations to level out the arrival of work, for many this variation in demand rates is difficult or impossible to control. However, once we have calculated the takt time for a process we can use it to calculate whether the process you are looking at is 'capable', meaning that it has the right number of people and right machine capacity to ensure that you can balance the incoming work with the work leaving the process.

Calculating minimum headcount

In Chapter 4 I introduced the concept of manual cycle time (MCT) as the amount of time required by humans to undertake a task. This is also sometimes referred to as 'touch time' as it is used to refer to the amount of time an operator in a factory would spend 'touching' the product – but in a lot of service environments this has no meaning so it is better to stick with MCT. Once we know the MCT of a process we can calculate the minimum headcount as follows:

> Manual cycle time/takt time: for example, if we have a process that requires 36 minutes of work to be undertaken (36 minutes of MCT) and that had a takt time of 8 minutes, it would mean our minimum headcount would be: 36 minutes / 8 minutes = 4.5 people

The term 'minimum headcount' is used because we have not added any allowance into the equation for holidays, absence, training, meetings, etc. You therefore normally need to add a safety factor to the minimum headcount that might be as low as 16 per cent, is most commonly 20–30 per cent and could be as high as 50 per cent, depending on how certain you are of your process and the times you have calculated for MCT and takt time. For the rest of this chapter I will assume that a suitable factor is added to every example given.

FIGURE 6.2   Example standard work loading chart

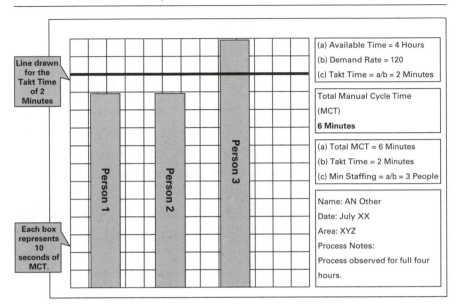

Line drawn for the Takt Time of 2 Minutes

Each box represents 10 seconds of MCT.

Person 1

Person 2

Person 3

(a) Available Time = 4 Hours

(b) Demand Rate = 120

(c) Takt Time = a/b = 2 Minutes

Total Manual Cycle Time

(MCT)

6 Minutes

(a) Total MCT = 6 Minutes

(b) Takt Time = 2 Minutes

(c) Min Staffing = a/b = 3 People

Name: AN Other

Date: July XX

Area: XYZ

Process Notes:

Process observed for full four hours.

To help visualize the concept of MCT and takt time we can use a 'standard work loading chart' as shown in Figure 6.2.

I want you to imagine that this process we are looking at in Figure 6.2 has three process steps that follow on from each other (ie Person 1 does their job and then passes it to Person 2, etc). The MCT for the whole process is six minutes and the takt time is shown as two minutes, meaning we have a minimum headcount requirement of three people calculated as follows:

MCT/takt time = 6 minutes/2 minutes = 3 people

On the left of the image in Figure 6.2 you will see a thick black line that has been drawn to show the takt time of two minutes on the graph. Each of the boxes up from the bottom represents 10 seconds of MCT so what this is telling us is that Person 1 and Person 2 both have 1 minute and 50 seconds of MCT to do, and Person 3 has 2 minutes and 20 seconds. Importantly, Person 3 will not be able to 'keep up' because their step takes longer than the takt time and they will fall behind by an average of 20 seconds for each piece of work done. Therefore, to bring this process back into 'balance' we need to reduce the workload on Person 3 to bring the total MCT under two minutes.

Another way of representing the bars on the standard work loading chart in Figure 6.2 is as a *yamazumi* chart, which 'stacks' activity to build up a picture of the structure of the work done by an individual or indeed a whole team. In Figure 6.3 I have shown a yamazumi representation of the work done by Person 3 that is shown in Figure 6.2. If we had been able to redesign the process followed by Person 3 we could represent the improved version on the same chart and through it see the amount of time saved for that step. Both the 'before' and 'after' for Person 3 is shown in Figure 6.3. This exercise of stacking the work done before and afterwards so that you can see the benefit is called a *paper kaizen*.

Now, you may say that this concept only works in factories but I can assure you it works across a wide range of sectors. The most common problem with applying it outside of a single production line is the fact that there is rarely only one type of work to be undertaken. For example, calls to a call centre can be simple or complex; patients coming into a hospital can have a variety of different issues, some that can be dealt with quickly and some that can't; a manufacturing plant may make a wide variety of products through the same processes, some that only require a minimal amount of work to make and others that

FIGURE 6.3 Paper kaizen example

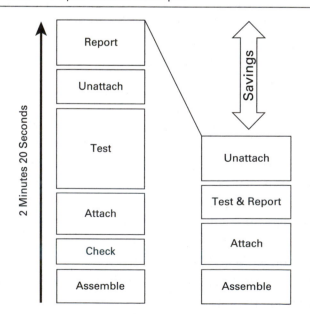

take much longer. This means that you won't just have a single MCT for the process but that each 'group' of products/people/calls will have a different MCT. This may be further complicated by the fact that you may also have different types of people in a process who undertake very different activities: for example, a nurse, physiotherapist and a doctor; or a planner, service engineer and quality control operator. To cope with this variation I will now show how you can use this to create a 'weighted manual cycle time' for any process.

The first step is to group together 'like' activities. Whilst you might argue that, for example, every product or every patient is unique, you will always find that you can put them together into groups that require similar amounts of work from different groups of people.

Imagine a theoretical process where there are four different staff groups, each with different skills and responsibilities (called Staff Groups 1 to 4). The process also has five different 'product' groups (for example different patient groups, call types or any other type of 'work' group) and all of this whole process information is summarized in Table 6.4.

TABLE 6.4   Example weighted manual cycle time starting template

	Column A	Column B	Column C	Column D	Column E	Column F
	Volume	% of total	Staff Group 1	Staff Group 2	Staff Group 3	Staff Group 4
Product Group 1	100	100/1500 = 6.7%	10 mins	30 mins	–	20 mins
Product Group 2	200	200/1500 = 13.3%	15 mins	15 mins	30 mins	15 mins
Product Group 3	300	300/1500 = 20%	20 mins	10 mins	20 mins	–
Product Group 4	400	400/1500 = 26.7%	25 mins	25 mins	–	5 mins
Product Group 5	500	500/1500 = 33.3%	30 mins	–	10 mins	15 mins

Table 6.4 may look complicated but try to stick with me for a little while. What it shows is the five product groups down the left hand side, the expected volume of each group (column A) and the percentage of the total that each of these volumes represent (column B). Table 6.4 also shows the manual cycle time, the amount of work done, for each staff group on each product group (columns C–F). You will see that for some of the product groups not all the staff are involved, for example for Product Group 5 it only involves Staff Groups 1, 3 and 4.

To calculate the weighted manual cycle time we multiply the MCTs in columns C–F against the per cent shown in column B. This is shown in Table 6.5 below.

Having done the calculations and added up the result we can see the weighted manual cycle time at the bottom of Table 6.5 for each

TABLE 6.5   Example weighted manual cycle time starting template

	Column A	Column B	Column C	Column D	Column E	Column F
	Volume	% of total	Staff Group 1	Staff Group 2	Staff Group 3	Staff Group 4
Product Group 1	100	100/1500 = 6.7%	10 mins x 6.7% = 0.7 mins	30 mins x 6.7% = 2 mins	–	20 mins x 6.7% = 1.3 mins
Product Group 2	200	200/1500 = 13.3%	15 mins x 13.3% = 2 mins	15 mins x 13.3% = 2 mins	30 mins x 13.3% = 4 mins	15 mins x 13.3% = 2 mins
Product Group 3	300	300/1500 = 20%	20 mins x 20% = 4 mins	10 mins x 20% = 2 mins	20 mins x 20% = 4 mins	–
Product Group 4	400	400/1500 = 26.7%	25 mins x 26.7% = 6.7 mins	25 mins x 26.7% = 6.7 mins	–	5 mins x 26.7% = 1.3 mins
Product Group 5	500	500/1500 = 33.3%	30 mins x 33.3% = 10 mins	–	10 mins x 33.3% = 3.3 mins	15 mins x 33.3% = 5 mins
Weighted manual cycle time			23.3 Mins	12.7 mins	11.3 mins	9.7 mins

staff group. Therefore, if the process had a takt time of four minutes we would need the following staff in each of the four groups:

- Staff Group 1 = 23.3 mins/4 mins = 5.8 people
- Staff Group 2 = 12.7 mins/4 mins = 3.2 people
- Staff Group 3 = 11.3 mins/4 mins = 2.8 people
- Staff Group 4 = 9.7 mins/4 mins = 2.4 people

We may also need to add a safety factor to these if we hadn't done so previously. We will also have to decide how to deal with 2.4 people (for example) by perhaps using part-time staff, only staffing that process for certain periods in the day or overstaffing it.

Time observation charts

In trying to create a standardized process it is often valuable to undertake some observation work to assess what is really going on within a process. There are a number of different ways of collecting this data. The first example I have shown in Figure 6.4 is a very simple process observation sheet that has space to observe three cycles of a process per page and the opportunity to identify whether steps are value adding or not.

FIGURE 6.4   Simple process observation sheet

Step Number	Activity Details	Task Done By	Time (1st View)	Time (2nd View)	Time (3rd View)	VA/NVA Task	Notes & Observations
Title/Area: Holiday Request Process						Sheet Number: 1 of 1	
1	Get File	Secretary	35s	39s	1m 15s	NVA	3rd Cycle had issue with finding file
2	Insert Notes	Secretary	44s	48s	47s	NVA	
3	Send to Ass't	Secretary	23s	35s	27s	NVA	
4	Sending (Post)	Post Team	125m	72m	188m	NVA	Waiting for porter
5	Wait for Ass't	Manager	2 Days	1 Day	15m	NVA	Manager on holiday during Cycle 1 & 2
6	Assessment	Manager	45s	1m 12s	5m	VA	Manager checked documents on Cycle 3
7	Return Item	Manager	25s	23s	28s	NVA	
8	Wait to Update	–	1 Day	1 Day	1 Day	NVA	
9	Update Files	Secretary	15s	25s	33s	VA?	
10	File Report	Secretary	44s	36s	23s	NVA	
11	Return	Secretary	5s	5s	5s	NVA	

FIGURE 6.5 Example activity charts

Step	Activity	Work Value Add	Work NAV	Work Run Time	Wait	Wait (Store)	Move	Yield %RTF	Dist (m)	Days	Hrs	Mins/ Secs	Notes
	Title: Production Process **Date: January XX**												
1	Move Item						●	25%	15			35s	
2	Check Forms		●									44s	
3	Send Item						●		25			23s	
4	Wait at Source				●					1d			
5	Wait at Destination				●					2d			
6	Assemble	●						87%				45s	
7	Return Item						●		25	1d			
8	Wait for next Step				●					1d			
9	Paint	●						47%			2m		
10	Dry in Store Area					●						44s	
11	Send to Despatch						●		15			5s	

The advantage of this simple process sheet is that you can see three cycles on a single sheet. The downside is that it is difficult to update or change. Another approach is shown in Figure 6.5. This is termed an 'activity chart' and makes it clearer what tasks are going on and also the yield, or probability that the work will be done 'right first time', as well as the distance travelled.

A more visual approach to displaying process information than either the activity chart or process observation sheet is a combination chart. As it implies, the name arises from the fact that it is useful for analyzing jobs that combine manual work with machine work and waiting time. An example combination chart is shown in Figure 6.6 for the simple process involving a client receiving some form of test. Also shown in Figure 6.6 is a line indicating the takt time for the process, showing that the combined time for all of the activities is less than the takt time and, therefore, the process is 'capable'.

In terms of ease of use, the simple observation form in Figure 6.4 is easiest to use and the combination chart in Figure 6.6 is hardest to use. Time observation is very useful if you want to get a real under-standing of what actually happens rather than what the instruction sheets say should happen. If you want to avoid arguments you should

FIGURE 6.6   Example combination chart

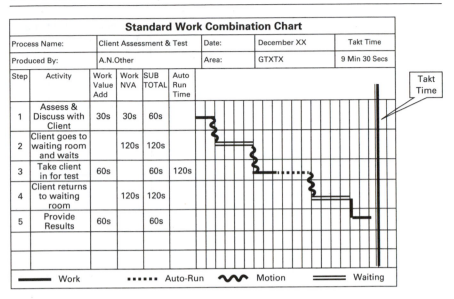

always tell people you will be observing them and why you are doing it. Also, for the first hour after you are there, be aware that people will be distracted by your presence and may go faster or slower than normal, so expect to have to wait for the second hour before you get realistic results that are reliable.

Before I finish the review of standard work there is one last concept to cover – and that is related to standard work instructions.

Standard work instructions

At their simplest, standard work instructions are the documented set of notes that outline how a process is undertaken. They can have a range of names such as method sheets, process instructions, or anything similar. An example template for a simple set of standard work instructions is shown in Table 6.6. A different style of standard work instruction template that includes both the process instructions and a standard work layout sheet is shown in Figure 6.7.

The myths of standard work

There are a number of comments, myths and objections that the introduction of standard work can generate. I have summarized below the ones that most commonly arise.

TABLE 6.6   Simple standard work instructions template

Step	Description of operation	Quality controls		Critical factors	Net time	
		check	measure		Min	Sec
1						
2						
3						
4						
5						
6						
7						
8						

FIGURE 6.7   Standard work instruction and layout template

	STANDARD WORK INSTRUCTION TEMPLATE			
Area		Issue Number		
Last Updated		Responsible Manager		
Step	Description	VA Time	NVA Time	
1				
2				
3				
4				
5				
6				
7				
8				
9				
10				
11				
12				
13				
14				
15				
16				

Safety Hazard   Inventory

Standard work deskills the task to a point where anyone could do the job

It is impossible to detail any task to the level that an unskilled person could undertake the task without training. Standard work simply removes the variation that occurs between people with a similar level of skill and helps them to find the most effective and productive way of undertaking tasks, whatever they may be.

Standard work should detail every aspect of the work standards into the process instructions

This has the effect of slowing down the introduction of standard work instructions because they are only adequate rather than excellent. It is better to achieve an 80 per cent improvement today than a 100 per cent improvement never.

Staff will look at the work instructions every day and follow them without question

I don't know where to start with this comment as it is so wrong. Standard work instructions that are posted on to walls, machines and notice boards will become effectively invisible within days. It is therefore important to continuously review how work is being undertaken.

Because we have standard work, operators won't make any mistakes

Human error will continue to occur whether you have standard work instructions or not. Standard work reduces the risk of errors arising but we can't assume there won't be any even with the most detailed standard work. What we can be sure of is that processes without properly agreed standard work will suffer more problems than those that do have standard work.

Staff will create their own work instructions

If individual staff members create their own standard work instructions then expect each to be different to each other. Standard work instructions are designed to be created by teams working together to identify the best and most effective way of undertaking tasks.

Cellular working

As I touched on in Chapter 4 when discussing mapping symbols, a *cell* consists of all the required equipment, tools, people and information required to deliver a product or service. Cells can be large, for example a Crown Court consists of all of the equipment, tools, people and information required to provide a court service; a supermarket has all the required equipment, tools, people and information required to deliver a retail service. However, cells in the context of Lean tend to be smaller, for example:

- An outpatients cell consisting of the clinical and non-clinical staff and all equipment.

- A manufacturing cell consisting of the manufacturing team, support staff and all of the production equipment.

- A trading standards cell consisting of the officers and support staff and their supporting equipment.

- A repair team cell consisting of the planners, mechanics and the associated equipment.

Cells originated in manufacturing, where it had traditionally been the way to organize factories by 'function' (for example, to have all of the cutting machines in one area and all of the forming machines in another area). It was noted that to complete a product in this type of environment meant there were a lot of delays as the parts were moved from, say, cutting to forming and then waiting for the part to be scheduled at the next stage, as shown conceptually in Figure 6.8.

This led to the development of a concept called Group Technology, where all of the equipment required to produce a product, or a closely related range of products, was grouped together into one team, or cell. This cut down both the physical distance travelled by the product and also the overall lead time by cutting out the delays between steps, as shown conceptually in Figure 6.9.

FIGURE 6.8 Functional factory layout

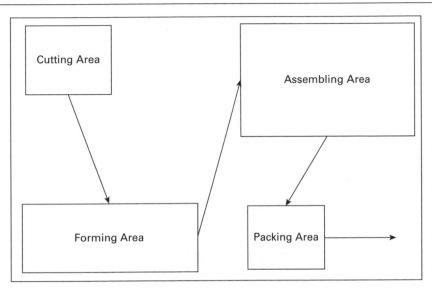

FIGURE 6.9 Conceptual cellular layout

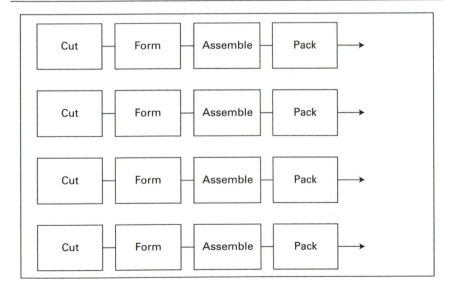

In addition to having all of the required assets to enable a product or service to be delivered, a Lean cell must have all four of the following aspects incorporated into it:

1 Flow: meaning small batch sizes and the elimination (or at least management) of bottlenecks.

2 Pull: meaning triggering activity on demand and having *kanbans* in place.

3 Standard work, as discussed earlier in this chapter.

4 Visual management (5S), also discussed in this chapter.

There is a very close association between rapid improvement events and 5S, standard work and cellular working, hence their inclusion in this chapter. Having discussed these critical issues we can now explore the typical life-cycle of a rapid improvement event.

Running rapid improvement events

Rapid improvement events (RIEs) can last anywhere between 30 minutes and five days or more. The most common duration of an RIE is two to four days. Often these days will be undertaken concurrently, for example a Monday to Thursday in the same week, but they could occur over a number of weeks if required. The actual RIE itself sits within a longer cycle that consists of the work done prior to the RIE, the RIE itself and the work done after the RIE to embed the changes. These additional 'wings' to an RIE can extend the whole process out to 9–12 weeks. This doesn't mean that people are working full time on the RIE for the whole of this period but that the time taken from initially deciding to undertake an RIE, until it is complete and many of the bugs and issues eliminated after the event has occurred, can take a long time.

In the following sections I will go through a hypothetical RIE that is planned over a nine-week period. The actual RIE will run during week five and will last for three days. For the purposes of this explanation it does not matter what the process is that the team are looking at.

Preparing for the RIE (weeks 1–4)

The kickoff for the RIE will normally be either the completion of a scoping paper (Chapter 2) or an event preparation form (Chapter 5). This will outline who needs to be involved and obviously some planning will need to be done to ensure these people are able to support the RIE in week five. They will also benefit from some basic Lean training covering the five principles, 5S and any other tools identified for use during the RIE if they don't already possess these skills. Other things that need to occur during this phase include the following:

- gathering any data and examples of any paperwork;
- walking the process to ensure you understand it;
- briefing the team affected so they know what to expect;
- identifying the 'Top 10 Hurts' for the process, these being the things that people really want to change.

In addition, you will need to brief the event sponsor who will be doing an opening brief on day one to set the scene, tell the team what the expectation is and to motivate them for the RIE. It is also often useful to do a pre-RIE 5S exercise.

Running the rapid improvement event (week five)

During week five we will be running the RIE and, as mentioned, I have assumed it will last for three days. The activities undertaken on each of the three days is described below. There should be time allowed during each day for the colleagues of those involved in the RIE to ask questions about what is going on. This is a hypothetical event; you have a lot of flexibility in how to structure the event and the example below should be used as an indication of the things that need to be done rather than a template of how to run your event.

RIE day one

The event sponsor should do an opening brief and there should be a very quick Lean refresher session. The team should be reminded of what the event is about and the expected outcomes. After that the team should go about mapping the current state of the process using the tools described in Chapter 5 when I discussed 'understanding the current state' and 'design and test options' for a 2P/3P event. If the RIE has been preceded by a 2P/3P event then it is not normally necessary to repeat the current state analysis unless there is a new team involved in the actual implementation event.

RIE day two

It is likely that the team will not have fully finished testing options until mid-morning and, after selecting the right way to go, the team should start moving/changing the process. If you are changing a physical layout of a process (as opposed to perhaps introducing new terms of reference) then you should undertake a 5S 'sort' exercise. Having got the basic process laid out in the way you want it to be, you should simulate the process again to ensure it works. This could mean pretending to build a real product, dealing with a pretend customer or even pretending to deal with a patient. Towards the end of day two the team should start creating a visual workplace (if applicable) and also looking to create the standard work for the process.

RIE day three

This will see the team finalizing the new process, documenting what they have done, producing a 'To Do' list and ensuring that the visual workplace they have created is correct. After lunch, the team should start preparing to deliver a closing brief to their event sponsor and the rest of their team about the new process, as outlined in Chapter 4.

Embedding the change (weeks 6–9)

Much of the work in this phase can be achieved through the use of *managing for daily improvement*, a concept we will discuss in Chapter 7. During this period the 'To Do' list needs to be closed off, the team should have opportunities to discuss issues and ideas for further improvements and the new performance needs to be managed. The purpose of the embedding phase of the RIE is to turn the short-term changes in the way the processes work into long-term changes in the way that teams and individuals work and behave.

Changing a process is easy; the difficult thing is to get people to work to the new process. Think of a time when you changed something in your own life, perhaps the route you take to get to work. How long did it take to stop feeling like the new route was 'different' and unfamiliar? Well, the answer is that for something to become a habit it needs to be repeated 30–35 times over a period of up to a month. This doesn't mean you can do 30–35 repetitions in a day and the habit will form. It means that you will need to repeat the way the work was done on that day 30–35 times (ie a month or more) before it becomes a habitual way of working.

Another analogy is that many people keep a pair of old shoes for the garden. Even though they are scruffy and dirty they don't throw them out because they are easy to slip on and are comfortable. When you change a process you effectively give them a new pair of shoes that feel 'different' to the old shoes. There is a natural inclination for people to want to put on the old shoes as they are more familiar and feel 'right'. To achieve a change in behaviour you either have to make it impossible for people to put on the old shoes or you have to keep reminding them to wear the new shoes until they are broken in and don't feel different any more.

In the next section I will explore a number of different RIE case studies from a variety of sectors to give you a feel for how they work. Because RIEs can vary in duration, content and outcomes depending on the organization(s) involved and the issues being tackled I have given four different case studies covering RIEs of four-day, three-day and one-day duration.

4-day RIE case study (manufacturing)

TABLE 6.7   Four-day RIE snapshot

RIE snapshot

The organization: manufacturing.

Duration of session: four days.

Present at session: Team leader and four production operators, operations planner, production engineering (two people), machine operators (two people) and a member of the procurement team (part-time).

Focus of RIE: the integration of a cutting and laser routing team into one production cell.

Prior to the RIE

This was part of an improvement programme covering the whole organization and was preceded by a scoping session and value stream mapping event. This was the first of the RIEs that arose out of the VSM event and the Lean facilitator put together an event preparation form to outline the specific objectives for this RIE. Due to the urgency of the changes required, the team mapped the current state and produced a spaghetti diagram prior to the event rather than during the RIE. The Lean facilitator also did a risk assessment and arranged for some heavy lifting equipment to be available for days two and three of the RIE in order to cope with shifting the machinery into a new position. The team also produced some extra stock to enable them to cope with a four day 'shutdown' during the RIE. Lastly, the Lean facilitator calculated the takt time and minimum staffing and did some Lean training with the team who would be involved.

During the RIE

On day one the Operations Director gave a short opening brief to the event. Having already identified the current state, the team were able to move directly into identifying options for the layout of the area using a paper doll, as discussed in Chapter 5. The team then cut out from large sheets of paper 'lifesize' replicas of the items to be moved in order to ensure that they would fit into the locations identified. By the end of the first day the team had identified the layout they were after.

Day two

Day two commenced with the team reviewing their decision from day one. After a few minor adjustments they started moving the equipment using the heavy lifting gear that had arrived in the morning. Whilst this was going on the rest of the team moved the remaining equipment into position. The movement of the equipment took most of the day, but towards the end of day two the team were able to do a dry run to confirm that the new layout worked appropriately.

Day three

During day three the team started putting in place a visual work-place and created shadow boards, these being boards containing all of the tools required to operate a machine or process. On the shadow board an outline of each item is drawn on the board so that when the item is removed you can see that it is missing. The team also marked out 'walking lanes' to provide a safe route through the cell. The machinery was installed and tested during day three.

Day four

Day four commenced with a full run through the process and some minor adjustments. The team then put together a summary of the new process including a standard work layout sheet for the area (an example of these can be seen in Figure 6.1) and undertook a 5S exercise. The last part of the day was taken up with preparing for the embedding phase and doing a short closing brief.

After the RIE

The team met weekly for four weeks after the event, during which they did a 5S exercise, and reviewed problems with the new process and opportunities for further improvement. This was in addition to daily team meetings (we cover this in Chapter 7). At the end of the four-week period, the project was deemed to be a success with a net reduction in the lead time through the new cell of 12 days (reducing from 15 days to 3 days).

Key learning point

Preparing for the event by 'building ahead' and also keeping the capability to produce any critical products during the RIE made a difference to the perception of the event within the wider organization.

3-day RIE case study (health care)

TABLE 6.8 Three-day RIE snapshot

RIE snapshot

The organization: health care

Duration of session: three days.

Present at session: Matron, Sister, Deputy Sister, ward clerk, nurse, health care assistant, Registrar (plus consultant, part-time), porter and two people from the facilities team.

Focus of RIE: improving the flow of patients with minor conditions in an emergency department (ED). The staffing of the department was specifically excluded from the RIE with the aim being to reduce the number of times that the team ran out of drugs and the time lost searching for information and equipment.

Prior to the RIE

This was a stand-alone event aimed at tackling a specific issue in an emergency department (ED), and prior to the event a short scoping session was undertaken. The team were identified and given some basic Lean training. A layout of the area was also identified and examples of the paperwork used in the 'minors' area gathered. The Lean facilitator also put together a spaghetti diagram for different patient journeys in the area.

During the RIE

The opening brief was done by the Chief Operating Officer and the team were broken into two groups. The first looked at the stock levels within the drug room and the process for identifying and dealing with broken equipment. The second team looked at the layout of the minors area with the aim of creating a visual workplace. The teams spent the first part of the day reviewing the current state before moving into designing and testing options.

The 'drug' team identified that they had £300 worth of excess stock and were out of stock on 12 drugs that they needed, plus they pulled together the equipment that was broken and worked through how the team currently reported these issues. The layout team walked various processes, including that for replacement linen, replacing consumables and putting a cast on a minor fracture. Day one ended with a discussion with the Head of Procurement and the Pharmacy Manager about whether it would be possible to introduce a '2 Bin Pull' system (see *kanban* in Chapter 13) for drugs, meaning that the team would reduce the number of 'stock outs' experienced.

Day two commenced with both teams presenting to each other what had been achieved on day one. Both teams then got on with putting in place a visual workplace and moving items so that the travel distance was significantly reduced. The afternoon saw the team labelling racks and locations for key equipment (such as blood-pressure-monitoring equipment). There was also a process developed with the Facilities Manager on how broken equipment would be identified and fixed within a reasonable period. At the end of day two the team did a dry run for a variety of different patient scenarios in order to test whether or not the new process worked.

Day three focused on improving the storage of documentation to make forms and patient notes easier to find and reduce the risk of the team running out of them. There were a number of discussions during the day with the pharmacy team, diagnostic teams (such as radiology and phlebotomy) who although not directly involved were going to be affected by subsequent events. The team did a short closing brief at the end of the session to all staff who were available and a selection of managers from across the organization.

After the RIE

The team struggled to hold a weekly meeting to review the changes, so a review was undertaken on an ad hoc basis over the following eight weeks. This led to some problems, particularly when the team weren't able to easily log operating problems – as this drove them to want to go back to the old way of doing things. However, the ED Manager managed to hold it together and at the end of the period the team had saved the equivalent of 200 hours per month, allowing them to spend more time with patients, and reducing the risks faced by both the team and patients.

Key learning point

Before you start out, make sure the team is completely committed to following up on their improvement activities for a number of weeks after the event is over.

1-day RIE case study (logistics)

TABLE 6.9   One-day RIE snapshot

RIE snapshot

The organization: logistics (warehousing).

Duration of session: one day.

Present at session: Team leader, two associates, planner and production engineer.

Focus of RIE: the focus was on reducing the distance travelled during picking from a 'pick face', a line of racks from which associates pick the requisite number of items prior to moving on to the next rack.

Prior to the RIE

Prior to the event the team produced an event summary form and the Lean facilitator also mapped the current process, producing a spaghetti diagram for how the associates currently walked the process. It was identified that they were travelling some 160m per 'pick' on average, because of the layout – an example of which is shown in Figure 6.10.

During the RIE

The team almost immediately identified that they could reduce the travel distance (and hence speed up the pick rate) by having the racks

FIGURE 6.10 Representation of the current pick face process

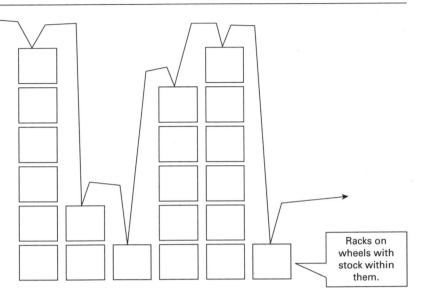

Racks on wheels with stock within them.

'in line' rather than having to walk up and down the aisles. However, the discussion was how to deal with bringing the racks forward and who would do the moving. The team worked through a series of options before finally deciding that the associate who took the last item from the rack would be responsible for pulling the next rack forward to the 'pick face'. The team leader would ensure that there were always racks available to be pulled forward. The afternoon of the event was taken up with putting in place the visual workplace (signs, floor markings, etc) to enable the new process to work. A representation of the new process is shown in Figure 6.11. The day ended with the RIE team discussing the new process with the outgoing and incoming shifts.

After the RIE

The process was monitored for a number of days after the event but there were very few teething problems. The monitoring was undertaken during the normal shift-start meetings that followed the process of *managing for daily improvement* (MDI) (covered in Chapter 7). The team reduced the overall travel distance per pick-run

FIGURE 6.11   Representation of the new pick face process

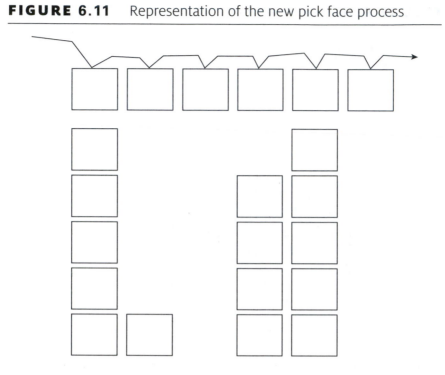

from 160m to 30m. Overall, this helped to improve pick rates by more than 6 per cent.

Learning points

A highly enthusiastic sponsor and the presence of a motivated team leader during the RIE make all the difference.

Closing thoughts

As I said at the start of this chapter, RIEs can vary in length from 30 minutes up to five days. The event could occur in 'one big bang' or be spread over a number of weeks, as needed. However you choose to proceed after your VSM events and 2P/3P events, unless you actually implement the changes all the work done up until this point will have been wasted.

Another of my interests is the science of astronomy. It is an area where new research is published daily and revolutionary research about the fundamentals of the universe are being actively pursued in areas as diverse as exoplanets (planets orbiting other stars), the nature of gravity, the age of the universe and many further areas. Careers are made on the back of leading edge research, but imagine that you have done all of the work and had discovered new and revolutionary things and are ready to present your findings to the world, but then didn't. All the work you will have done will have been for nothing – and this is the same as failing to turn your plans into actual improvements in a Lean context.

In the next chapter we review the concept of managing for daily improvement, the key to the longer-term process of embedding the changes made during RIEs.

Managing for daily improvement (MDI)

In this chapter I aim to answer the following questions:

1 How do you define managing for daily improvement (MDI)?

2 What does MDI involve?

3 How can you use it to help turn process changes into behaviour changes?

In any organization looking to create an environment where improvement occurs every day there are a number of routines that need to happen every day, every week and every month. In addition, leaders at all levels will need to behave in a manner that supports a culture of continuous improvement. Collectively these routines and behaviours are called *leader standard work*. The aspects of leader standard work that relate directly to daily activities are called *managing for daily improvement* (MDI) (which is also sometimes referred to as simply 'daily improvement'). These daily routines are at the heart of continuous improvement and are also key to embedding any changes that are made to the way things are done. Most frequently MDI is practised by front-line teams – and that will be the focus of this chapter. However, as you will see when we discuss the remaining aspects of leader standard work in Chapter 8, daily routines don't just apply to front-line teams. The principle of MDI is to involve 'everybody, every day' in improving the way things are done.

In this chapter I start with an overview of the structure of MDI and end with a discussion of how MDI also forms the basis of embedding changes made after RIEs.

Managing for daily improvement: everybody, every day

How do you get everybody thinking about improvement every day? That is the question that MDI attempts to answer. It consists of the four routines that are shown in Figure 7.1.

These are not stand-alone routines and often overlap. For example, you may undertake some problem solving as part of a team meeting, or whilst undertaking 'management by walking about' it is common to uncover information that requires the information centre to be updated. We will explore each of these four routines in more detail below.

FIGURE 7.1   The four routines of MDI

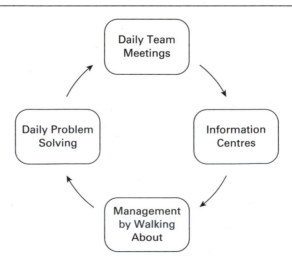

Daily team meetings

Many organizations already have regular (if not quite daily) meetings that have names such as toolbox talks, shift handovers, scrums, daily accountability meeting, morning briefings or similar. There are normally three objectives of these meetings:

1 What happened yesterday?

2 What do we need to do today?

3 What problems/issues or ideas do we have to deal with?

Daily team meetings can vary from 5 minutes to 30 minutes depending on the environment and organization. As long as you cover all the ground, shorter is better than longer. The difference between a good daily team meeting and a bad one normally comes down to issues such as:

- Ensuring the maximum number of people attend (or indeed the full team if possible).

- People come with data already prepared, and also prepared to discuss it.

- Having a defined agenda that you stick to ruthlessly.

- Giving everyone an opportunity to participate.

- Logging issues and ideas and giving feedback on the progress of dealing with issues and ideas logged previously that are still outstanding.

- Focusing on action rather than moaning or an extended discussion that doesn't lead to any conclusion.

Having the meeting standing up rather than sitting down will help to keep it short, and inviting guests to attend will help to keep things fresh. By guests, I mean people who have an input to make to the team such as a specialist engineer invited by a plant servicing team to discuss a technical issue, or a member of a procurement team invited by a manufacturing team to discuss the delivery of key parts.

Most people associate daily team meetings with front-line operational staff, whether it is a construction team or a shift in a fire station, but the concept of 'everybody, every day' means just that. Daily team meetings should occur in every team area, from a sales team to human resources and from a hospital ward to a call centre. It is common to hold a daily team meeting around an information centre as these contain all of the information required by the team and provide a useful place to log ideas and issues.

Information centres

Information centres provide a centralized place for displaying information relevant to a team. They may be called team boards, production boards or Lean boards but they aim to serve three purposes:

- Provide information on current performance against the team's measures.

- Provide information on team deployments for the day or week and details of the forward work plan.

- Provide a place for people to log ideas and issues and for them to be tracked as they are improved.

Some people have opted to have a Lean board that contains details of all things Lean related and to have a separate 'control board' or production control board that contains details of staff deployments, but I would suggest it makes sense to put them in the same area and have them reviewed at the same time in order to avoid Lean being seen as 'something else to do' rather than 'the way we do things around here'.

One possible layout for an information centre is shown in Figure 7.2. This example contains all of the information most commonly found on information centres. I have grouped this information together under three headings.

Performance data

This section needs to contain the team targets. Every team should have a range of targets that are linked to the overall corporate strategy (we will discuss this more in Chapters 8 and 9) and these targets normally drop into five areas:

FIGURE 7.2   Example information centre layout

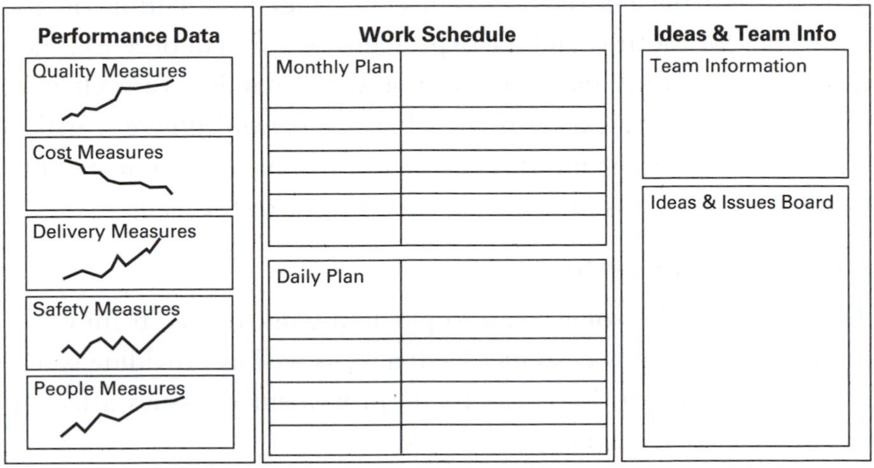

Performance Data	Work Schedule		Ideas & Team Info
Quality Measures	Monthly Plan		Team Information
Cost Measures			
Delivery Measures			Ideas & Issues Board
Safety Measures	Daily Plan		
People Measures			

- **Quality** – measures related to such things as scrap/rework, customer satisfaction and similar issues.

- **Cost** – measures related to the financial performance of the team such as their costs against budget, profit centre performance or team surplus.

- **Delivery** – measures related to the operational performance of the team such as patients discharged, units made, calls taken, sales made, etc.

- **Safety** – measures related to incidents and accidents.

- **Morale** – measures directly related to people. This could include absence rates or something more positive such as staff survey results or the number of improvement ideas logged per team.

You may have one, two or more measures against each area but the idea should be that every team have measures that cover all five of the QCDSM (quality, cost, delivery, safety and morale) as part of your MDI programme.

One final thing to say on the performance data section is that you don't need to put them up in this order. You will probably have a personal preference for putting (for example) safety as the top measure and that's fine. I have simply shown them in the most commonly occurring sequence.

Work schedule

This area of the information centre provides information on the daily plan for the area and the expected forward plan of work, such as shift deployments and changes, expected demand and any changes to demand that are expected for whatever reason. Where it makes sense, this area of the information centre will have an hour by hour summary of progress towards the daily target for the team.

Ideas and team info

This area provides somewhere to put non-work-related team information including any customer feedback, as well as providing somewhere for people to log ideas for improvement or issues affecting performance that need to be addressed.

A more detailed version of the ideas and issues board is shown in Figure 7.3. This area not only provides a place to log ideas but

FIGURE 7.3   Ideas and issues board

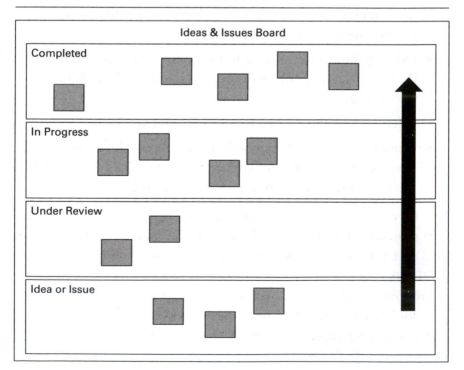

also gives an instant visual indication of the progress made towards resolving them or implementing them.

An issue or idea can be logged on the board by anyone. As soon as possible it should be picked up and allocated to someone to review the issue and develop a plan (at which point it is moved into the 'under review' section) or a response if the idea or issue cannot be taken forward. Ideas and changes that are actively being implemented are then moved into the 'in progress' section and the final part of the ideas and issues board is for actions that are closed.

Every idea and issue that is raised should be acknowledged and the person who raised it should be thanked for their contribution. If it isn't going to be taken forward, a reason should be provided as to why.

Management by walking about (MBWA)

MBWA is a well-established management concept that involves managers actively spending time 'on the floor' talking to staff, solving problems and checking on performance. In Lean terminology these are also called *gemba* walks, where gemba (also sometimes written as *genba*) generally translates as 'the real place' and is used to mean the place where work is done.

One of the best examples of MBWA that I have seen was a chief executive of a large organization (4,000 employees working 24/7) who, when not with clients, would park his car in the car park furthest from his office and then spend the first hour of every day walking through the organization taking time to speak to staff, find out what was going on and meet with customers who were on-site. It was not only inspirational for staff but informative for the chief executive, as the person in overall charge.

Another concept related to MBWA is to occasionally use a *gemba square* (or circle). These are areas where people stand and watch what is going on in operational areas without being able to interact with people. The aim is for those in the gemba square to look for waste and opportunities for improvement. You will also be able to gather a lot about team morale by watching behaviours of a group for 15–20 minutes. The gemba square doesn't need to be fixed and you could either mark it out in chalk on the floor where you want it to be at that time, or simply just practise it without necessarily making it clear that you are stood in the gemba square.

Daily problem solving

The fourth routine within MDI is to practise daily problem solving. This means that problems that are logged either at the daily team meeting or during the day are dealt with that same day. The ones that can be fixed quickly could form the basis of mini rapid improvement events (RIE), or could indeed be a 'do it'. Those that need a more detailed response need to be discussed with relevant specialists and an implementation plan put together. The aim should be to fix at least 50 per cent of the issues raised on the same day, with the vast majority fixed within five days. To aid with the identification of problems (and ideas for improvement) teams should undertake a 5S exercise (see Chapter 6) at least weekly.

A supply of 'log sheets' needs to be made available for people to complete whenever they encounter a problem or have an idea for an improvement, which they then attach to the ideas and issues board. A typical log sheet needs to contain the following information:

1 Name of the person suggesting the idea.

2 Date/time of logging.

3 An outline of the issue or idea (and details of the expected benefits).

4 Name of person dealing with the issue/idea and the date they had it allocated to them.

5 An area for a response/implementation plan to be recorded.

6 Some way of tracking the progress.

One way of achieving all of this would be to use an A3 as outlined in Chapter 3 or to create a simple issue and idea log sheet. An example log sheet is shown in Figure 7.4.

A closing thought on the four routines of MDI is that it can take a while to get going and become established as a series of daily routines when working with people who are not used to this way of working.

FIGURE 7.4   Example issue and idea log sheet

Issue & Idea Log Sheet

Name

Date Logged

Outline Issue/Idea

Allocated To

Date Allocated

Response Section

Expected Close Date:

Actual Close Date:

It is normal to encounter teething problems and you should treat these as learning points rather than as a reason to give up on MDI.

Embedding the change after an RIE

As discussed in Chapter 6 when we met rapid improvement events (RIE), there is a need to embed any changes that are made. This is about changing the habits and ways that teams and individuals perform tasks in order to prevent old practices from creeping back in.

When an RIE is finished there are normally four embedding issues that have to be tackled:

- Training or at least informing everyone affected by the new process.
- Ironing out the teething problems that occur.
- Closing off the actions on the 'To Do' list that will inevitably exist.
- Quantifying the benefits of what has been achieved.

For organizations that are practising MDI, dealing with all of these four issues will easily drop into the MDI cycle. It will take at least four to five weeks, and 30–35 repetitions of the process, before the changes start to embed themselves. In addition, you should aim to get all of the actions on your 'To Do' list finished during this period.

If you don't have MDI in place, then after you have completed your RIE you will need to undertake a number of tasks to ensure the changes become embedded. In Chapter 6 I introduced you to a nine-week cycle for an RIE that is summarized as:

- Weeks 1–4 – preparing for the RIE.
- Week 5 – RIE.
- Weeks 6–9 – embedding the changes.

Weeks 1–5 were covered in Chapter 6. I have summarized the actions that need to occur in weeks 6–9 in Table 7.1. By doing these tasks you will ensure that benefits don't just slip away. If you are not practising MDI you probably don't have an information centre where ideas/issues and actions can be logged and that has been assumed in the list of tasks in Table 7.1.

Whether or not you are practising MDI, you will need to undertake a 'closing off' process for the RIE. Typically this means organizing a 30-day post-implementation review to confirm benefits and 'close off' the RIE. The aim is that within 30 days (sooner for smaller changes or longer for bigger ones) all of the major tasks on your 'To Do' list will be closed off and you will have some confidence that the new process is generating benefits that are at the level you expected/required.

A checklist for closing off an RIE is provided below:

- the benefits arising from the RIE are at the correct level;
- all the 'To Do' actions have been implemented (not always possible, but this should be the aim);

TABLE 7.1   RIE weeks 6–9

RIE Week 6	• Create an 'embedding phase' information centre to track post-RIE tasks and the performance of the team. • Document the 'To Do' list after the RIE and allocate tasks to individuals. • Aim to close off one or more of your 'To Do's every day. • Start updating documents affected by the changes. • Hold a review session with the team to capture issues and ideas. • Do a first check that the benefits you expected to realize are going to come. • Undertake a 5S audit (if your RIE was focused on a layout change). • Arrange for a senior manager to do a walk through and thank the team.
RIE Week 7	• Update your 'embedding phase' information centre. • Review the outstanding 'To Do' actions. • Hold a review session with the team to capture issues and ideas. • Undertake a further 5S audit.
RIE Week 8	• Update your 'embedding phase' information centre. • Review the outstanding 'To Do' actions and aim to have 80% closed off by now. • Hold a review session with the team to capture issues and ideas. • Undertake a further 5S audit.
RIE Week 9	• Update your 'embedding phase' information centre. • Review the outstanding 'To Do' actions. • Hold a review session with the team to capture issues and ideas. • Summarize the benefits realized and confirm whether you are on-track. • Undertake a further 5S audit. • Arrange for a senior manager to do a walk through and thank the team. • Undertake a 'close of' review at 30 days post the RIE.

- team trained and completely familiar with the new process;
- all documentation modified;
- the team has been recognized for their input during the RIE.

In terms of recognition, I would avoid cash incentives and focus on public recognition and praise as a more sustainable way of recognizing input to any Lean activities. After the RIE is finally closed off, whether at 30 days or earlier/later, you will need to have a process to capture any further improvements. Obviously, the best way to achieve this is through using MDI.

Closing thoughts

Both MDI and embedding changes after an RIE, if done properly, will lead to people consistently and permanently adopting new practices and behaviours. If changes are not embedded, old and inefficient ways of working will resurface and this means that the only way to realize benefits from Lean in the long term is to embed the changes. The problem is that embedding changes is hard and requires time and effort – and that is where it starts to go wrong. Sometimes this is because no one thought to allocate the time and effort to this phase, but more commonly it is that no one manages the embedding phase. To overcome this issue you need to plan how you will manage the embedding phase when you first sign up to the RIE, including having nominated roles and getting managers to plan regular reviews if they are not practising MDI already. If you don't put the effort in to embed the changes you will join the legions of organizations that have put all the effort into a Lean programme and then failed to realize any (or only very little) long-term benefit.

As I mentioned at the start of this chapter, MDI is only part of the story of leader standard work and should not be undertaken in isolation. We will cover the remaining aspects of leader standard work, along with how to shape a culture that supports Lean, in the next chapter.

Leader standard work (LSW)

In this chapter I aim to answer the following questions:

1 What is leader standard work?

2 How do you create a culture to support continuous improvement and Lean?

3 What routines do you need to put in place to ensure that Lean embeds itself?

*L*eader standard work (LSW) describes the daily, weekly and monthly routines that need to occur within organizations to ensure that Lean moves from being 'something else to do' to 'the way things are done around here'. More than simply the structure and content of meetings, LSW is concerned with creating an organizational culture that supports Lean. The routines of LSW provide a structure to managing Lean on a day-to-day, week-to-week and month-to-month basis, but it is the behaviours of leaders at all levels that will determine whether Lean becomes embedded as a way of working. This chapter therefore has two main purposes. The first is to explore how organizational culture is formed and how you can shape it; the second focuses on the routines that define LSW.

Creating a culture to support Lean

An organization's culture comprises all of the values, beliefs, assumptions, principles, myths, legends and norms that define how individuals and groups of people think, make decisions and perform. The MIT Professor Edgar Schein, who is credited with inventing the term 'corporate culture', wrote in his book *Organizational Culture and Leadership* (1992) that culture was 'a basic set of assumptions that defines what we pay attention to, what things mean and how to react emotionally to what is going on'. Schein went on to state that an organization's culture will also define what actions are taken in reaction to various situations, for example the introduction and adoption of Lean.

Another popular definition of culture is that it simply defines, 'The way we do things around here.' This simplistic definition describes the reality of a culture that manifests itself in the form of behaviours and the thought patterns of individuals and groups and whether or not they will embrace or reject Lean.

Putting this in simple terms, organizational culture will impact positively or negatively on everything you try to do whether you want it to or not.

Describing organizational culture

The culture of an organization is learnt over time. It can be taught to new employees through formal training programmes but is more generally absorbed through stories, myths, rituals and shared behaviours within teams. The five aspects of organizational culture are shown in Table 8.1.

Edgar Schein described how the five aspects of culture described in Table 8.1 manifest themselves at three levels within organizations, as outlined below.

Level 3 – surface manifestations and artefacts
These are the most visible and accessible form of culture in terms of the jargon used, how conflicts are managed and the decision-making processes. In addition, you will also see the manifestation of

TABLE 8.1   Aspects of organizational culture

Aspects of culture	Description
Values	These describe the ways in which individuals assess certain qualities, activities or behaviours as good or bad and are based on how an individual or a group of individuals perceive the organization they work for.
Beliefs	These reflect an individual's understanding of the way their team and organization works and the probable consequences of the actions they take. For example, in some organizations people adhere rigidly to rules because that is how they believe you get ahead, or alternatively people resist taking risks because they believe that 'risk minimization' is the way to manage a process. What a person believes directly affects how they behave.
Myths	These are the persistent stories or legends that provide clues or signals about the behaviours that are expected of team members. Myths are often based on a mix of truth and fiction and become embellished over time.
Traditions	These are events that occur on a repetitive basis and that include such things as parties, social events, celebrations and similar activities that are a basic way of communicating cultural values. Traditions highlight to groups what is held in high esteem by the organization.
Norms	These are the informal rules that define the work of individuals, such as dress code, work habits, work/life balance, communication styles and the power of the grapevine or gossip. Norms are rarely, if ever, written down and are accepted often without question by people as the 'way things are'.

an organization's culture in such things as working hours (is it expected that people work excessive hours or not), formality, performance against standards, flexibility, etc.

Level 2 – espoused values

These are the stated values and rules of behaviour within a team or organization. They are often stated in terms of official policies, public statements and local working instructions. They can be written either to describe what you have today or written to describe how you hope a team will work in the future. An example of the official statement of an organization's values is:

> We treat one another with respect and communicate openly. We foster collaboration while maintaining individual accountability. We encourage the best ideas to surface from anywhere within the organization. We appreciate the value of multiple perspectives and diverse expertise.

There is a difference between a statement of values and the actual adoption of them, and there is a definite need to close the 'values gap' (the gap between the values that are stated and how they are adopted). For example, you may have a statement that says you value ideas from your staff but have supervisors who knock back ideas from their staff, or you may state that you will adopt the safest practices in the industry and then allow people to circumvent safe practices for 'rush jobs'. This difference between how you have said you will act and how you actually act undermines people's confidence in your motives and the belief in what you are trying to achieve through Lean.

Level 1 – shared basic assumptions

The lowest of the three levels described by Edgar Schein concerns invisible, unconscious and taken-for-granted assumptions held by individuals. They are often so well integrated into a team's behaviour that they are hard to recognize from within. For example, it may be taken for granted that no one will act on problems that are identified, or that any attempt at discussing issues with 'team X' will result in an argument and therefore no one tries. What we believe affects how we behave – and how we behave affects the outcome. If people believe that Lean is a waste of time and will not lead to any real improvement then they will behave accordingly. And, of course, if people believe that Lean is here to stay and is beneficial to the long-term organization then they will behave very differently.

Shaping a culture to support Lean

To be able to shape organizational culture we need to understand the difference between culture and climate. We can compare this difference by using an everyday analogy with a person's personality and mood. Someone's personality is enduring and difficult to change, whilst their mood may change many times during a day. Based on this analogy, culture is the equivalent of personality, whilst climate is the equivalent of mood.

Another analogy that provides insight into the difference between climate and culture, and how climate affects culture is taken from nature: imagine you want to grow a flower that is strong, colourful and formed correctly. The flower represents the organizational culture we are looking to 'grow'. To enable us to grow the flower we need to provide the seed with a number of climatic factors such as light, heat, water, food, nutrients and so on. If we provide the seed with the right climatic factors in the right quantities then we will get a strong flower that closely matches what we were expecting. However, if we deprive it of something it needs or provide it with too much of something (for example water) then we run the risk of killing the plant or at best creating something that does not meet our expectations.

Fundamentally, a change of culture occurs when people start behaving differently as a result of a change in the climate of the organization. There are many different models of how an organizational culture is shaped by the prevailing climate and how it can be assessed. In terms of assessing current culture I have selected to focus on the work of Swedish Professor Göran Ekvall (1995), which I have found both easy to understand and directly relevant to the introduction of Lean.

Ekvall spent many years investigating climatic factors and how they affected the ability of organizations to be creative and adopt new methods and processes. His work identified 10 climatic 'dimensions' that could be used to define the ability of an organization to adopt creative methodologies such as Lean. These dimensions are described below.

Challenge

How challenged, emotionally involved and committed are employees to their work? For example, do people just do the minimum amount of work or will they go the extra mile if it is needed?

Freedom

How free are your staff to decide how to design their work? This is different to people not being managed and is about whether staff feel they have any freedom to change their working practices.

Idea time

Is time allowed for people to consider different ways of working? For example, are people allowed time to participate in rapid improvement events?

Dynamism

Do people feel positive and motivated in their work? This is different to chaos, highly stressed or energetic environments where there is a lot of 'running around' but little in the way of positive feelings.

Support

Are there resources available to enable staff to give new ideas a try? Are people supported by their managers when they make decisions?

Openness

Do people feel safe speaking their minds and offering different points of view? Is there trust and respect between team members and between staff and managers?

Playfulness

How relaxed is the workplace in terms of people's relationships with each other and is it okay to have fun (in a professional or business-like context)?

Conflicts

Do people discuss contentious issues without the discussions getting out of control? Does the organization prevent tribes from forming and also prevent 'open warfare' between departments?

Debates

To what degree do people engage in lively debates about the issues faced by the organization? Is any debate of a difficult or contentious topic encouraged or avoided?

Risk taking

Is it okay to take calculated risks and even to fail? This is different to negligence and describes the attitude towards employees who want to try new things to help improve performance – and whether managers are prepared to 'stick their necks out' on issues or not.

Each dimension defined by Ekvall exists on a scale that extends from 'supports improvement' to 'undermines improvement'. For example, risk-taking would be given a score of minus 10 if every time someone tried to do something that did not fit within the 'norm' they were punished, whether or not the outcome was successful. On the other hand it might score plus 10 where time and resources are allocated to enable people to proactively take risks – and whether or not they worked out would contribute to organizational learning. Organizations normally exist between these two extremes on all 10 of Ekvall's 'climatic' dimensions.

Climatic factors (or dimensions) are in turn primarily affected by the leadership environment and, to a lesser degree, factors such as the systems and processes within the organization, physical working space, design of processes, equipment, etc. The leadership environment of an organization is described by such things as:

- what leaders pay attention to, measure and control;
- how leaders react to critical incidents;
- how resources are allocated by leaders;
- the role played by leaders in promoting effective behaviours and coaching others;

- how rewards and status are allocated;
- recruitment, selection, promotion and exit policies.

I have found that the best leaders for Lean programmes have high levels of 'emotional intelligence'. Emotional intelligence, or EI, is the ability to identify, assess and control the emotions of oneself, of others and of groups. There are a number of competing models of EI and, for simplicity, I have used that of Daniel Goleman (1996), who has done much to popularize the topic. Goleman describes the 'emotionally intelligent manager' as having capability in five different 'domains' that are described below:

Self-awareness

The ability to read your own emotions and recognizing when they are negatively affecting performance and when 'gut instinct' can be used to guide decisions.

Self-regulation

The ability to control your emotional responses and avoid impulsive behaviours. Self-regulation allows you to adapt to changing circumstances appropriately.

Empathy

The ability to sense, understand and react appropriately to the emotions of others.

Social skills

The ability to communicate with people, inspire them, influence them and effectively manage conflict.

Self-motivation

The ability to remain outwardly motivated even when under pressure, tired or faced by complex challenges.

The more senior a person is, the more important it is that they have mastered and understood emotional intelligence. Without EI it will be very difficult to implement Lean successfully, because the behaviour of leaders will work against its adoption.

Monkey business: a light-hearted look at how cultures form

The following is a light-hearted look at how team cultures form. Of course, any experiment undertaken in the manner described below would be cruel, but as a simple explanation of how culture forms I hope you will indulge me.

There were three monkeys in a cage in a zoo. Hanging from the roof of the cage was a bunch of bananas beneath which was a ladder to enable the monkeys to climb up and reach the bananas. One of the monkeys saw the juicy treat and decided to climb the ladder to get to them.

As soon as his foot touched the ladder, the remaining two monkeys were sprayed with water from high-pressure hoses. Having retrieved and eaten his first banana the first monkey went to climb the ladder again and immediately his fellow monkeys were again drenched. As the first monkey went for his third banana, the two soaked monkeys grabbed him just as he reached the ladder and threw the third monkey to the ground. It didn't take long before all three monkeys learnt to stay away from the ladder to avoid the wrath of their comrades caused by the associated drenching.

Unbeknown to the monkeys, the high-pressure hoses were then turned off but as the monkeys no longer went near the ladder they didn't realize this. A few days later a fourth monkey is introduced to the group. This new monkey is completely unaware of the issues the other three have experienced, so when he sees the bananas he goes to climb the ladder. Before he gets anywhere near the bananas all of the other three monkeys attack him. Having experienced this aggressive behaviour the new monkey also quickly learns not to go near the ladder.

Time goes by again and a fifth monkey is introduced. As this new monkey goes to climb the ladder all four monkeys attack him, including the fourth monkey, who has never experienced the 'drenching' and is just reacting to the 'way things are done round here'.

In effect, the monkeys have formed a new set of cultural behaviours, even though some of the group have no idea why things are done the way they are.

Developing your culture so that it can support Lean

In this section I have highlighted seven practical actions that you should consider undertaking if you want to shape your organizational culture so that it supports Lean.

Become aware of your current culture

You should start to notice your existing culture. Listen to how people express themselves and the stories they tell about successes and failures. Pay attention to shared values and watch how teams behave. Over a few days this will give you a good feel for your 'cultural current state'. Remember, whatever you may believe, you are part of a team with a group of norms and behaviours that you may not even realize exist unless you undertake this activity. You will gain a lot of information about your current culture by practising *management by walking about* (MBWA) and using the *gemba square* that I mentioned in Chapter 7.

Assess your cultural 'current state'

There is a need to identify the cultural aspects you want to retain from your current culture. For example, you may want to keep motivated teams, a commitment to achieving excellent performance, flexible working practices and a desire to deliver exceptional customer service. You will also need to identify the things that need to go, for example a 'norm' of not sharing performance data or covering up safety issues. Lastly, you will need to identify the things that are missing, for example 'individual accountability' or the need to take more risks in developing new products and services.

Create a cultural 'future state'

Imagine your ideal culture. For example, how do you want people to behave and to react when things go wrong? Fine tune it with colleagues until you have a clear picture of what you want from your organizational culture in the future.

Share the vision

Communicate openly, frequently and consistently. Describe your cultural vision in letters, e-mails, briefings and put it on notice boards, in newsletters and everywhere else you can. Do not be afraid that you will 'overcommunicate' your vision – because you can't.

Align your leaders
There is a need for leaders to do more than just agree about the future state. Alignment is about leaders at all levels 'living the cultural future state' for the organization. You and your fellow leaders should constantly be working together to learn and reflect on how things are going. You want leaders who can model the culture you are looking to create, meaning they can display the behaviours you are looking for.

Treat culture as a strategic issue
Culture may be perceived as 'pink and fluffy' but it has a real impact on organizational performance. Changing a culture can change the fortunes of the entire organization and is therefore a senior management team issue and should be discussed regularly at management meetings. In Chapter 9 I will introduce several different ways of creating a Lean strategic plan.

Keep it fresh and up to date
Culture can take a long time to change. Celebrating every success along the way has the effect of keeping things fresh during this extended period of time, as well as reinforcing the behaviours you want in the future. You will also need to keep your cultural future state up to date, based on any changes in your organization's market or operating environment. In Chapter 12 I discuss how different communications and celebrations can be used to help embed a culture of Lean.

The behaviours of Lean leaders

In Chapter 2 I introduced you to Toyota's 4Ps. The 4Ps define the commitments that need to apply to leaders at all levels within a Lean organization. The physical manifestation of the commitments can be seen in the way that leaders behave and these form the basis of the list shown in Table 8.2.

TABLE 8.2   The behaviour of Lean leaders

Lean supporting behaviour	How to spot if you have Lean leaders or not	What it means for senior management
Passionate about Lean.	They speak with enthusiasm about Lean and are keen to 'get on with it'.	There is a need for leaders to have been involved in Lean activities that have gone well and to understand what the organization is trying to achieve.
A disciplined approach to implementing Lean.	They are visibly committed to leader standard work and follow a structured approach to any implementation activities. They also set standards for their team and regularly follow up on performance.	The organization needs a structure for LSW and a defined set of standards and procedures that local leaders can adopt and manage.
A desire to improve performance.	There is a keenness to make tomorrow's performance better than today's.	There is a need for clearly defined objectives that are easily understood and collected by leaders.
Direct involvement in Lean activities.	They turn up and actively participate in Lean activities and also practise MBWA.	Time needs to be allocated to allow local leaders to participate in Lean and also to practise MBWA.
Taking a long-term view.	They do not sacrifice the long-term success of Lean by adopting unnecessary short-term 'anti-Lean' practices.	The behaviours of senior leaders when a 'crisis' occurs will set the standard for how other people react and whether or not Lean gets shelved in difficult times.
A passion to communicate with and coach others.	Regularly communicates the objectives and achievements of Lean and keen to spend time working with individuals who are struggling.	Communication of Lean is a two-way process and having some structure to it helps. I will discuss this in Chapter 12.

TABLE 8.2   *continued*

Lean supporting behaviour	How to spot if you have Lean leaders or not	What it means for senior management
A desire to learn more.	An understanding that you are on a continuous journey towards Lean and that there is always something new to learn and there are always better ways of doing things.	You will need to invest in training and also to have a process to continuously review your Lean practice and how to improve it.
A detailed knowledge of activities.	An in-depth understanding of how the activities undertaken by their team and where/how problems can arise.	There is no implication for senior managers on this one, other than to set it as a minimum standard for all leaders within the organization.
Keen to solve problems rather than work around them.	A passion for solving problems and using problem-solving tools rather than just applying 'quick fixes' that don't last.	Again, the actual practice for this will be set by senior management and how they behave when a problem occurs.
Effective at building relationships and managing conflicts.	Keen to build effective working relationships within their areas and with other leaders to create powerful 'Lean coalitions'.	Good relationships between individuals and teams start at the top and encouraging people to work together, and engineering activities when they can work together, will be key to this.

Daily, weekly, monthly LSW

LSW defines the daily, weekly and monthly routines that need to happen inside organizations that are looking to adopt Lean. LSW therefore helps eliminate guesswork for leaders at any level about how to approach issues/ideas and problems and also defines the behaviours and ways of working that are expected of them. The structure provided by LSW also means that you are less likely to 'forget' to do an essential forward planning task and also introduces consistent management practices between teams. In this section I explore the essential daily, weekly and monthly routines that need to be established in any organization wishing to adopt Lean.

Daily routines: the three tiers of daily meetings

The daily routines of LSW occur at three levels in most organizations.

First level: managing for daily improvement (MDI)

As I mentioned in Chapter 7, MDI is a key part of leader standard work. MDI provides the daily structure to enable individual teams to tackle local problems and improve performance. MDI should be practised within every team within an organization on a daily basis, or as near to daily as you can get.

Second level: team leader meetings

Second level meetings should occur daily between team leaders running departments. The purpose of the team leader meetings is to discuss cross-cutting issues between teams. This could be a discussion between team leaders involved in different aspects of a construction project to discuss availability of people and materials or a discussion between team leaders in a health-care organization to discuss bed availability, theatre scheduling or diagnostic capacity. Team leader meetings are held after the MDI is held so that team leaders are equipped with the issues that need to be addressed within their area of responsibility. In addition to the team leaders, a department or divisional manager should be present as they will then participate in the third level meeting.

Third level: department/divisional manager meetings

Third level meetings are between department or divisional managers who have attended the second level team leader meetings. The purpose is to discuss cross-cutting issues between departments such as priorities, resourcing, capacity, equipment availability and similar issues that go outside the scope of responsibility of individual departmental managers. In addition to the department/divisional managers, a director or the equivalent level person responsible for the managers in the room should attend. In larger organizations there may also be a need for a fourth tier of daily meetings.

Important points about daily meetings

The purpose of the daily routines is not to have meetings for meetings sake – and they are also not intended to be moaning sessions. People must come prepared, and be willing to listen and act. The principles for all daily meetings should be:

- **Duration** – less than 20 minutes is good but less than 10 is better.
- **Position** – standing up, ideally, to reduce the desire to extend the meeting.
- **Agenda** – a fixed agenda that people stick to rigidly.
- **Location** – at or near the place where work is being done.
- **Attitude** – people need to attend with the aim of seeking solutions.
- **Style** – people should be friendly and professional without the need to seek blame.
- **Preparation** – people need to turn up with the data and be prepared to speak about it.
- **Pace** – keep the meeting flowing and don't debate things for too long.
- **Outcomes** – focus on identifying actions and then go and get things done.

As a flippant final point I would also add:

- **Waffle** – have it for breakfast but don't 'waffle on' in the meeting.

Weekly routines

Whilst the daily routines focus on short-term performance and problem solving, the weekly routines are concerned with reviewing progress towards longer-term performance and planning for the next few weeks' activities. There are two types of discussion that should occur weekly – operational planning and improvement planning – and these are described below.

Operational planning

This is about planning the deployment of staff and resources in response to the expected operational environment for the next few weeks, with the duration that you can 'look ahead' normally dependent on the industry. This means looking at previous or planned demand and discussing any issues that might be important, such as audits, reviews, customer visits or similar activities, and then planning any necessary changes.

Improvement planning

This is concerned with reviewing any improvement activities that are due to occur in the next week (or few weeks) and how they need to be dealt with. This is about planning value stream mapping events, rapid improvement events, 2P/3P events and discussing how you will be able to support them and work through them.

As you can see, operational planning and improvement planning are not mutually exclusive. For example, a planned rapid improvement event might have a significant impact on the operational planning for an area and changes in demand may impact when you undertake a 2P event. It is therefore normal for these issues to be discussed at a single meeting at team leader level and another single meeting at department/divisional manager level. It is good practice to have front-line staff in attendance at these meetings normally on a rotational basis (meaning different people each week).

Monthly routines

There are two key routines that should occur on a monthly basis as part of your LSW: 1) a steering board session to discuss overall progress and update objectives; 2) longer-term operational planning covering the next quarter at least.

Unlike the weekly routines, where it makes sense to combine the two aspects into a single meeting, it is more likely that there will be a need to run the two monthly routines as two distinct meetings because of the differences in attendance.

Steering boards

A steering board should be established to provide the overall guidance to your Lean programme. The steering board should be chaired by your overall sponsor for Lean within your organization, who should be on your senior management team and be the person responsible for dealing with your board on issues related to Lean. It should also have within the steering board a cross-section of people including representatives of your 'Lean team' (the people who train and support Lean activities in your organization), various department managers, front-line staff and team leaders as well as invited guests when you have a specific issue to discuss.

The purpose of a steering board is to review the objectives for Lean within the organization and to discuss the day-to-day practices that are going on. For example, are people preparing effectively for rapid improvement events? Is MDI occurring regularly in all areas? Steering boards (also called 'transformation boards' or 'improvement boards') aim to set the pace for the adoption of Lean, tackle issues with implementation and continue to keep Lean high up the agenda for managers, so that it isn't seen as something only done by a small group of enthusiasts within the organization.

A monthly steering board session should also review the positive aspects of Lean such as achievements, case studies and feedback.

Longer-term operational planning

This should be occurring within your organization every month as common routine. An operational planning meeting also needs to take into account any major changes that are planned, disruptions expected and changes in demand that are likely over the following quarter (or longer), and undertaking the planning that is required to achieve them. In a Lean context, the operational planning team is normally made up predominantly of departmental/divisional managers and directors plus a few invited guests (and again I would recommend opening this up to front-line staff to avoid any mystique arising about it).

Structured problem solving in LSW

One thing that any organization cannot escape is the need to deal with problems that arise. Creating a structure to deal with any problems or issues that arise is essential for any organization and also contributes to LSW as it provides an 'off the shelf' structure for staff of how to deal with a problem.

One popular approach to structured problem solving is called *8D* (standing for the *Eight Disciplines*). This approach to problem solving originated in the automotive sector but has spread since then to any organization that needs a structured approach to dealing with medium- to large-scale issues. The eight disciplines (well, nine really when you include D0) are described in summary below:

- **D0: Prepare (or plan):** decide whether 8D is the correct approach and raise awareness of the problem.

- **D1: Establish your team:** identify and assemble the team of people with product/process knowledge needed to tackle this issue.

- **D2: Describe the problem:** specify the problem by identifying in quantifiable terms – the who, what, where, when, why, how and how many (called the 5W2H) of the problem.

- **D3: Develop and implement interim containment plan:** define and implement containment actions to isolate the problem to protect customers and staff until a permanent corrective action can be implemented.

- **D4: Identify and verify root causes:** identify all causes that could explain why the problem has occurred and, if it wasn't picked up till later, why it wasn't picked up when it first occurred. All causes shall be tested to verify whether your assumptions are correct. Corrective actions should be developed for any potential root causes that have been verified as being real.

- **D5: Choose and verify permanent corrections:** confirm that the corrective actions will resolve the problem and will not give unwanted or unexpected side effects. If there are potential side effects, develop a contingency plan based on the severity of the side effects.

- **D6: Implement and validate corrective actions:** implement corrective actions and ensure that the root cause has been eliminated. Monitor the process over an extended period of time to confirm that the problem has been resolved permanently.

- **D7: Prevent recurrence:** modify the management systems, operation systems, practices and procedures to prevent recurrence of this problem or similar problems.

- **D8: Congratulate your team:** recognize the collective efforts of the team. Publicize what they have achieved and share your knowledge and learning.

Most of the 8D describe general actions, such as identifying the relevant people and assembling them, and do not rely on tools and concepts. However, you will notice that in undertaking the second discipline (D2) you would use the PDCA A3 described in Chapter 3, and in the eighth discipline (D8) you would want to consider how you communicate and celebrate the results achieved, as described in Chapter 12.

In the very first discipline – actually D0 – it says to identify whether 8D is the right approach. What it is asking you to do is to distinguish between the following two types of problems: *JDI* (just do it) improvement, and extended improvement, as outlined below.

JDI (just do it) improvement

These are ones that can be dealt with by a team without external input from specialists or other teams. They need to be 'low risk' (so you might have to create a short risk assessment for teams to help them make the right decision) and should not require investment that is outside of the budget of the local team leader. Any improvements that drop into this category do not need to go through a full 8D cycle.

Extended improvement

Any high-risk, multidisciplinary or difficult problems can be classed as requiring some form of extended improvement process and, therefore, are suitable for using an 8D approach.

Lastly, there are some additional tools and concepts that are commonly used to support some of the other disciplines within 8D that I will describe in the following section.

8D additional tools and concepts

In this section I have outlined two additional tools and concepts that are useful for supporting the structured approach to problem solving that 8D provides. These two concepts are: the *5 whys* and *cause and effect diagram*, both of which are useful for D3 and D4 of the 8D cycle.

5 Whys: root cause analysis

It is common for people to react to the immediate symptoms of a problem rather than trying to uncover the root cause of the problem. However, by just tackling the surface problem we are at risk that the problem could occur again and again because the root cause still exists. For example, if a machine breaks down (surface problem) then we would immediately call for someone to fix it (immediate solution). However, we might wonder why the machine has broken down by using a tool referred to as the *5 whys* that might go as follows:

Q1: Why is the machine not working?

A1: Because it is broken.

Q2: Why is it broken?

A2: It has jammed.

Q3: Why has it jammed?

A3: Because debris is trapped inside.

Q4: Why is debris trapped inside?

A4: Because it wasn't cleaned properly.

Q5: Why wasn't it cleaned properly?

A5: No one has been shown how to clean it.

It is only when we get to the fifth answer (A5) that we find out that the root cause is that no one knows how to clean the item, so a root cause solution is to train people and then monitor that they are following the new process. If the team had just dealt with the surface problem and fixed the machine it is likely that it would need to be fixed again in a few days time.

Cause and effect diagram

Another way of identifying the root cause of a problem is to use a *cause and effect diagram*, also known as an *ishikawa diagram* or *fishbone diagram*. An example of this is shown in Figure 8.1.

FIGURE 8.1   Cause and effect diagram

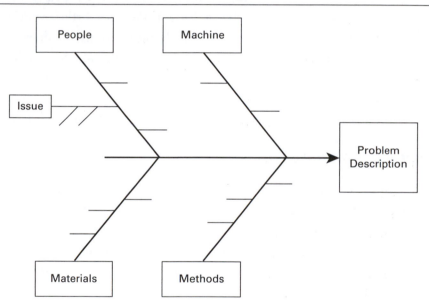

Figure 8.1 shows the problem described on the right-hand side and then the potential root causes broken into four areas: machine, material, methods and people (sometimes called the 4Ms when people is replaced with man). Under each of these four headings the team look for related issues that could have caused the problem. For example, under people they might identify working practices, training or access to information as potential root causes. These level one issues, such as the lack of training, might then be drilled into further so that we might identify 'inadequate induction' or 'poor planning' as the root causes of the level one issue, and so on.

Managing the process

Before I conclude this chapter some of the issues that come up in practice need to be addressed, if not these issues will undermine your attempts to embed Lean.

Ad hoc not every day

One of the first issues that you will encounter is that LSW is seen as something that can occur 'as and when' there is time. There is never time, so very quickly teams stop doing it as a routine. When it does occur it is haphazard and takes a long time with little resulting output. The reasons you will get for not doing the daily routines are usually very well articulated: urgent orders, exceptional demand, key information missing, etc. What will happen if this is not addressed is that more and more things 'come up' that will prevent your team from reliably undertaking their daily (or weekly or monthly) LSW.

Dealing with absences

Sometimes the team leader or other crucial people will be away and the LSW will not occur. You need a contingency for when people are not available, by perhaps having a deputy team leader or nominated stand-in. Also, you have to accept that sometimes people cannot participate in the LSW because of a crisis issue that is genuine, but unless it is a real crisis then you should expect people to turn up and get on with the daily routines of LSW.

'One off' workarounds that aren't

It is a constant source of amazement to me that people are prepared to spend 1,000 hours doing the wrong things but will struggle to give up one hour putting it right. Perhaps there is the sense of achievement in working 10 times harder than you expect? What I am talking about is people not wanting to deal with the problems and finding 'quick workarounds' rather than tackling the root cause of a problem. They perceive the introduction of a quick fix, or simply just working around the problem, as quicker and somehow more effective than dealing with the problem for good. I remember one of my managers working late in the evening and I watched him remove a component from a printed circuit board and attach it to another board. The conversation between us went like this:

Me: 'Hi. What are you doing?'

Him: 'Hi. I am removing a switch from this board that has only just started production so that I can put it on that board which is nearly finished so I can get it out of the plant tomorrow.'

Me: 'Why is the board you're attaching it to missing a switch?'

Him: 'Well, when it was first starting production I removed its switch to use on a different board.'

Me: 'So why not order another switch?'

Him: 'Well, I just haven't got the time.'

Me: 'But you seem to have the time to keep removing and reattaching switches?'

One-off workarounds lead to increased workload and undermine LSW. Get people to fix problems not work around them.

Closing thoughts

Hopefully you will realize that LSW is a strategically important issue for any organization attempting to implement Lean. Without routines that get Lean 'into the muscle' of an organization it is likely to either remain a side issue or simply not deliver medium or long-term benefits. In fact, I can comfortably state that, without the routines of LSW, there is an 80 per cent plus chance that your organization will have stopped Lean within a year.

A key aspect of getting Lean from being seen as 'something else to do' to being a core part of the way the business operates is to ensure it is seen as a strategic issue. This means creating an integrated strategic plan – and that is the subject of the next chapter.

Strategic planning

In this chapter I aim to answer the following questions:

1 Why is it important to have a strategic plan for Lean?

2 How do I create an integrated strategic plan?

3 How do I create a strategic picture of my whole organization?

There are normally many projects, priorities and initiatives being undertaken concurrently within any organization all of the time. A failure to coordinate these various activities can lead to them competing for management time, duplicating effort and wasting resources. The focus of this chapter is on creating an integrated strategy that avoids Lean being 'something else to do' and puts it at the heart of 'the way we do things here'. If Lean is treated as just another initiative in the minds of managers it will always take second place to more important operational problems and issues, even when Lean can be used to help stop them arising in the first place. The absence of an integrated and aligned strategic plan leads directly to my observation that people are quite happy spending 1,000 hours doing the wrong thing but aren't prepared to invest one hour putting it right, because they always perceive managing day-to-day operations as more important than actually making improvements.

Creating an integrated strategic plan has two main benefits. The first is that it aligns the goals of individuals, teams, departments and divisions with the overall goals of the organization; the second is that it prioritizes the right things within the organization, avoiding duplication and saving time in the long run. I have deliberately provided two different approaches to creating (and managing) a strategic plan. The first approach is *policy deployment* (also called *hoshin kanri*) and this is the true Lean approach to creating alignment but can take a long time to produce and requires a rigid approach to be followed. The second approach is called *transformation mapping* (*T-map*) and achieves the same aims as policy deployment but is generally quicker to produce, more visually appealing and is easier to read and update, albeit with a potential loss of detail. I have used both approaches and find them equally viable, so have no preference apart from the visual appeal of a transformation map over the policy deployment X-matrix that you will see later in this chapter. I will leave you to decide which one works better for your organization.

Before we get into the detail of either approach I will first mention the basic strategic actions that need to be undertaken prior to the creation of any form of strategic plan.

Strategic preparation

Both policy deployment and transformation mapping begin with describing your organizational vision. However, before you are able to do this there are a number of strategic actions that need to be undertaken to gather the information needed to enable you to fulfil the rest of the process. I have identified three key tasks that should not just be undertaken annually as part of the updating of a strategic plan but that should be an ongoing priority for management teams. These three tasks are:

- Environmental scanning – trying to spot trends and changes in the marketplace.
- VotC (voice of the customer) – listening to what customers are really telling you.
- Gap analysis – continuously reviewing the gap between what you are capable of and what the market needs from you.

I will now explore each of these in turn.

Environmental scanning

This activity is concerned with understanding what is going on in the marketplace and trying to spot trends, threats and other changes that might affect the organization. Scanning is concerned with understanding the marketplace from two viewpoints. The first is the viewpoint of what is currently happening in your local marketplace; the second is what is happening in the more remote wider economy. Not unsurprisingly, these two viewpoints are called the 'near environment' and the 'far environment'.

The near environment

The tool frequently used to look at the near environment is called 'Porter's Five Forces'. This was developed by Michael Porter, a Harvard professor, in 1979 and is shown in Figure 9.1.

FIGURE 9.1   Porter's Five Forces

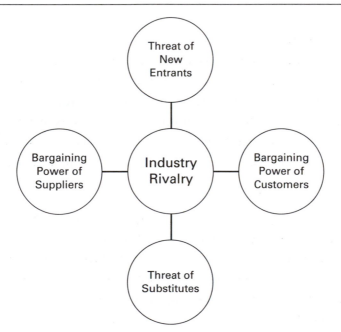

The five forces that this model describes are:

Industry rivalry

How are your competitors changing what they do in order to create a competitive advantage? For example, are they shortening lead times, lowering costs or offering more flexible services?

Threat of new entrants

How easy is it for new competitors to 'open up shop' in your marketplace? Some industries have high barriers to entry, such as regulated health care provision and the energy industry, but others are much easier to break into and organizations need to develop sources of competitive advantage to keep new entrants out.

Bargaining power of customers

Do your customers have choices about who to use and how easy it is for them to switch to another source? This describes the ability of customers to put your organization under pressure so that, for example, you cannot increase costs in line with inflation without risking losing key customers.

Threat of substitutes

Can your customers switch what they are buying from you to a completely different product or service? If so, how easy is it for them to switch? If the costs of switching are low and the perceived difference is negligible then the threat of substitution is high. For example, Pepsi is a substitute for Coca-Cola. If the price of Coca-Cola increases too much then a lot of people will switch to Pepsi without too much trouble at all.

Bargaining power of suppliers

What power do your suppliers have over you? Can you switch the source of your supply easily and with low cost and risk? If so, then the bargaining power of suppliers is low, but for many people it can create a real barrier to moving to a new supplier and therefore gives that supplier a lot of leverage over you to increase their costs and restrict supply.

The solution to these five issues involves activities such as brand development, supplier selection, product/service design as well as the use of Lean. Specifically, Lean can help you deal with the five forces by developing new sources of competitive advantage, including lower costs, shortening lead times, improving flexibility, increasing reliability, etc. It can also help in other indirect areas such as streamlining purchasing processes, thus allowing more time to be spent developing supplier relationships. Collectively, Lean can make you more competitive in the market, create barriers to entry for new entrants, increase switching costs for customers and reduce your exposure to the power of suppliers.

The far environment

In the far environment you are concerned with understanding longer-term changes that will affect your organization. This is often referred to as STEP (or PEST) analysis, or the slightly more extended PESTLE analysis. PEST (and PESTLE) are explained below.

PEST stands for changes in four areas:

- **Political** – new legislation, taxes or other politically led changes that could affect you.

- **Economic** – changes to funding, economic growth, interest rates, exchange rates, etc, that could affect you.

- **Social** – changes in the population such as an ageing population or reducing numbers of younger people, career attitudes, concerns about health and population growth rates that could affect you.

- **Technological** – new technologies that could revolutionize (or harm) your organization.

In addition to the four categories above, PESTLE adds in two further considerations:

- **Legal** – legislation related to such things as discrimination, consumer law or employment law, etc, that could affect you or your marketplace.

- **Environmental** – ecological or environmental issues such as weather patterns and climate change, which could affect you directly or indirectly either by changing patterns of demand or increasing your business costs.

VotC: voice of the customer

The second of the three 'pre-strategy' tasks that need to be undertaken is to listen to the voice of the customer and understand what they want, how these 'wants' are changing and what they would value from you if you could provide it.

Gap analysis

The third preparatory task that needs to be undertaken prior to the creation of a strategy is to undertake a gap analysis. The only purpose of a strategy is to match what your organization is capable of to the needs of your market. This is shown in Figure 9.2, which is based on the Resources, Capabilities and Competitive Advantage Model created by Robert Grant.

Gap analysis in the context of strategy is the process of understanding what the key success factors are in the market you operate in (through environmental scanning and VotC) and ensuring that your organizational capabilities are organized so that you can react to these. For example, if the market wants a shorter lead time then you will need to invest time in developing the capability of your processes to respond to this. To achieve this change you may also need to 'up skill' your staff and work on your organizational culture.

FIGURE 9.2   Resources, Capabilities and Competitive Advantage Model (Grant)

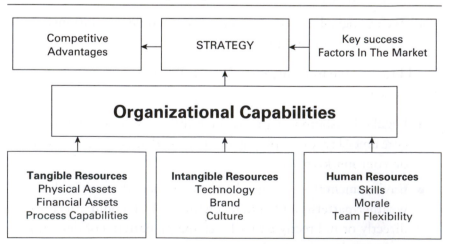

SOURCE: Grant, R (1991) The Resource-Based Theory of Competitive Advantage, *California Management Review* **33**(3) 114–135

Collectively, the three tasks described in this section provide you with the background information you need to undertake either a policy deployment or transformation mapping exercise.

Policy deployment (*hoshin kanri*)

Policy deployment, which is also called *hoshin kanri* or *hoshin planning*, is a strategic way to align activities in organizations so that everyone is pulling in the same direction. An analogy of this is that of coordinating a fleet of ships so that they all arrive at the correct destination at the correct time. Another analogy I have found useful is that of the 'elephant movers' shown in Figures 9.3a and 9.3b.

The purpose of policy deployment is therefore to align individual, team, departmental, divisional and organizational objectives so that everyone is pulling in the same direction. It is different to traditional management by objectives (MBO), in which targets are not aligned and often the objectives are developed in isolation by departmental managers, leading to the promotion of both individualism and short-termism. The most important problem of MBO is that it can drive destructive behaviours, and I have directly experienced these negative

FIGURE 9.3a   Poor alignment slowing the movement of the block

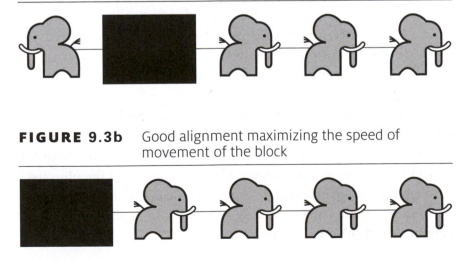

FIGURE 9.3b   Good alignment maximizing the speed of movement of the block

behaviours driven by MBO on a number of occasions. One such occasion was an organization where the purchasing team were measured on purchase price variance (PPV) as their key measure. To achieve a PPV you had to buy items cheaper than the stated standard cost, so if something was listed as £10 and you bought it for £9 then you had made a PPV of £1. This had the effect of encouraging the team to buy cheaper quality parts in large quantities from far away. This would not have been a problem had the organization not been in a very volatile market, where a good review led to an increase in demand of up to 10 times the demand, and vice versa for a bad review. By purchasing from far away the organization lost a lot of sales and also created problems of excessive stock that they couldn't sell. A bigger problem was caused by the poor quality of the parts that were being purchased, and subsequently required a team of 40 people to rework parts, which more than negated the few thousand pounds that were saved each month through PPV. A failure to align the organization increased costs over three years by almost £10 million and also led to lost sales that were conservatively estimated at £11 million over the same period.

Overview of the policy deployment 'catchball' process

One of the key aspects of policy deployment is the concept of *catchball*. This is a process where the person initiating a key part of the process then 'throws' the ideas to other stakeholders for feedback, support or action. In policy deployment this normally occurs at two levels: 1) the three- to five-year breakthrough objectives are passed by the senior team to managers to comment on; 2) one-year objectives are passed by managers to front-line teams to comment on and create a plan.

The process of catchball means that policy deployment is a far more interactive process than traditional strategic planning. It also becomes more iterative, therefore requiring more time, but with the benefit that teams are much more likely to commit to the objectives through the simple observation that if people don't understand what an objective means and how they are meant to achieve it then you cannot expect them to commit to it.

Seven stages of policy deployment

Figure 9.4 shows the seven stages of policy deployment. The normal way for recording information is on a policy deployment X-matrix as shown in Figure 9.5, although you may find some variations in how these are designed in practice to meet the needs of individual organizations.

The seven stages provide a structured approach to policy deployment whilst the X-matrix provides the structure for recording the outcomes of the seven stages. An example semi-complete policy deployment X-matrix is shown in Figure 9.6, with nine areas highlighted with the letters A to I.

FIGURE 9.4   The seven stages of policy deployment

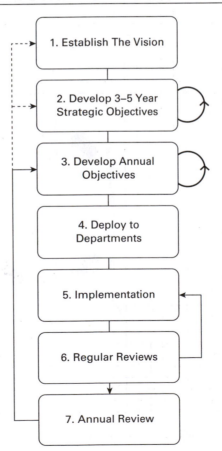

FIGURE 9.5 Policy deployment X-matrix

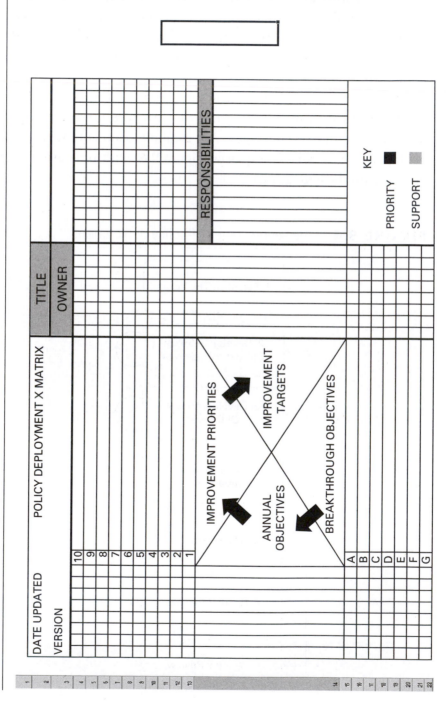

FIGURE 9.6 Policy deployment X-matrix (part complete)

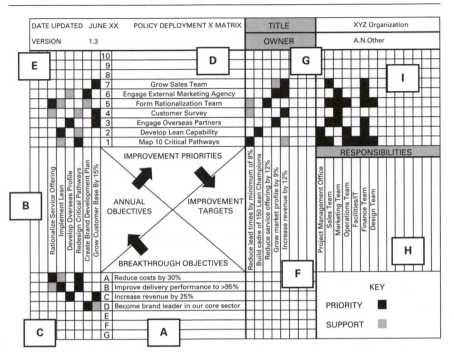

We can now go through the seven stages of a policy deployment exercise and see how we use the X-matrix to record the data.

Stage 1: establish the vision

The first stage is concerned with creating a vision for the organization to work towards. Visions outline what the organization is striving to be and provides a long-term view for teams to work towards. There is a distinct difference between a vision that states an aspiration such as, 'We are working towards a world without violence', and an operationally focused vision such as, 'We will be the leading provider of services in our core markets.' In both cases you will need to provide contextual information to help people understand the vision. For example, by when will it be achieved? What will the organization look like at that time (size, number of people, etc)? What are the boundaries of the vision (for example the regions or markets you will be a leader within)?

Two example vision statements are shown below:

Pfizer

At Pfizer, we're inspired by a single goal: your health. That's why we're dedicated to developing new, safe medicines to prevent and treat the world's most serious diseases. And why we are making them available to the people who need them most. We believe that from progress comes hope and the promise of a healthier world.

DuPont

DuPont's vision is to be the world's most dynamic science company, creating sustainable solutions essential to a better, safer and healthier life for people everywhere.

Behind both of these statements is an explanation of what this means, a description of how success will be measured and a plan to realize the vision. The purpose of a well constructed and well-explained vision is to align the direction of travel of everyone towards *true north*. True north is commonly associated with the phrase; 'What we should do, not just what we can do.'

Stage 2: develop three- to five-year strategic objectives

This stage is concerned with developing BBIGs (big, beautiful improvement goals) for the organization. These are the longer-term goals for the organization and are normally created by the senior team and then, using catchball, passed to managers for comment and refinement. Having agreed the three- to five-year strategic objectives they are then recorded in the area marked 'A' in Figure 9.6. It is important to provide details to explain each objective, as putting targets such as 'improve quality by 30 per cent' doesn't mean anything without some additional information such as 'this applies to the combined costs of rework, wastage and customer returns'. Therefore, there is normally additional information provided to explain the detail behind everything listed in the X-matrix. Ideally there should be no more than five to seven strategically important objectives. In policy deployment, less is more.

Stage 3: develop annual objectives

The third stage is concerned with defining the objectives that will be undertaken this year towards achieving the three- to five-year objectives. For example, a three- to five-year strategic objective may be to grow sales by 40 per cent, and this year we might aim to work towards this longer-term aim by growing sales by 12 per cent. Using catchball this is then passed to local teams to agree how they will achieve these objectives and develop the plans. Once agreed, this information is logged in the area marked 'B' in Figure 9.6. The box marked 'C' in Figure 9.6 then shows how each of the three- to five-year strategic objectives are linked to the annual objectives.

Stage 4: deploy to departments

Department teams finalize the plans that were created in Stage 3 and list these 'improvement priorities' – that they will undertake in order to deliver the annual objectives – in the area marked 'D' in Figure 9.6. Again, the overlap between the annual objectives and the improvement priorities is shown in the area marked 'E'. For example, we can see in Figure 9.6 that the annual objective 'grow customer base by 15 per cent' is linked to three improvement priorities: grow sales team, customer survey and engage overseas partners. Individual improvement priorities may need further scoping work and the creation of an A3 or PID (as covered in Chapter 3).

In addition to listing the improvement priorities it is also important at Stage 4 to identify what the expected outcomes are for each activity. This information is listed in the area marked 'F' in Figure 9.6. We also need to list the people who will take the lead in each improvement priority and this is shown in the area marked 'H' in Figure 9.6. To show the overlaps between the improvement targets and the improvement priorities we complete the box marked 'G', and to show the overlap between the improvement priorities and the responsibilities for delivering them we complete the area marked 'I'.

Stage 5: implementation

Having created the X-matrix there is then a need to actually go ahead and implement the improvement priorities using the Lean concepts such as value stream mapping (VSM), managing for daily improvement (MDI), rapid improvement events (RIE), etc.

Stage 6: regular reviews

Monitoring progress on a monthly basis forms the basis of the sixth stage. This can be done using any number of different reporting mechanisms, such as RAG Charts (red, amber, green) or Bowling Charts, with an example of the latter shown in Figure 9.7. The aim of Stage 6 is to ensure that you are on track to deliver your annual objectives and thus should be integrated with the monthly routines of leader standard work.

Stage 7: annual review

The last stage is concerned with creating an annual routine to update the objectives and improvement priorities, effectively returning you to Stage 1.

The benefits and limitations of policy deployment

There are a number of benefits of the policy deployment process. For one thing, it brings into focus the vision and future of the organization and, through catchball, helps to achieve consensus. It can increase the commitment to implementation and the ability of teams to work together to achieve them. More importantly it can be deployed at a number of levels so that you can have annual objectives for the organization that are then used in place of the three- to five-year strategic objectives listed in area 'A' of Figure 9.6. These are then linked to departmental annual objectives, and so on, until you reach individual objectives.

The main limitation of policy deployment is the lead time required to create it. For larger organizations it is not uncommon for it to take up to three months to create the plan for the next 12 months. Another limitation is that the use of the X-matrix can be difficult to read and also makes it very difficult to update.

Whilst policy deployment is the appropriate Lean tool for creating a strategy, I am also going to introduce a different approach drawn from strategic planning that provides a more visual, more easily updated approach to aligning organizations, albeit with a certain loss of information when compared to the X-matrix.

FIGURE 9.7 Example bowling chart

Policy Deployment Bowling Chart	Status		Month 1	Month 2	Month 3	Month 4	Month 5	Month 6	Month 7	Month 8	Month 9	Month 10	Month 11	Month 12
Quality		Plan												
		Actual												
		Plan												
		Actual												
Cost		Plan												
		Actual												
		Plan												
		Actual												
Delivery		Plan												
		Actual												
		Plan												
		Actual												
Safety		Plan												
		Actual												
		Plan												
		Actual												
People		Plan												
		Actual												
		Plan												
		Actual												

Transformation mapping

A conceptual transformation map is shown in Figure 9.8. It is also referred to as a sunray diagram (for obvious reasons) and aims to provide a visual picture of how tasks and objectives are aligned in delivering a corporate vision.

The process for creating a transformation map (T-map) follows the same process as policy deployment, namely to establish the vision and develop the three- to five-year objectives (shown in Figure 9.8 as key objectives). Also, as per policy deployment, you should aim to keep the number of key objectives to no more than seven. Along the top edge of the T-map are 'phases' and these can be as long as you need them to be, although they are commonly 0–3 months, 3–6 months and 6–12 months or Year 1, Year 2 and Year 3. The phases are the equivalent of the annual objectives section used in policy deployment.

What we can now show are the specific tasks that are needed in each phase in order to deliver each of the key objectives. For example,

FIGURE 9.8   Conceptual transformation map

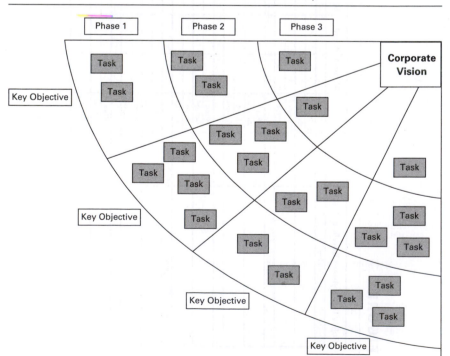

you may have a key objective of reducing lead time by 40 per cent. In Phase 1 you may aim to achieve a reduction of 10 per cent and the tasks that may be undertaken to deliver this could be, for example, a redesign of key pathways, installation of monitoring system and the introduction of *kanban* on all key components.

Tasks will often have an overlap with multiple measures and, unlike policy deployment, we cannot easily show this overlap on the T-map. However, you should always put tasks under the key objective it has the biggest impact on (you can list the other objectives that it will affect in the details about each task).

Applying the same seven stages introduced for policy deployment to the creation of a T-map gives us the following:

Stage 1: establish the vision

This is an identical process to policy deployment and the resulting vision is listed in the top right of the T-map in the corporate vision area.

Stage 2: develop three- to five-year strategic objectives

These are placed around the outside of the T-map, where you will see the words 'key objectives' in Figure 9.8. It is often necessary to add additional information to these objectives to explain them. For example, you may have a key objective of 'becoming market leader' and this might have the following explanation attached to it:

To become a market leader we need to:

- *grow market share from 16 per cent to 21 per cent;*
- *increase share value by 14 per cent;*
- *etc.*

Like policy deployment, this process benefits from a catchball process.

Stage 3: develop annual objectives

Unlike policy deployment, it is possible to show on a T-map objectives that span the whole three- to five-year period by having three to five phases along the top edge, or to provide more detail than the X-matrix by breaking down the year into smaller periods (for example

0–3 months, 3–6 months, etc) for a more detailed view of a single year, if required.

Stage 4: deploy to departments

In Stage 4 we identify the tasks that populate the T-map. The normal starting point is to collate the actions that are already under way within the organization and place them on the T-map. This normally highlights that around 30 per cent of the projects that are already under way are either not required or are duplicated. Having populated the tasks on the T-map with existing activities there is then a need to explore and fill the gaps. As in policy deployment, individual tasks will normally also need to be scoped in their own right using an A3 or PID, as covered in Chapter 3.

Stage 5: implementation

This is identical to policy deployment and involves a mix of value stream mapping (VSM), rapid improvement events (RIE) and managing for daily improvement (MDI).

Stage 6: regular reviews

Monthly progress reviews need to be undertaken. An advantage of T-maps is that typically the completion of one task triggers the need for others, for example the use of VSM can trigger the need for a number of RIEs. On the T-map we would add additional tasks to reflect these additional tasks, and also move things forward and back through the different phases as things get done earlier than expected or delayed.

Stage 7: annual review

As with policy deployments, T-maps benefit from a quarterly overhaul and an annual review.

The benefits and limitations of transformation maps

Like policy deployment you can have T-maps that cover the whole organization, or specific divisions and departments. T-maps are more visually appealing than an X-matrix and can normally be displayed on a single (if large) sheet of paper, but you lose the detail of the overlaps between objectives and tasks that you would see in an X-matrix. Further benefits of a T-map are that they are generally much quicker to produce than an X-matrix, can be implemented on a running basis by considering existing initiatives more easily than you can achieve with policy deployment and can be operated more fluidly. However, it is not an 'official' Lean tool and I will leave it up to you to decide whether policy deployment or T-maps are the best way forward for your organization.

Enterprise level value stream mapping (ELVSM)

In Chapter 4 when we explored value stream mapping I mentioned that we would return to one final type of value stream map, namely ELVSM. Sometimes it is important to get an in-depth view of the whole organization (or its entire supply chain) before you can create your strategic plan. The purpose of ELVSM is to identify the linkages between teams within an organization as well as with customers, suppliers and other partners. ELVSM provides a '10,000 foot view' of an organization, meaning that you imagine you are looking down on your organization from 10,000 feet above it, so you can't see the fine detail only the key highlights.

ELVSM is closely related to the concept of a SIPOC chart that is used to give you a high-level overview of an organization, with SIPOC standing for:

- suppliers;
- inputs;
- processes;
- outputs;
- customers.

Typically ELVSM uses only a few of the value stream mapping symbols, namely those shown in Figure 9.9.

An example ELVSM is shown in Figure 9.10. The process of each of the five steps involved in creating an ELVSM is outlined below.

FIGURE 9.9   The normal symbols used in ELVSM

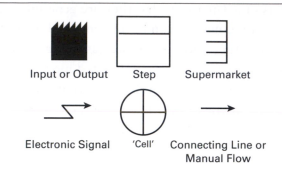

FIGURE 9.10   Example simplified ELVSM

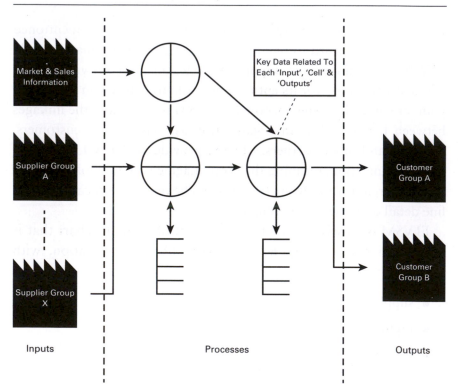

ELVSM Step 1: identify your outputs

This first step is concerned with identifying the markets/customers you serve and providing key information about what is going on. For example, is that group growing/shrinking and what percentage do they represent of your organization's turnover? You may also have other 'outputs' from your organization such as statutory reports or reports to your parent organization that should be shown.

ELVSM Step 2: identify your inputs

This step is concerned with grouping together different types of input, whether that is suppliers, patients, requests, etc. You will often find you have more than one type of input, for example materials and specifications in manufacturing or patients and reports in health care. Again, you should add key information to each input such as expected changes, volumes, issues and opportunities. Remember that the whole purpose of ELVSM is to give you a '10,000 foot view' of your organization.

ELVSM Step 3: identify your internal processes

The third step is to focus on your internal processes and the various teams that exist (shown as 'cells' in Figure 9.10) and how these teams interact with each other to convert 'inputs' to 'outputs'. You should also add key information to the ELVSM for each team, particularly focusing in on any problems or opportunities for improvement that exist, changes that are occurring and any key performance data. I have also shown in Figure 9.10 that several of the teams (cells) are putting information or products into a *supermarket* and this is used when it is important to show that information and/or materials are being placed into storage for later use or retrieval.

ELVSM Step 4: analysis stage

This requires you to analyse your ELVSM and understand the changes that are likely to occur. This is used to help you prepare for Step 5.

ELVSM Step 5: create future state

This last step is concerned with creating an ELVSM that shows the expected future state for your organization. This needs to show the outputs you want to have (for example, 35 per cent of sales in Europe, 45 per cent in North America and 20 per cent in the rest of the world), the inputs, and any changes you need to make to your internal processes. Internal changes normally appear as changes to the flow from inputs to outputs. For example, doing away with a planning team or reducing lead time through team X by 25 per cent.

The purpose of ELVSM is to aid the strategic planning process and feed into your annual objectives and improvement priorities within policy deployment; also to help you identify the tasks that are needed when creating transformation maps.

Closing thoughts

One of the aims of this chapter has been to show that strategic planning is essential in aligning the work of individuals and teams with the overall direction of the organization. Alignment is part of the overall process of engaging staff in the journey to Lean. Something I tell people regularly is that the tools of Lean are 'blind', meaning that the application of tools alone cannot affect the success of Lean (although they can negatively impact if done inappropriately or incorrectly). The only thing that makes the difference between those who will attempt Lean and fail, and those who succeed, is the engagement of everyone in the organization: this is covered in the next chapter.

Engaging the team

In this chapter I aim to answer the following questions:

1 How do you engage and motivate people?
2 What specific things do you need to do to keep people engaged with Lean?
3 How do you deal with the most difficult types of people you will meet?

In Chapter 8 I covered how organizational cultures form and are shaped, with the most important driver being the prevailing leadership style. This chapter builds on the work in Chapter 8 but is focused on how to engage and motivate individuals, what drives them to either resist or engage with Lean, the specific things that can be done to build a core of motivated individuals, and what normally happens to turn them off.

Engaging individuals

Edgar Schein, the MIT professor who has had a major impact on the thinking associated with organizational development, once said that, 'People don't resist change, they resist being changed.' In this section I am going to explore why resistance occurs and what can be done to engage the majority, if not everyone, on the Lean journey.

FIGURE 10.1   Factors affecting engagement

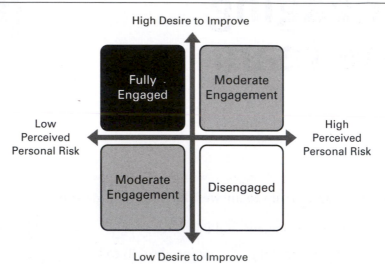

Why do people resist change?

Everyone has the capability to engage with Lean if they want to. There are two main factors that seem to affect whether people will or won't engage with the Lean process and these are summarized in Figure 10.1.

Figure 10.1 contains two important terms 'desire to improve' and 'perceived personal risk' and we can look at each of these in turn. At this stage I want to exclude those people who might be classed as 'nay sayers' or people who will also seek to obstruct the Lean process and will return to them later in this chapter.

Creating a 'desire to improve'

People develop a desire to change and improve a situation if they are unhappy with the status quo. This is sometimes referred to as creating a 'burning platform' to indicate something that motivates people for change. In a business context, people will have a high desire to improve if most of the following exist:

- They are unhappy with the status quo.
- They believe that it is not possible or realistic to keep the status quo.
- They believe that now is the time to change.

- They understand what the change will involve.
- They are capable of implementing the changes (ie they have the skills to do it).
- They believe that the future state will be better than the current state.
- They believe that the change can be undertaken successfully.

Part of the role of preparing a team for engaging in a Lean activity is to consider each of these elements and how you might address them. It will probably need a good compelling need to be created along with obtaining customer feedback (or even feedback from ex-customers) to say why the changes are required. Obviously, there is a need to explain what will happen and to provide people with the relevant training so they are capable of implementing the changes required of them.

Lowering 'perceived personal risk'

Put yourself in the shoes of people about to engage in a Lean programme and think why they might view engagement as a high personal risk. If you do this for a couple of minutes you will find that the reasons you come up with cover areas such as:

- They don't trust the motives of the people leading the change.
- Previous change programmes have 'gone wrong'.
- They stand to lose something they value.
- They don't understand what is required and are afraid of what has been asked.
- They feel they will be 'shown up' through the process in some way.

Some of these issues can be addressed through an effective communications programme that has clearly stated, honest, objectives. I was witness to two different Lean projects that came to a grinding halt and will explain each of them below.

'Bank the cheque'

In the first programme, which was in health care, the CEO had signed off the A3 for a Lean project and agreed that its focus was on releasing nurses' time so that they had more time to spend dealing with patients. Having checked with the CEO we were assured that there was no financial target at all and that this was purely about improving the quality of care. The team involved in the project undertook a great piece of work in which the equivalent of six nurses' worth of time was released back to giving care across three wards. On the day the team presented the results to the CEO he sat through the presentation with a face that looked like a bulldog chewing a wasp. At the end of the session his only words were, 'So, when can I bank the cheque?' It was clear that he meant 'when can I get rid of people'. Given that the project had no financial targets, and certainly no headcount reduction targets, this unexpected statement caused an unseemly outburst from the Nursing Director and also demoralized the team involved. The Lean project stopped very soon afterwards, as other teams found suddenly that they were too busy to get involved anymore.

Had the CEO been open from the start that there was a financial and headcount target then this problem could have been avoided, but in discussions afterwards he had felt that had he been honest then the teams would not have engaged so positively. The problem was that by not being honest he had demonstrated that people could not trust his motives and therefore Lean moved into the 'high perceived personal risk' area of Figure 10.1.

Unexpected headcount reduction

In a second Lean programme at a housing association the focus was on growing the organization without growing the admin support-team size. This meant reducing the time taken to do the routine tasks so that individuals had more time available to deal with the new work that the organization would pick up. The team engaged enthusiastically and achieved savings that amounted to an almost immediate 13 per cent saving in the time taken by the admin team to deal with routine tasks. When we looked in more detail at the teams that dealt with these everyday activities, which included such things as gas servicing and rent arrears, this meant that some individuals were 40 per cent or more productive than they had been. Within a few weeks of the changes I received a strange phone call from one of the team to say they had been unexpectedly made redundant. Checking in with the management team I discovered that they had down-graded the growth potential and had decided instead to get rid of nearly 20 per cent of the admin team. Unsurprisingly, this generated some fairly robust feedback and, even less surprisingly, the Lean programme came to a grinding halt.

Snap decisions made by managers who were only semi-committed to Lean resulted in the programme coming to an end, and to Lean being referred to as 'mean' (in the term 'Lean is mean'). This created a legacy for the staff involved that will last for years.

Both of these examples demonstrate that you can kill Lean through not considering the people aspects. This means having honest and clearly stated targets, an explanation of why those targets have been set and details of what will happen in the process. You also need to consider how you will change your plans due to market changes, and, for those people with genuine concerns, you need to also provide an opportunity for them to raise their concerns with you, something we will cover in the next section.

The distribution of people

When you first announce your plans for Lean you will find that your existing workforce will divide into the three groups, as shown in Figure 10.2.

FIGURE 10.2   Distribution of people in initial Lean activities

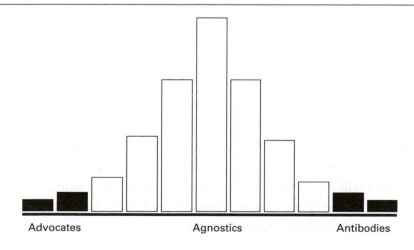

Advocates   Agnostics   Antibodies

Advocates are people who are positive about Lean and are keen to get involved. By contrast, antibodies are people who are actively against the implementation of Lean for a variety of reasons. In the middle are the agnostics, who form the bulk of your workforce and are initially neither positive nor negative about Lean and are simply looking for leadership. The problem at the start is that the advocates tend to be quiet, because they have nothing to shout about, whilst the agnostics can be very 'noisy'. The antibodies can spread doom and gloom that can adversely affect the morale of the agnostics, who then perceive involvement in Lean as a negative thing.

There are at least three different types of antibodies, but unfortunately you can't tell them apart because they behave in the same way. They raise objections, fail to get involved, put up obstacles and seek to keep others from participating. The three groups can loosely be described as:

- Those who are afraid because they fear they will lose something they value such as status, or that they will need to work for a different manager they don't like. I will call these people 'Wendy' because the first person I realized was in this category was called Wendy.

- Those who don't understand the need for Lean or indeed what you are trying to achieve. I will call these people 'George'.

- Those who have lost out in previous initiatives. For example, losing status. I will call these people 'Polly'.

Within each of these three groups there will be extremes, with most people capable of engaging with Lean if you work with them correctly, and a very, very small number who will never engage in Lean irrespective of what you do:

- A Wendy will need reassurance and an opportunity to explain their concerns. You should aim to listen to Wendy's concerns and act on those that are reasonable whilst explaining the reasons why you can't act on the others.

- A George will need some additional information about what you asking of them and how you expect them to be involved. This will normally be in addition to the general information given to everyone and they might benefit from talking to you one-to-one about the programme.

- A Polly is normally harder to deal with because it doesn't matter what you say they have heard it all before. They are jaded by change initiatives and sometimes are concerned about losing out even more. For example, further shrinking their sphere of influence or status.

Most Wendys and Georges can be converted into agnostics, and some will become your most ardent advocates. Pollys are harder to bring round and you may have to take steps to isolate those who continue to object so that they do not demoralize everyone else. An interesting observation is that most of the Pollys I have ever come across have been middle managers and above.

As time goes on, the number of advocates in your team will increase and you will also find them more and more vocal in their support. From the start you should be aiming to use advocates to help promote Lean. Get them to talk to their colleagues about why they are interested in Lean. Write case studies about the work done by advocates in order to give them recognition (and promote knowledge sharing). Ask them to speak about Lean at briefings and contribute to articles. Whatever you do, as long as you have made good progress your workforce distribution will have shifted by the end of the first year to look more like that shown in Figure 10.3.

FIGURE 10.3   Conceptual workforce breakdown at the end of your first year

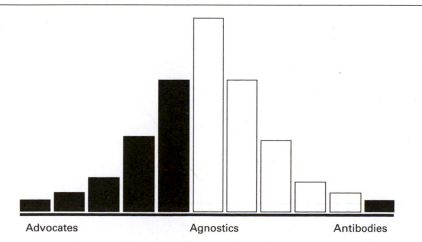

Antibodies will often go quiet as time goes on and as you start clocking up more and more success. There will be a slight resurgence of antibody behaviour in Year 2 of your Lean journey, with comments like, 'I thought we were already Lean,' and 'Wasn't that something we did last year?' Perhaps the most important management skill when dealing with this type of resistance is perseverance.

Dealing with the 'U-curve'

Many of you will already be familiar with the concept of a change curve that describes how people go through an emotional 'swing' as they manage the change. The late Elisabeth Kübler-Ross, a psychologist working in the area of bereavement, discovered that people go through a sequence of emotions when a loved one dies. She devised the Kübler-Ross model to explain these emotions. It is possible to extend the use of her work to explain the sequence of emotions that people go through during any major change in their life, which can include the introduction of Lean. A version of the Kübler-Ross model is shown in Figure 10.4 with the word 'impact' used to describe your decision to 'go Lean', with the rest of the emotions following on.

FIGURE 10.4   Adapted Kübler-Ross model (the U-curve)

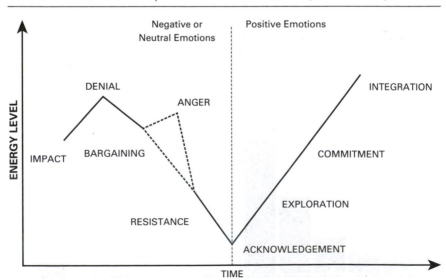

After the announcement that you are about to introduce Lean, people will go through the emotional U-curve shown in Figure 10.4 and you will hear them saying the following things:

- **Denial** – 'This won't affect me.'

- **Bargaining** – 'Okay, if we do A then can we avoid doing B?'

- **Anger** – 'I can't believe you are forcing me to do this.'

- **Resistance** – 'Go on then, show me this Lean thing.'

- **Acknowledgement** – 'Okay, I accept this is not going away.'

- **Exploration** – 'Okay, show me what Lean is all about.'

- **Commitment** – 'Wow, this is great.'

- **Integration** – 'Did we ever do it a different way?'

The problem is that some people (mostly advocates) will go through all of these emotions in a matter of hours whilst others, such as a few of the antibodies, could still be in denial after a year or more. You need to take into account that different people will be at different stages in the U-curve and will therefore need different things from you.

Engaging people during Lean events

Within any group of people involved in Lean there will be a mix of skills, motivations and beliefs as well as each person being at a different point in their U-curve. Being technically competent in the tools of Lean is less than half the story for a Lean practitioner, with the rest of it being concerned with the ability to motivate others and manage a fluid plan that may be changing every few minutes during a complex and fast rapid improvement event.

In addition to an overall U-curve that people will go through on the longer-term journey to Lean there will also be a separate U-curve that everyone (and that includes you as a Lean practitioner) goes through during Lean activities and events.

Taking a 4-day value stream mapping event as an example, people will start out generally not knowing what to expect, or being neutral about the whole thing. As they get into reviewing current state, the emotional state will often drop so that by the end of the first day they will be both tired and demotivated. This demotivation carries on into day two but by the start of day three they will have started to pick up. By the end of the event, the majority of people will have become very motivated by what has taken place (assuming the event has gone well).

Now, it is one thing to affix sticky-notes to a process map (such as you might find on a roll of brown paper) and completely another when you are physically changing work areas as you might do in a rapid improvement event. This means the emotional swing is even deeper (and more negative) during RIEs. I flippantly call day two of an RIE either 'Tearful Tuesday' or 'Weepy Wednesday' as it can be extremely emotional for people (and tiring) to undertake an RIE.

There are three things I have found that really help to manage people through this emotional roller-coaster and these are described below.

Tell them about the U-curve

Telling people that they may feel stressed during the process, but reassuring them that things will improve, genuinely helps people to self-manage their emotions during the event. It also gives you something to comment about when you start to see or hear negative emotions coming to the surface, because you can remind people that it is a natural part of the Lean journey to feel the way they do.

Team rules

Getting Lean teams to decide the rules that they will follow is another way of helping them manage their emotions during the change process. First allow people to decide the rules they will follow as a team. Common rules include such things as:

- Only one person speaking at a time.
- We will turn up on time.
- Everyone's opinion is equal.
- We will remain positive.

Put each on a sticky note and place it on a flipchart or blank A3 paper. When the team are doing well against one of their rules they move it to the top half of the paper to show they are 'positive' about that rule, and when they feel things aren't going well they move it to the bottom half of the paper, as shown in Figure 10.5.

FIGURE 10.5   Team rules chart

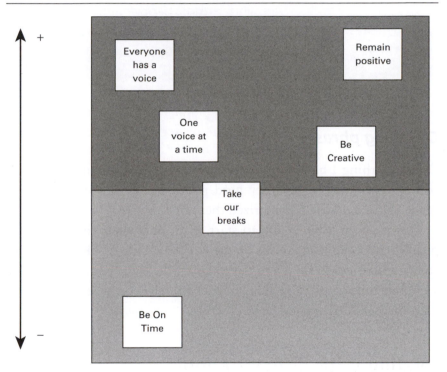

You should encourage people to update their chart after every break; you will find it useful in spotting when the team are reaching the bottom of their U-curve as they will move all of the rules to the bottom of the page. This gives them all something to laugh about and helps raise spirits.

TABLE 10.1   Replacement phrases

Replace this term	With this term
Yes, but...	Yes, and...
We don't...	We could...
It won't...	It could if...
We can't...	Why can't we...
We mustn't...	You might if...

Changing phrases

One final thing I have found useful to tell people about at the start of Lean activities is that they need to replace certain phrases with other phrases. I have summarized these in Table 10.1.

This is again a bit of fun to start with, but when you are facing people who keep using terms on the left-hand side of Table 10.1 you can remind them to switch to the terms on the right-hand side. It may seem flippant, so use it wisely in order to help you when stuck with a group that is struggling to be creative.

Dealing with difficult people

Whilst this is not a book on facilitation skills there is a need for a great Lean practitioner to also be a great facilitator of people. This last section is concerned with providing practical advice on how to deal with specific types of people that you will encounter in Lean activities, whether you are working with them one-to-one or in a group. I have summarized the strategies in Table 10.2.

TABLE 10.2   Tactics for dealing with difficult people

Person type	How they behave	Managing them
Bulldozer	Hostile, pushy and often sarcastic.	Avoid confrontation with them. Let them have their say without interrupting them (to avoid inflaming them further). Ask clarifying questions to ensure you fully understand their point before answering. Remain unemotive when dealing with them.
The talker	Loves to speak and is often quite arrogant.	Let them finish what they are saying without trying to interrupt them (unless you're in a rush, in which case just tell them that time is short). Then make your point without allowing them to interrupt you or put you off.
The fire hose	A doom merchant who cannot see anything positive.	Avoid being dragged down by them. Listen to them and ask for alternative solutions. Remain focused on getting results and do not agree with any points they make that are factually incorrect.
The waffler	Wants to be liked but is unable to make decisions.	You will have to make the decision for them and then seek their confirmation. You also need to ask questions that can surface their hidden concerns because they won't tell you otherwise.
The sleeper	Lacks energy for Lean and doesn't communicate or respond to communications.	Meet with them individually if possible and ask them open questions (ie where they can't just give you a yes or no answer) and then wait for them to respond.

TABLE 10.2   *continued*

Person type	How they behave	Managing them
The sniper	Withholds information and tries to cause problems.	The sniper will normally be aiming at the person leading any Lean activity rather than the rest of the group. If you can, discuss their behaviour and how it makes you feel. Do not react aggressively or become embroiled in a lengthy discussion with them. Use others to help you deal with the sniper if you are working in a group. For example asking, 'What does everyone else feel about the point that has been made?' is very useful.
The super-agreeables	They are keen to please, promise everything but generally fail to deliver anything.	Show them you like them (they want to be liked) and prevent them making unrealistic commitments. That means sometimes turning down their offer to do certain things so that they only have a small number of things to work on for you.

Closing thoughts

Engagement is key to the success of Lean. You cannot impose Lean on people; you need the support of the majority to get things done. Earlier chapters focused on the daily, weekly and monthly routines that help to build engagement over time as well as the creation of an integrated plan to help align everyone in the organization. This chapter has focused on motivating and engaging individuals. The next chapter explores some of the warning signs that your Lean programme is going off the rails, before returning to one final strategically important issue, namely communications and celebrations, in Chapter 12.

Ensuring success 11

In this chapter I aim to answer the following questions:

1 What problems might you encounter on your Lean journey?

2 How do you ensure Lean success?

3 What is the journey towards Lean really like?

Your improvement efforts can be subjected to a variety of problems that can arise during or even before you have started your Lean journey. Some of these problems will be minor teething issues that are a natural part of the learning process, whilst others present the first signs of a problem that could cause you major difficulties if not addressed. This chapter explores the most important warning signs for your Lean programme and the elements that are needed to ensure success. I will then introduce you to what the real journey towards Lean is like and the various crisis points you will encounter on the journey.

The top three warning signs

This section highlights the top three things that signal you have a significant problem with your Lean programme. Ultimately, all three are related to problems with the leadership of Lean activities but manifest themselves in three distinct ways.

Leadership disengagement

When senior managers and directors stop demonstrating an interest in Lean it is only a matter of days before this will permeate the whole organization. There are a number of different ways of spotting that leaders are 'cooling off' in their support for Lean such as:

- not responding to e-mails or other communications about Lean;
- being 'no shows' at Lean meetings;
- preventing or significantly delaying Lean activities and events;
- pulling resources from Lean activities;
- reducing the amount of time allocated to Lean activities;
- complaining continually about Lean.

These issues arise for one of two reasons:

Reason 1: failing to integrate Lean

In the first case there has been a failure to integrate Lean into the strategy of the organization, or a failure to update the strategy when something significant has changed for the organization, and you will find that senior managers and directors have been put under pressure to achieve other targets.

Reason 2: perceived lack of progress

The second issue arises when there has been a perceived lack of progress with Lean. For example, targets that were set may not have been achieved or more problems with implementation may have occurred than had been expected.

The impact of leadership disengagement can be profound and long lasting. In particular it can lead to a whole range of issues:

- staff disengage because they see their leaders disengage;
- increasing resistance because people perceive Lean as no longer a priority;
- programme slowdown because people find reasons to do other things instead;

- programme fragmentation because Lean has not been integrated into the strategy.

Obviously, solving the first reason for leader disengagement can be achieved by going back to your strategy and ensuring that Lean is not simply 'something else to do' but is seen as an integral part of achieving the overall objectives. I accept that to achieve this in practice is not as easy as it sounds, but if Lean is simply treated as another initiative then it is in real danger of just dying away over time as other initiatives take priority.

The second reason for leadership disengagement, concerned as it is with a perceived lack of progress, is itself related to one of four things:

- setting targets that were too ambitious or beyond the capability of the organization to deliver;
- being unrealistic, or simply unprepared, to cope with teething problems;
- choosing the wrong projects to focus your improvement efforts on;
- delivering Lean badly.

The first two of these issues are about senior leaders setting an appropriate and realistic pace for the programme, based on the current level of Lean capability within the organization and also accepting that problems will occur. The third often happens when people want to choose 'simple projects' to try out their Lean skills and then forget that this is what they were doing by continuing to tackle only minor issues. Alternatively, this can occur when there is a level of nervousness about using Lean to tackle the 'big ticket' items, so it gets relegated to low-level unimportant areas that cannot deliver the big returns that senior leaders are looking for. The last issue occurs when Lean has been badly planned or badly implemented and has therefore lost credibility in the eyes of senior managers.

These problems can be avoided by:

- setting realistic targets and an appropriate pace for your programme;

- treating problems that occur as learning experiences;
- integrating Lean into your overall strategy;
- planning and scoping activities properly;
- having a little faith that it does, and will, work if you do all of the above.

Lack of action or a lack of sustainability

The second issue that will signal a major problem is that either things don't progress beyond the planning stage or things don't stick after you have made the change. It is quite common for organizations to have rooms full of brown paper covered in post-it notes, and very detailed implementation plans, but to have not moved into action. It is also common amongst those who do move into the practical deployment phase for Lean, whether it is through managing for daily improvement (MDI) or rapid improvement events (RIEs), to find that within a few weeks things have returned to normal and that all traces of Lean have either disappeared or have started to gather dust in a corner.

There is something therapeutic about producing a plan without having the stress of actually implementing it. Many people find it very exciting to create grand plans that encompass huge organizational changes. The problem comes when you actually want to move someone's desk so that they can no longer sit facing a window, or when you try to change a form that has been used for a long time. It is then that people realize that this is for real, and you will initially encounter quite a lot of resistance for what might appear relatively small and insignificant changes. The emotive aspect of implementing changes – and the fear that people have of managing the complex mix of emotions and actions that occur during implementation – is a key reason why so many Lean initiatives end up simply providing sticky-note-covered wallpaper.

Having moved from the planning phase into the implementation phase, and actually made the changes – whether they occurred through daily problem-solving activities or a fully planned RIE – can be very rewarding for people. There is definitely something exciting about having worked in a team to deliver improvements and often people leave such activities with very positive feelings about Lean. However, the initial implementation of the changes is only half the problem because you don't start to realize the benefits until you have made those changes 'stick' and ironed out all of the initial teething problems. The problem is that managing the transition from the old state to the new state can be very tedious. It is certainly much less exciting than participating in a five-day RIE. The embedding phase of Lean requires as much planning effort as the actual implementation phase and may require even more management time than the implementation phase, but it is often forgotten.

The lack of action in terms of failing to implement changes gradually builds up negative feelings towards Lean that it is simply a 'waste of time', and the failure to embed changes means that senior managers never see the return on their investment in Lean. Both of these issues will lead directly to the slowdown and eventual stoppage of your Lean activities.

These problems can be avoided by: 1) ensuring that dates for all implementation activities are planned with realistic dates set and that the accountable individuals are supported to move from planning into action; 2) ensuring the embedding phase is planned as robustly as the implementation phase and that there are processes in place to enable people to flag up problems they see with the changes made, and provide them with support to implement further improvements.

It's not my problem

The third major warning sign is where there is a lack of ownership for Lean. People are happy to pass responsibility for delivery to other people and to find reasons not to engage with Lean activities. There are two interrelated problems that arise from a lack of ownership, which are summarized below.

Problem 1: facilitation versus programme management

Many organizations that are looking to adopt Lean will often have a small team of people (or even a single person) who will provide expertise and training to the rest of the organization and will help facilitate Lean activities. This 'Lean team' could be part-time, full-time or a mix of both depending on the size of the organization. In reality they should be facilitators for the Lean process, but in an environment where ownership is lacking they can often end up being treated as the project managers for improvements. The difference is that in the latter case they will be held accountable for the improvements realized, even though they normally do not have responsibility for the budgets, the people or any of the equipment and facilities. This enables individual managers to blame the Lean team for failing to deliver, whilst at the same time preventing them from actually doing anything meaningful by withholding resources, information and people.

Problem 2: the never-ending 'other priorities'

A second way that a lack of ownership can manifest itself is in the list of never-ending 'other priorities' that need to be tackled before you can get on with your Lean activities. Here is a true-to-life sequence of 'never-ending priorities' that you might encounter and that are used to prevent the implementation of Lean for a year or more:

- Winter: we can't start our Lean activities now because we are expecting a rush of orders over the winter months.

- Spring: we need to delay our Lean activities now because we are trying to recover from the winter rush.

- Summer: well, now we have a problem because so many people are off on holiday so we can't afford to divert resources at this time.

- Autumn/fall: we have to prepare for the winter rush during this period.

An important point to make is that there never will be a right time to start improving things. There will always be 50 or more reasons not to do something today and to delay it till tomorrow or next week, next month or next year. A lack of ownership, which is related to a lack of interest or perceived need for Lean, will slow your adoption of Lean and could quite easily knock it off the management agenda for the organization.

Solving these problems requires you to:

- Ensure there is a clearly understood pressure for change in the organization.
- Create a sense of urgency for getting things done.
- Set a realistic plan for Lean with clear accountabilities.
- Be clear about your expectations for your 'Lean team'.
- Get into implementation in pilot areas quickly to demonstrate that you are serious.

As I said at the start of this section, ultimately all three of these problems are related to leadership engagement and it is the role of senior leaders and Lean practitioners within organizations to ensure that the six elements of success we will cover in the next section are in place if you want a successful Lean programme.

The six elements of success

This section focuses on the six elements that, when combined, will ensure that your Lean programme is a success. The six elements are shown in Figure 11.1, along with the six effects that arise if any one of them is missing.

Pressure for action

It is basic human psychology that people do not change the way they do things unless there is a pressure for change. Outside of a work

FIGURE 11.1 Six elements of success

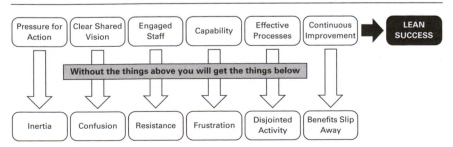

context, the pressure for people to change comes from laws, advertising, life experiences and from advice received from books, articles, TV programmes or conversations. Think of something you changed in your life, such as your attitude towards poverty that led to you giving money to charity on a regular basis. You perhaps started to feel the pressure for change when you saw the living conditions of homeless people and perhaps read an article on it and then lastly saw what could be achieved through charitable donations. Whatever the route, you certainly did not just wake up without any knowledge of poverty and the negative effects it can have on people's lives and decide to give money. You felt a pressure to change your life from a position of not donating to charity to donating.

The same applies to Lean. You are asking people to change the way they do things and for this to work there has to be a pressure for change that they believe in. This could be that by adopting Lean it will lead to greater job security or improve job satisfaction. It could also be that by adopting Lean you are going to help customers and the public in some way or increase the recognition of individuals within the community, for example by becoming a flagship organization within a group of companies. Whatever the pressure for change is – and sometimes it is a negative pressure such as 'If we don't do this then we are going to have to make 50 per cent of the people redundant' – people will not want to participate.

An example I use is that of someone I worked with who had a diary full of meetings for at least eight weeks in advance. This meant if you wanted to schedule some time with him then you had to wait for up to two months before he could fit you in. I used to wonder what would happen if his partner rang up and said, 'Darling, we are all safe but the house is on fire.' Would he say: 'I am really sorry but I have a day full of meetings'? Or would he say: 'I am coming home now'?

The answer is clearly 'I am coming home now'. In this case the pressure for change, ie to change his plans, is greater – the house on fire takes precedence over meeting someone.

You need to carefully and realistically communicate the pressure for change. Don't exaggerate or lie about the pressure by making unrealistic statements. For example, don't say, 'If we don't do this then we will close' if you know that you won't.

Clear shared vision

A clear shared vision means that there is broad consensus for what you are going to do, when you are going to do it and what the expected benefits will be. The more complex the change, the more important this is. I once got involved with a programme in health care that was focused on 'improving urgent care'. This change spanned nine different organizations each employing more than 1,000 people. The chief executives had been working together for a period of time before requesting support and what was immediately clear was that there was no agreement on what 'improving urgent care' actually meant. For example, to the hospital involved it meant rapidly admitting patients into a bed, but to most of the other teams it meant avoiding people ending up in hospital in the first place. Without a clear shared vision they had created confusion and a complete lack of progress.

Engaged staff

We covered how you could go about engaging staff in Chapter 10. Without people being engaged in Lean and wanting to participate you will simply encounter resistance.

Capability

Do you remember how stressed you felt when you had your first swimming or driving lesson? You knew what the aim was (to swim or drive) but not how to do it – and you felt stressed. Do you also remember when you had a piece of new technology or equipment that you simply didn't know how to use and it caused you a lot of frustration? This element of success is concerned with training people and giving them the skills to enable them to participate in Lean activities. As you go through your Lean journey you will encounter the need for people with differing levels of knowledge about the tools and approaches to Lean. These groups and what they need to know is summarized in Table 11.1.

Part of your Lean plan will be to provide each of these groups with the relevant skills. I am sometimes asked how many people should

TABLE 11.1   Lean capability groups

Group	Who are they?	What they need to know
Lean sponsors	Senior managers and directors who will sponsor programmes and activities.	An understanding of Lean and the role of sponsorship, as well as the behaviours needed for success.
Lean leaders	The people who lead your Lean programme and are responsible for training others, developing your portfolio of tools and managing the rollout of Lean.	Experts in Lean with the ability to train others, along with a good mix of interpersonal and project management skills.
Lean practitioners	People with at least a percentage of their time allocated to leading small- to medium-scale Lean activities and events.	A good understanding of Lean and a knowledge of the activities they are supposed to lead, as well as the same mix of interpersonal and project management skills as above.
Lean participants	People who will participate in Lean activities either day-to-day or via Lean events.	The tools and concepts relevant to their involvement.
Lean aware	Everyone else not included above.	A basic understanding of Lean and what you are trying to achieve. Over time this group will disappear as they all move upwards to participants and above.

you have in each category, and whilst there is no definitive answer I would suggest the following targets for the end of Year 1 and Year 2 of your journey:

- Lean sponsors – at least two director/board-level sponsors for Lean in Year 1 increasing to three or more in Year 2.

- Lean leaders – at least two people but ideally aiming for a minimum of 0.1 per cent of your workforce in Year 1 with an aim to increase this to at least 0.3 per cent in Year 2. Putting real numbers on this for an organization employing 2,000 people means a target of two people in Year 1, increasing to six people in Year 2.

- Lean practitioners – typically this will include all of your team leaders, supervisors and managers plus a number of motivated front-line staff as well, as these make up somewhere between 5 per cent and 10 per cent of most workforces that is the target for the end of Year 2.

- Lean participants – if you roll out managing for daily improvement (MDI) across your organization it is realistic that within two years 100 per cent of your workforce will have had to have been trained to participant level. If you adopt an approach more biased towards involvement only in rapid improvement events and other Lean events then you might only be able to involve 20 per cent to 30 per cent of the workforce directly in Lean events by the end of Year 2.

- Lean aware – obviously the aim is to achieve 100 per cent awareness within Year 1 and to reduce the size of this group (by having them become participants, practitioners or even leaders) through Year 2 and beyond.

Effective processes

The aim of this book has been to provide you with a structure for running many different types of Lean activities and to give you the processes to follow. Without effective processes – for example trying to skip the scoping of a project and to move straight into implementation – you are likely to encounter a range of unexpected problems.

At the organizational level, without an effective process to manage your overall programme for Lean you are likely to have lots of projects all being handled differently, and managed without any consistency of approach. This means that you cannot share learning and will also waste a lot of time doing the wrong things.

Continuous improvement

Whilst running a rapid improvement event is very exciting, without following through afterwards and dealing with the issues that arise – as well as focusing on continuously improving it – you will find your benefits just slip away.

The bumpy road to Lean

Figure 11.2 shows a typical adoption curve for Lean within organizations. As you can see, there are four zones that you will pass through on your journey, as well as three points at which performance can drop off (marked 1, 2 and 3 in Figure 11.2).

FIGURE 11.2   Lean adoption curve

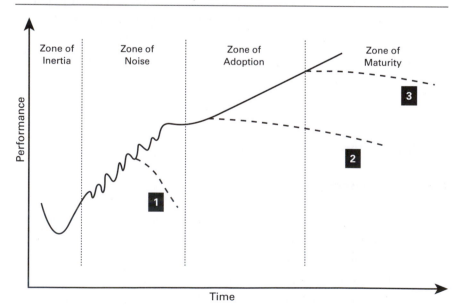

Zone of inertia

When a decision to adopt Lean is first announced within an organization there can be a small dip in performance caused by stress, concern or the legacy of previous initiatives that have failed. You will have to overcome this through frequent communications. It is also important not to be dragged down by the many reasons that people will come up with to 'put off' the implementation of Lean to another date. That is a normal response during this zone.

Zone of noise

As you start your first activities some will go well and others won't. This is a normal learning curve for an organization doing something new. You will encounter people who will use every little setback as a reason to abandon Lean – and when these concerns are raised by senior managers there can be a crisis of confidence that leads to the decline in the use of Lean that returns performance to previous, or slightly below previous, levels (indicated as the line marked 1 in Figure 11.2).

Zone of adoption

During this zone you will have overcome your initial teething problems and the bumps will become fewer in number and smaller in size. It is at this time that the enthusiasm for Lean begins to slow down and the pace can drop significantly. There is a related problem in that Lean will still be seen as a process rather than a natural way of working, in effect you will not yet have changed the behaviour of the organization, only changed a few processes within the organization. Changing processes is easy but changing behaviours is a lot harder; it is the lack of commitment to adopting Lean as a way of doing things that leads to the slowdown and gradual decline in the use of Lean. Performance will also decline slowly back to previous performance levels but the drop could occur over an extended period of time, as indicated by the line marked 2 on Figure 11.2.

Zone of maturity

By now Lean will have become embedded within the organization and it is likely that performance will continue to improve, albeit at a slower rate than earlier in the journey, until something changes again. This change could be the arrival of a new senior manager, an unexpected change in the organization or market forces. How the organization responds during such a change determines whether they continue to improve, stagnate or even decline in performance (indicated by the line marked 3 on Figure 11.2). If the change results in the strategic plan being updated and then the changes communicated to the team, along with details of how this will affect the development of Lean, then you can reasonably expect Lean to continue onward. However, often a significant change leads to the plan being abandoned or re-created and Lean being sidelined. Because by this time you will have embedded many changes, if Lean is sidelined then performance will begin to drop off: the change may be imperceptible to start with and might never return to its previous level, but will also be unlikely to improve further.

Closing thoughts

In Chapter 8 I discussed how you might create an organizational culture that supports Lean, whilst in Chapter 10 I discussed how you might engage individuals in Lean. This chapter focused on the key elements that will ensure the success of your Lean programme. In particular, the six elements of success that define whether you will have a great, good, average or poor experience of Lean. One final aspect of ensuring success that has been mentioned but not fully covered is the importance of communications and celebrations in the success of Lean – this is the subject of Chapter 12.

Communications and celebrations 12

In this chapter I aim to answer the following questions:

1 Why do you need to communicate?

2 How do you go about communicating in a Lean programme?

3 What celebrations should you consider?

This chapter brings together the two remaining important aspects that are key to the success of any Lean programme, namely the need for communications and the role and purpose of celebrations.

The purpose of communications

Communications in the context of a Lean programme is concerned with everything from the face-to-face aspects of daily team meetings to discuss operational problems through to the use of case studies to share knowledge. Communications is a 'force multiplier' in Lean programmes, as effective communications can help you to spread your message quickly, engage staff more proactively in Lean activities and share knowledge so that teams can learn from each other more quickly.

Communications within a Lean programme serve seven distinct purposes, each of which are described below.

Demonstrating commitment

Communications, when coupled with appropriate actions such as practising MBWA (management by walking about) demonstrate that senior leaders are committed to Lean and this helps reassure people that it is not just a passing fad.

Creating clarity

Communications can create clarity about the objectives, plan and progress of Lean.

Removing fear

Without communications, rumours will spread and fears will develop in your team. Clear and honest communications can help to remove that fear for most people.

Promoting behaviours

Communications in the form of case studies and other updates help to reinforce for people the things that are being recognized in the organization. For example, if I hear or see that my colleagues are being recognized for doing certain things then, over time, I will start to emulate those behaviours.

Demonstrating progress

Achieving things helps to create ongoing momentum for Lean, and communications plays a key role in helping keep Lean 'fresh and alive' within the organization through a constant stream of updates on progress. The key here is that 'success breeds success'.

Creating a sense of urgency

Communications should also be used to help create a sense of urgency for getting things done. Without a sense of urgency then everything can be delayed.

Sharing knowledge

Sharing knowledge is a key aspect of Lean. Whether that is sharing details of what one team has done so that another team can apply the same principles, or sharing the lessons learnt from an activity so that others don't need to spend time learning the same lessons: communications are key.

The purpose of celebrations

Related to communications is the need to celebrate successes, as this tells people about the things that are important and creates new stories and myths for people to talk about. It is these stories and myths that build teams and help shape the culture of the organization.

Organizational cultures are shaped by the stories and myths that are told. I worked with one organization that had manufacturing plants around the world. A key story amongst the 10 plant directors was how one of the previous chief executives had brought them all into a room in January of one year and opened a suitcase that held US $2 million. He said that any of them who had achieved 20 per cent EBITDA (earnings before interest, tax, depreciation and amortization) by 1 June would share the money, with those falling below the 20 per cent limit not getting anything from this additional bonus. By 1 June, 6 of the 10 plants had achieved an EBITDA of 20 per cent and the relevant plant managers each had a bonus of more than $300k. The problem was that to achieve the EBITDA they had all had to adopt some pretty unpleasant practices, including changing schedules to prioritize high-value orders, which annoyed key customers who had their orders delayed, and also shipping substandard products. They also undertook excessive rework to get products out, even at the expense of the long-term reliability of the product.

This story was repeated numerous times at plant manager level and within their senior teams. The problem was that the messages it contained included such things as:

- It is okay to upset customers.
- Who cares about quality? Ship it anyway.
- Short-term profit is more important than long-term business.

Organizations like this have a real problem with adopting Lean because they celebrate the wrong things and promote the wrong behaviours. Many other organizations also promote the 'hero culture' where people are recognized for having sorted out a crisis whilst others are ignored for managing day-to-day performance effectively. You will hear people talk about how somebody 'really kicked the team to deliver X' or 'rushed to the rescue of struggling Y', but no one will be saying how good it was for 'Z to have managed performance within budget and targets'. 'Hero cultures' affect the long-term stability of Lean because people learn that it is only through being in crisis that they get recognition. I know that sounds weird but it is true. Any organization that – through the things it celebrates – encourages people to do the 'wrong thing' at the expense of the 'right thing' will have people who don't want to introduce stable, well-organized and efficient processes, because they see that they will not get recognized for doing so. This isn't saying that you don't want to celebrate those people who go above and beyond, but by only celebrating them you are sending a clear message to everyone else.

Celebrations therefore shape the stories and myths of organizations and you will probably want to change the stories that people talk about so that they say things like:

- We really got that process under control.
- I can't believe how much more efficient things work now.
- We have achieved so much more with our available resources.
- People feel a lot happier about their work now.
- I am really proud to work with this team.

In deciding what to celebrate you will probably need to understand what things you want to stop celebrating. We will return to celebrations later in this chapter.

The style of communication

Different people like different things. Different people also have different styles of learning and preferred forms of communication. We have all met the person who would rather send an e-mail than pick up a phone, or the person who stands really close when they are talking to people. You will also know from your own experience the preferences you have for communications from people. Perhaps you like the rough and tumble of open two-way debates, or you might like reading notice boards or attending conferences. In a Lean programme, communication plans need to take into account these differences between individuals along with some key principles that are outlined below.

Communications should be two-way

There should be opportunities for people to comment and give feedback on what they are being told. It is a key part of the process of catchball (explored when discussing policy deployment in Chapter 9), but applies equally to all forms of communication.

Communications should be ongoing

The idea of a monthly team-briefing with no information in between is not likely to keep Lean at the top of people's agenda. Ideally you will adopt the daily team meetings that are a key part of managing for daily improvement (MDI) but without this structure you should consider other ways of communicating regularly, if not daily.

Multiple formats

For maximum effect, communications should occur via a number of different formats. Information centres, team briefings, e-mails and conferences are four different ways of getting your message across – and each will appeal differently to every individual.

Clear and consistent

For people to believe something they must first understand it, so it must be clearly communicated in language that the team understands; second, it must be communicated consistently over a period of time. If you hear a message once that your organization is going Lean you are unlikely to believe it. However, if you hear the same message over a number of weeks, whilst at the same time colleagues are being trained and you are also hearing that Lean activities are occurring, there is a good chance you will begin to believe what you have been told.

Types of communications

There are a range of communication activities that you need to consider as part of your overall Lean programme. The most important are listed below.

MDI and LSW

The daily, weekly and monthly routines of managing for daily improvement (MDI) and leader standard work (LSW) are key aspects of your communications strategy. These include the information centres, daily briefs, problem solving, steering groups and many other aspects of communication.

Case studies

It is important to create case studies for things you have achieved. These case studies have a two-fold benefit. First, they reinforce that things are actually happening and, over time, this will start to bring around some of the antibodies. Second, they help to disseminate learning across the organization. Case studies should contain the following as an absolute minimum:

- an overview of the problem the team tackled;
- what was done;
- any before/after photos that are relevant;
- how performance has improved (include numbers if possible such as '30 per cent more productivity');
- the names of people involved.

Newsletters

Less important than the two above but still useful is to produce a newsletter summarizing progress and recognizing the success of individuals.

Intranet site

Another form of communication, and something very useful for creating consistency, is to host an intranet on which people can get access to templates, training materials and other similar collateral for use in their Lean activities, and at the same time provide a place for them to put information about what has been done and to pose questions that need to be answered.

Types of celebrations

Recognition is a form of celebration: by recognizing the contribution of individuals to Lean you are also sending a message to the organization about the behaviours that are wanted. In addition to recognizing people through case studies and newsletters you should also consider the types of celebratory activities listed below. In the first few months of Lean I would suggest you adopt the mantra of 'celebrate every success, irrespective of size or impact' because one success promotes people to achieve another. As I have already said, success breeds success.

Event celebrations

The closing briefs of Lean events are an opportunity for senior managers to thank teams for their input and for the team to celebrate what has been achieved. In some organizations they like to hand out T-shirts and caps to people who have participated in Lean, whilst in others they may organize some refreshments such as cakes and biscuits. I personally don't like these types of rituals as it sets a precedent that is then hard to remove later on but you will have to make the judgement call of what will work best for your organization, given that cultures vary not only between organizations but also between countries and between continents.

Recognize people

You need to start creating new stories within the organization to replace the old ones. One of the best ways of achieving this is to recognize the commitment of people who have really bought into the concept of Lean. That means identifying people who have done things that support the adoption of Lean and then telling others what they did (with their permission, I would suggest). For example, I was working with a company and had led a few Lean activities in their call centres that had standardized the work done and also reduced the amount of time people spent having to do activities not concerned with client contact. One of the managers for a different call centre within the group saw what had happened and whilst he was scheduled to start his Lean implementation some months ahead he pulled the whole programme forward so it could start very quickly – as he was keen to involve his team as soon as possible. His enthusiasm for Lean was contagious and was certainly worth recognizing, as it was the type of behaviour that the organization needed.

The power of 'thank you' and 'well done'

It is impossible to underestimate the power of the phrases 'thank you' and 'well done' when said with conviction to someone who deserves it. It recognizes that the individual has contributed something of value and also helps to motivate them for further participation. When practising MBWA (management by walking about) I would urge you to find a reason to thank at least two people every day.

Presenting Lean topics

This chapter ends with a brief overview of some of the things that will benefit you when you are presenting Lean to other people, whether this is at a conference, training session or at the start of a discussion.

Interact every eight minutes

If you have been speaking for eight minutes without interacting with people you will find that 30 per cent of the people are no longer listening. By the time you have spoken for 15 minutes without an interaction almost 100 per cent of the people will be thinking about their next shopping trip, holiday, the children or anything other than what you are saying. An interaction keeps people engaged in what you are saying. It could be as simple as asking a question and getting people to raise their hands, or a full interactive mapping exercise.

Pictures are generally better than words

When presenting Lean topics in presentations try to show pictures rather than words. If you are talking about 5S show examples of each of the 5Ss. This is where photographs for case studies are really useful to have – as you can drop them into your presentation. Pages of text that you just read aloud certainly should be avoided. If you want people to read lots of text then print it out and give them a handout instead.

Use real life examples

Intersperse theory with real-life examples, ideally from your own organization but if not then from similar organizations that have done what you are trying to teach people.

Be enthusiastic

Your enthusiasm for Lean will rub off on others. Whether presenting Lean to others or leading Lean activities and events, it is your enthusiasm and that of the managers and other influencers you are working with that will set the tone for everyone else.

Closing thoughts

Communications are at the heart of both the routines of leader standard work and in engaging staff. Ensuring you communicate the right things, and that you are celebrating the right things too, help to create a commitment to Lean. The timescales involved can be extensive and need consistent management interest and input for a significant period of time if you want them to succeed. To achieve this commitment ensure that communications appears in your strategic plan and also that it appears in your weekly and monthly routines for leader standard work.

The majority of this book has been focused on the processes of Lean. I am conscious that most of the tools of Lean would benefit from a book each but I am also conscious that without an effective process for Lean then it doesn't matter what tool you use because it won't work. The last chapter is a review of the main tools of Lean that have not been covered elsewhere in the book.

Key tools and concepts

This chapter gives a short description of all of the common tools used in Lean that have not been covered elsewhere in the book. In Chapter 6 I provided an overview of the three tools and concepts that are most commonly used in Lean implementation: 5S/visual management, standard work and cells. This chapter provides an overview of a further seven most commonly encountered Lean implementation tools and why you might want to use them:

- *Total Productive Maintenance (TPM)* – to maximize equipment 'up time' and reduce maintenance costs.

- *Overall Equipment Effectiveness (OEE)* – used to describe how effectively equipment and resources are being used.

- *Single Minute Exchange of Die (SMED)* – used to reduce the amount of time spent changing over from one activity to another.

- *Kanban* – used to control the flow of materials (and information) within a process.

- *Poka yoke (mistake proofing)* – used to reduce the risk of mistakes occurring and to detect and mitigate the damage caused by mistakes.

- *Jidoka (autonomation)* – a discipline to stop and investigate problems and selectively automate the detection of problems.

- *Heijunka (levelling)* – used to level out volume and mix variations in a process.

Each of these tools could be explored in an entire book on their own but I have provided a distilled version of each to highlight what they are and how you might use them. All seven are implementation tools that you would use to improve operational processes, so you often find them at the heart of a rapid improvement event (RIE) or other form of implementation activity. A more detailed description of each of these seven tools can be found in the following sections.

Total Productive Maintenance (TPM)

Even today a lot of organizations still operate a 'breakdown mainte-nance' policy, meaning that they will fix machines when they break down but unless it breaks down there is no active servicing. The motto for breakdown maintenance is 'if it isn't broke, don't fix it'. A more advanced type of maintenance is preventative maintenance by which you either try to predict when equipment will fail and organize a maintenance schedule that hopefully gets to it before it fails or simply have a time-based maintenance schedule that services equipment at set intervals. Both breakdown maintenance and pre-ventative maintenance work to the assumption that operators work the machines and do not maintain them, and maintainers fix the machines and do not operate them. TPM blurs the lines between oper-ators and maintenance staff and involves both groups in ensuring the effective performance of equipment.

The three main aims of TPM are to achieve:

- zero defects;
- zero unplanned equipment failures;
- zero accidents.

There are two additional aims that arise indirectly from the three main aims and these are to extend the life of the equipment and reduce the overall operating costs. TPM is used to reduce the six types of losses that are found in most organizations where equipment is used, these being:

- Breakdowns – lost time due to a complete stoppage of equipment.

- Setup and adjustment – lost time due to having to set up equipment and adjust it.

- Minor stoppages – lost time due to an interruption in the equipment that is not a breakdown.

- Reduced speed – lost time due to the slow running of equipment.

- Start-up rejects – rejects during warm-up or initial production.

- Defects – rejects during steady-state activities.

Figure 13.1 shows that TPM is built on the base of 5S (see Chapter 6) and that the roof of the 'house of TPM' is supported by eight pillars that are described below.

FIGURE 13.1 House of TPM

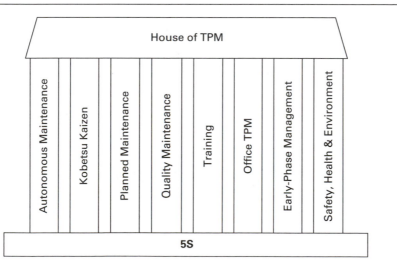

Autonomous maintenance (*jishu-hozen*)

Most of the breakdowns that occur with equipment can be traced back to minor issues such as the accumulation of dust and dirt and the poor lubrication of moving parts. Normally a major breakdown is preceded by warning signs such as unexpected noises or frequent minor interruptions. Take your car as an example, if you didn't put oil into it or if dirt and dust was allowed to clog the engine it is likely your car would break down. You would know that it was going to break down because you would notice such things as increasing engine temperature, unusual noises and warning lights appearing on your dashboard. *Autonomous maintenance* (AM) is the principle of involving operators in routine maintenance activities in much the same way that you might look after your car. For example, you are responsible for cleaning it; putting fuel, oil and water into it; checking the tyre pressure; etc. However, when it needs a full service or develops an unexpected knocking sound you will normally take it to a maintenance yard to be fixed. This is the same principle for TPM, the operator is responsible for day-to-day servicing and monitoring of the equipment 'health' and the full servicing is done by a specialist such as the maintenance team. The specialists are also responsible for writing the operating and routine servicing instructions for the operators and carrying out the training of operators so that they know what to do.

AM aims to involve the equipment operator in helping to keep it clean and ensuring it is properly lubricated. AM goes on to also train operators to undertake first-line or minor maintenance issues when they notice something is wrong and equips them with the relevant spare parts and tools to enable them to undertake these tasks. This often requires the use of *shadow boards* to reduce the amount of time spent looking for tools and equipment.

You may encounter resistance from people who feel that they should be paid as maintenance staff if they are doing maintenance jobs. I have found the car analogy very useful in diffusing these situations: you are not asking people to become fully qualified engineers just to take additional responsibility for keeping things from breaking down.

Kobetsu kaizen

Kobestsu kaizen means 'focused improvements' and is used to imply the small improvement in a very focused area often undertaken by a small group or even an individual. The focus of this is to continuously work to identify improvements that will reduce the six losses. This should form part of daily problem solving that is a key routine of MDI, covered in Chapter 7.

Planned maintenance

This is the systematic management of maintenance activities that uses predictive tools, information from operators and regular inspections of equipment to plan maintenance activities. A lot of maintenance time is freed up through AM, because there are generally fewer breakdowns so it gives maintenance staff more time to be proactive in scheduling and servicing equipment. The aim of planned maintenance is to have trouble-free equipment that is used to produce defect-free products. Planned maintenance consists of six steps:

1 Evaluation of equipment and recording of current status.

2 Restoration of deteriorating parts and improving weaknesses.

3 Building up an information management system.

4 Preparing a time-based information system to select equipment for servicing.

5 Introducing diagnostic techniques and equipment to help predict maintenance needs.

6 Evaluation of your planned maintenance programme.

Quality maintenance

This is concerned with improving equipment to eliminate variability in the outputs so that there is much more consistency in the product quality. This requires sources of variability to be identified and controlled and often requires the modification of equipment to ensure that better and more consistent outputs can be achieved.

Training

The aim of training is to develop multiskilled and motivated staff who are capable of supporting autonomous maintenance (for operators) and planned maintenance (for maintenance staff), as well as both groups contributing to quality maintenance activities.

Office TPM

This involves applying TPM to offices as well as operational or production areas. The aim is to eliminate the various losses that occur within offices which include:

- processing loss due to equipment unavailability;
- communications loss;
- set-up losses;
- idling due to minor breakdowns;
- accuracy loss;
- retrieval of information loss;
- customer complaints;
- expenses because of emergency purchases or couriers.

Office TPM is built on the same principles of autonomous maintenance, kobetsu kaizen and planned maintenance that non-office based
TPM activities are based on.

Early-phase management

Sometimes referred to as development management this is a learning
process that happens when TPM is first introduced with the following aims:

- make the work as easy to undertake as possible;
- determine the standard work for the new processes;
- iron out the problems that occur after the initial introduction
  of new technology or equipment;
- continuously improve what you do.

Safety, health and environment

This last pillar of the 'house of TPM' is concerned with achieving
zero accidents and health damage, and minimizing the environmental impact of equipment and technology. This involves such
things as ensuring guards are fitted, people are trained correctly, risks
are assessed and any rubbish or waste materials are minimized.

Overall Equipment Effectiveness (OEE)

OEE is a concept closely related to TPM and provides a way of
measuring the impact of the 'six losses' on equipment effectiveness

and productivity. In effect, OEE gives you a measure of the amount of value-adding activity that is occurring.

Calculating OEE takes into account three variables – availability, performance and calculating OEE – as outlined below.

Availability

This is the amount of time that the process was working against the total amount of time available and is calculated as follows: (time available – downtime)/(time available) × 100%. For example, if an office was due to be open for 10 hours but because of a late start and an early finish, and also some lost time during the day when equipment broke down, the team were only able to work for 8 hours then the 'availability' would be 80%: (10 – 2) / 10 × 100% = 80%.

Your available time is the actual time that you were expecting the equipment to run. For example, you may not run machines during breaks and in this case you would need to remove breaks from your available time. However, if you operate a continuous process and expect machines to run through breaks, perhaps by having people take overlapping breaks, then you would include the break times in your available time calculation.

Performance

This measures the productivity of a process against the expected output and is calculated as follows: actual output/maximum possible output × 100%. Again, imagine the office described earlier and looking at people working we found that because the computers were running slow they were only processing 50 items per hour instead of 100 items per hour. The performance this would give is therefore only 50%: 50 / 100 × 100% = 50%.

Quality

This measures the percentage failure or defect rate of the work done and is calculated as follows: (total work done – defects/rejects)/total work done × 100%. Again, in our example from the office imagine that of the 50 items processed in an hour that 5 of them had been wrong, then our quality rate would be 90%: (50 – 5) / 50 × 100% = 90%.

Calculating OEE

To calculate OEE we multiply the three results for availability, performance and quality using the equation: OEE = availability × performance × quality. Using the figures for the office discussed above our OEE is therefore: OEE = 80% × 50% × 90% = 36%.

OEE results of 40–50% are quite normal whilst results of >80% would be approaching world class.

Single Minute Exchange of Die (SMED)

A die is a specialized tool used in manufacturing to cut or shape material using a press. Imagine the shape of a door on a car. This originally began as a flat piece of metal and was then pressed using a die (and possibly more than one) into the shape it has now. The concept of SMED therefore arose in manufacturing with the aim of reducing the time taken to change over from using one shape of die to another. The term 'single minute' means to achieve a change-over in less than 10 minutes (ie single digit) rather than to achieve this in one minute.

SMED breaks activity into two types:

Internal activity: those that can only occur when the equipment is stopped (normally because you need to get your hands into the equipment).

External activity: things that can occur whilst the equipment is still running. For example, locating the next item for processing, finding instructions and tools, obtaining materials and preparing tooling by heating it up so it is at the correct temperature.

Typically, changeovers from one job to the next are extended because external activity is occurring whilst the process is stopped. I have listed how SMED might be used in a traditional manufacturing environment as well as in two less common environments, namely Formula 1 and hospital theatres.

SMED in manufacturing

Manufacturing is the traditional home of SMED. Its use has expanded out of the automotive sector and the use of dies into a wide range of different environments and equipments. The typical application of SMED involves five key things:

- *Shadow boards* near the equipment so staff have rapid access to the tools required for a changeover.
- The use of *kanban* in supplying consumables and other materials.
- The use of *visual management* and kanban to control the flow of jobs and information about the next job to be undertaken.
- Training of staff so they know the best way to change over from one job to the next.
- The utilization of *TPM* to maintain equipment up-time.

It is not unusual to find an 80 per cent or greater reduction in change-over times through the application of these five things. This means that more products are made and operations are therefore more productive.

SMED in Formula 1

The whole aim of Formula 1 is to win. The difference between winning and coming second can amount to millions in lost sponsorship and winning fees and therefore every second counts. You want to have as little 'internal activity' as possible, as in you want to stop the car for as short a period as possible. This is why you can drive into the pits and have your tyres changed, engine fuelled and give the driver a drink in under eight seconds. The things they have done in the pits include:

- detailed and standardized work that everyone has been trained to use;
- the design of the wheels, etc, to enable swift removal and replacement;
- the use of visual management to show the driver where to stop;
- all equipment stored at the point of use;
- rapid access to spare equipment if something goes wrong;

- the use of radios so that the team are ready when the car comes in;
- a culture of practice, learning and reviewing what they have done to improve it.

Often people will comment that a pit team has a lot of people; my response is that if you could save one second from your changeovers – and from this increase income by more than £1 million – how many people would you have in your pit team?

SMED in hospital theatres

It costs a lot of money to have a theatre team standing around idle waiting for the next patient to arrive. The aim of SMED in a theatre is to reduce the lost time between operations so that theatre teams can get through their list of patients in the time planned and, therefore, not need to cancel or delay operations or work extra hours, often incurring extra cost. Some of the things that can be done in theatres to ensure this happens include:

- Setting up a preparation and recovery area next to the theatre with a team responsible for:
  - bringing the next patient down to theatre in a timely manner;
  - getting the next patient ready for theatre including getting changed, signing consent forms and doing pre-theatre checks;
  - managing the recovery of a patient after theatre before they are returned to a ward.
- Having all the equipment ready and checked for the operation to ensure nothing is missing.

Sometimes the application of SMED in a hospital setting may require additional staff, such as an extra anaesthetist, but the impact on throughput can be profound.

Implementing SMED

The use of SMED is justified wherever delays occur changing over from one activity to the next. Its implementation consists of four steps, as listed below.

Step 1

Review the current process. This might mean using a camcorder to film what is really happening, or mapping it out. Please don't make the mistake of not telling people you will be filming what they are doing!

Step 2

Maximize the amount of external activity by doing as much as you can whilst the operation is running. For example, getting the next job ready, collating equipment and gathering information. This frequently relies on the use of visual management and kanban.

Step 3

Convert internal activity to external activity by redesigning the process and changing the way things are done. For example, in Formula 1 they only have one bolt holding the wheels on – in order to reduce the amount of time that is required to get the wheel off. Reducing the number of steps required to undertake a changeover is therefore key to Step 3.

Step 4

Streamline the whole process and return to Step 1.

Kanban

Kanban comes from a Japanese phrase meaning 'signal' or 'signboard'. A kanban helps to schedule activity so that work is triggered when required. Often this involves a visual trigger or signal that something is needed, such as the replenishment of stock. Interestingly the concept of kanban originated not in manufacturing but in supermarkets where it was used to trigger the restacking of shelves. Figure 13.2 shows how this worked.

The sloping shelves would be stacked with goods and a 'flag' (actually a red slip of paper) would be put in at approximately the half-way point. As people purchase items, the flag would slowly move towards the front of the shelf. The supermarket would have people called 'water spiders' who had the job of circulating to look for the red flags as they appeared at the front of shelves and to obtain the relevant goods from stores to restock the shelves.

FIGURE 13.2   Supermarket kanban

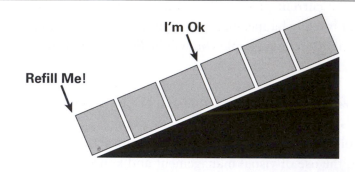

This was adopted and improved within manufacturing (specifically Toyota) when it was realized that the same principle could be applied to the replenishment of any parts on a 'demand' basis, meaning that you only need to replace parts that are being used. This is why kanban is so closely related to the concept of *pull*, being that it triggers activity only when there is a demand and not in advance of the demand occurring.

Although over the last twenty years or so the use of kanbans have been automated, initially through the use of such things as 'faxbans' where operators would request a refill of materials from suppliers by sending a fax, and the equivalent 'e-Ban' with the utilization of e-mails. Even with the advent of technology, the majority of kanbans remain visual and normally take the form of a card that provides all of the information required to trigger activity such as:

- part numbers;
- quantity required;
- who requires it;
- when it is required by.

A very common way of deploying kanban is to utilize a 'two bin kanban' system where you have two identical 'bins' or boxes that contain equal amounts of material to start with. The boxes are either numbered or have different colours and are arranged so that only one can be used at a time, often by having one sat behind the other. As the first bin is emptied, the second bin can then be pulled forward and, because it is

FIGURE 13.3 Conceptual two-bin kanban system

different to the first (ie a different colour), it creates a visual trigger that a replacement is required. A conceptual example of this in action is shown in Figure 13.3, where the appearance of the black bin in the second row creates a visual trigger to replenish the stock levels.

In any kanban system the aim is to minimize the stock levels whilst at the same time ensuring that a process is never stopped or interrupted because of a stock shortage. In the case of the two-bin kanban, the idea is to ensure there is sufficient stock in the second bin to keep the process going whilst the first bin is refilled. This means that some calculation is required to work out how much stock to request with each *pull*. For example, if I am using 1,000 parts per hour and the replenishment might take three hours to achieve then I will need to resupply a minimum of 3,000 parts. However, I may also want to add a safety factor to allow for any delays that might take this from three hours to perhaps four hours.

There are a number of different ways of calculating the required quantity, with one of the simplest being to calculate the following – kanban quantity = demand rate × (processing time + queue time + safety stock):

- Demand rate: the rate at which items are 'consumed' in the process per hour/day/week, etc.

- Processing time: the time taken to replenish the material.

- Queue time: any lost time, perhaps waiting for the kanban to be picked up.

- Safety stock: an allowance for any 'lumps or bumps' in the process.

For example, imagine a process using 50 parts a day that takes two days to replenish (processing time). Prior to the kanban being collected there is typically a half-day wait for someone to collect it (queue time) and the manager has determined that they want a further half-day worth of safety stock. This means that the kanban quantity would be: kanban quantity = 50/day × (2 days + ½ day + ½ day) = 150 parts.

If you refer back to Chapter 4 you will remember that there are two types of kanban symbol used in a value stream map. The first is a withdrawal kanban that requests that something is moved from one point to another. The second is a production kanban that triggers work to be undertaken. Figure 13.4 shows how you might show a production and a withdrawal kanban on a value stream map.

In Figure 13.4 you can see that there is a request from a customer to supply something that uses a 'withdrawal' kanban. The parts are supplied from a *supermarket*. The act of removing the item triggers the 'production' kanban' to be sent to the assembly team for them to resupply the supermarket with a replacement part.

FIGURE 13.4   Example use of production and withdrawal kanban

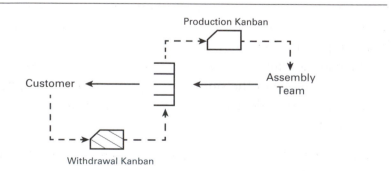

Poka yoke (mistake proofing)

Poka yoke, or *mistake proofing*, describes any behaviour-changing constraint that is built into a process to prevent an incorrect operation or act occurring. The three aims of mistake proofing are:

- To reduce the risk of mistakes or errors arising.
- To minimize the effort required to perform activities.
- To detect errors prior to them impacting on people, materials or equipment.

In our normal lives we are all familiar with very many different mistake-proofing concepts, such as windows that don't open fully in order to prevent people falling out, self-closing fire doors, lights that turn themselves off when they detect no one is there, and so on. You will also have seen warning instructions and traffic lights, as well as having read work instructions, all of which aim to reduce the risk of error. However, you will also notice that some of these are more effective than others. For example, the windows that don't open on the 15th floor of a hotel to prevent you falling out are likely to be more effective than leaving the windows able to open fully and providing an instruction pamphlet in one of the drawers that tells you to be safe when opening the window. This shows there is a hierarchy of mistake-proofing concepts, with a decreasing level of effectiveness. The five levels of the hierarchy of mistake proofing is shown below.

Hierarchy of mistake proofing

1 **Eliminate** – the most effective but also normally the mostly costly level involves eliminating the source of risk completely. In reality, it is very difficult to completely remove risk. An example that comes close is the UK 3-pin plug that must be supplied fully wired up (except in very limited situations) with all electrical equipment. Previously people had started fires because of having wired the plugs up incorrectly, so the law was changed. As I said, it is close to eliminate but not quite there because you could still cut off the plug and try rewiring it yourself – but I hope you get my point.

2 **Redesign** – if you can't eliminate the risk then you might try to replace it with a less risky process. For example, lawn mowers used to kill a lot of people after the wires were cut because it left the electrical supply still exposed and people would accidently touch the supply. We can't eliminate the error of cutting lawn mower wires but we can redesign the lawnmowers so that they have circuit breakers that cut the supply if the cable is cut.

3 **Reduce** – when it is not possible to redesign the problem you need to think about reduction techniques. For example, we cannot redesign all of the roads to make them safer but we can reduce the risk of accidents by introducing traffic lights and signs.

4 **Detect** – here we are no longer trying to prevent mistakes: we are trying to detect when they have occurred. For example, a warning system that sends an alert when pressure drops unexpectedly.

5 **Mitigate** – at this lowest level we are simply trying to reduce the damage caused by the mistake arising. For example, airbags do nothing to stop drivers having an accident but aim to reduce 'damage' done to the driver if an accident does occur.

Some common examples of mistake proofing that most people should be aware of – and the levels they probably occupy in the mistake-proofing hierarchy – include:

- Fuel low warning lights on cars – detect;
- safety glasses – reduce;
- standard operating instructions – reduce;
- lift door sensors that detect an obstruction – redesign;
- blood-pressure monitoring equipment – detect;
- variable speed limits on roads – reduce;
- filing cabinets that won't allow you to open more than one drawer at a time – redesign;
- hard hats – mitigate;

- electronic door locks on cars – redesign;
- the little hole at the top of a sink to prevent it overflowing – mitigate;
- irons that turn off automatically – replace.

Guiding principles

The guiding principles of mistake proofing should be as follows:

- Errors are inevitable.
- Errors can be eliminated.
- Defects are preventable and zero defects can be achieved.

There is a perception in some organizations that particular people are 'error proof' and that they do not and cannot make mistakes. If you believe that anyone is immune to making mistakes then you will be sorely disappointed in the very near future.

Jidoka (autonomation)

Sometimes referred to as 'automation with a human touch' as well as the less than elegant term *autonomation*, *jidoka* is concerned with the detection and prevention of problems. It is based on four guiding principles:

1 Detect that something has gone wrong.

2 Stop.

3 Fix the immediate condition.

4 Investigate the root cause and install a countermeasure.

In this way, jidoka is often used in conjunction with the structured problem-solving tools described in Chapter 8. The implementation of jidoka relies on a mix of cultural concepts and Lean tools that are summarized below.

Developing a jidoka mindset

Many people are trained to react to problems and to put in place quick fixes. The concept is to keep things running for as long as possible and work around problems as quickly as possible. A jidoka mindset is different in that it says that, in the long run, efficiency will come from addressing the root cause of problems and that investing time in solving problems is a valuable investment.

Empowering staff to 'stop the line'

Do your staff feel that they are empowered to say 'stop' when they see an unsafe act or a problem occurring? Many organizational cultures, through the words and actions of managers, disempower staff from stopping a process. Developing a culture where people feel that they are able to raise a real issue – and that far from being penalized they will actually be thanked for raising the issue – is very important in jidoka.

Installing andons

Andon are audible, or more commonly visual, signals that something has happened. The aim is that andons quickly alert managerial and technical staff to a problem having arisen so that they can get to the source of the problem and begin to investigate it.

Solving the root cause

Quick fixes are typically just that. Jidoka relies on the implementation of an immediate fix to stem the potential damage and on the longer-term fix that comes through root cause analysis.

Utilizing standard work

Having implemented the changes it is vital to document what has been done and to carry out any training required on the new process.

Selective automation

Selective automation is about investing in technology to detect – and more ideally prevent – errors arising wherever there is a business case to do so. This means wherever there is either a high probability that things will repeatedly go wrong, or where a problem arising has a significant impact (such as the ability to cause harm), then it means investing in sensors and other systems to enable you to control the process and detect problems as early as possible.

As you can see, jidoka combines the concepts of mistake proofing, TPM, standard work, structured problem solving and the creation of a Lean culture – the clustering of concepts under one heading is a feature of many higher level Lean tools and concepts.

Heijunka

Large variations in demand or the mix of work done on a frequent basis lowers the overall productivity of individuals and processes. The aim of *heijunka* is to level workload by controlling both the volume of work and the mix of work done. Many organizations suffer from a 'hurry up and wait' culture that has people rushing one minute and then waiting for work the next. This creates stress for people and extra costs for organizations. Whilst it is an objective of Lean to only build 'on demand' and then to build in batches of one, this may not be the best way to organize your workforce in the long run if volume and mix varies significantly. Heijunka aims to provide a balance between responding only to customer requests in the sequence they arise and the need to obtain efficiency from your people and processes.

In a normal process the split of work over a week could be as shown in Figure 13.5. The demand every day is different and there are frequent and long changeovers from one process to the next.

FIGURE 13.5 Typical operational activity sequence

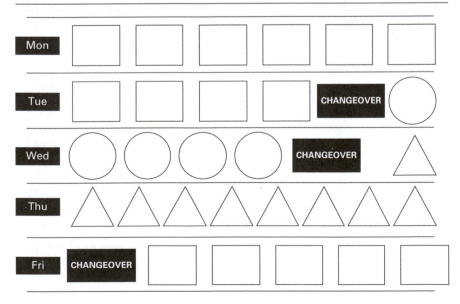

FIGURE 13.6   Example activity plan within a 'levelled' process

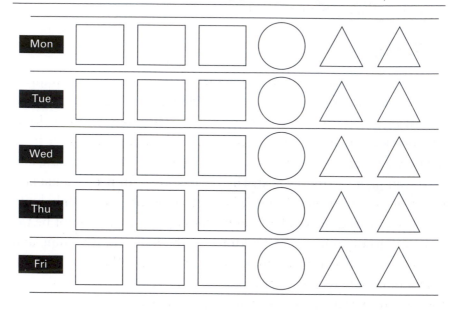

Heijunka encourages you to create regularity in workload in what is called a levelled, mixed-model line as shown in Figure 13.6. Obviously, to achieve this you will need to apply concepts such as SMED to reduce the changeover times and to probably change the mix on a weekly or monthly basis, but from a working-pattern perspective it is much more effective to build 'every product, every day' to a regular pattern than to have a 'lumpy' demand pattern.

Heijunka box

A *heijunka box* is a specific tool used within heijunka to provide a visual picture of activity. The box consists of a number of pigeon-holes with the horizontal rows representing each type of activity and the columns representing identical time 'slots' (called a *pitch*) as shown in Figure 13.7.

Work is allocated into each time slot until such time as the slot is 'full'. As in Figure 13.7, each slot is two hours long and in the first column there are plans to make two of Item A (which takes one hour to make), whilst in the second column there are three item Bs (1.5 hours total) and two item Cs (30 minutes total), so again column two is

FIGURE 13.7   Heijunka box

full. The heijunka box prevents overloading and underloading on a process.

Heijunka, and the heijunka box, aim to balance the competition between the need to undertake work only on demand and the most efficient way of organizing the work of people and machines. Without some form of levelling you will create additional stress and incur additional costs in managing your organization, but with too much you will become unresponsive to customer needs. Getting the balance right is an art form in itself.

GLOSSARY

2P (process planning) A 2P event is used to prepare an area or process for improvement by removing risks and preparing an implementation plan. A 2P event will be followed most commonly by a rapid improvement event.

3P (product and process planning) A 3P event is used in the same way as a 2P event but additionally focuses on the design/redesign of products and services as well as the processes that are used to deliver the product/service.

4M The 4Ms are the main categories used on an ishikawa diagram (or cause and effect diagram) to assess the source of 'issues' (effects) that drive problems in processes. The 4Ms stand for material, method, machine, man.

4Ps The Toyota 4Ps define a number of management commitments required to ensure the success of an improvement project.

5S The elimination of waste through creating a visual workplace. The 5Ss are: sort, set, shine, standardize, sustain – although variants exist with 'safety' sometimes being added as a sixth 'S'. These originate from the original Japanese words *seiri, seiton, seiso, seiketsu, shitsuke*.

5-second rule A key concept of the visual workplace in that problems/ issues/status should be visible to an informed person in less than five seconds. Sometimes reduced further to give a 3-second rule on the same basis.

5 whys Also known as root cause analysis, the 5 whys tool is used to uncover the root cause of a problem.

8D A structured problem-solving concept originating from the automotive industry.

A3 A document used to structure and plan a Lean activity or to solve a problem using Lean that encapsulates all information on a single A3 sheet of paper.

andon   A visual system (often a light) that provides a signal to managers/supervisors when abnormalities occur within processes.

autonomation   See jidoka.

autonomous maintenance   This is also referred to as *jishu-hozen* and is a concept from TPM (Total Productive Maintenance) in which the person responsible for a part of a process also takes responsibility for the basic maintenance and servicing of the equipment they use in order to reduce 'downtime'. This includes cleaning, oiling and checking to ensure correct functioning of the equipment.

batch processing   The act of undertaking work in batches or groups rather than one at a time. This is the antithesis of *one piece flow*.

blue sky diagram   Also known as *ideal state*, this is a process used by teams engaged in value stream mapping to create ground-breaking solutions.

car park   An area on a wall or flipchart used to capture ideas and questions raised by a team.

catchball   A process used in *hoshin kanri* to create a general agreement on a strategic plan by 'throwing' the strategy and ideas to different people to comment on.

cause and effect diagram   See fishbone diagram.

cells   A collection of people, equipment, machines, materials and methods such that a product or service (or products or services) can be delivered. A Lean cell will also incorporate the principles of flow, pull, standard work and visual management.

chaku-chaku   Also known as *load-load*. Normally used in one piece flow systems where machines automatically unload parts so that a worker can rapidly move a part through a process from one machine to the next without having to go through a lengthy unload of parts.

concurrent engineering   Also called concurrent design, this is a concept designed to reduce the lead time for the development of new products and services through the use of multidisciplinary teams and ensuring that activities occur concurrently rather than sequentially.

continuous flow Also known as *one piece flow*. A process where items or people are processed and moved to the next stage of a process one at a time rather than in batches.

current state mapping An activity involved in determining what is really happening in a process 'today'. Sometimes also referred to as 'as is'.

cycle time This is the average time between the completion of successive items at a step or steps in a process. Cycle time is directly related to the output rate so that if a process outputs 4 items per hour then it has a cycle time of 15 minutes. Cycle time is normally measured using 'time per unit' measures such as minutes/customer or hours/part. Do not confuse with lead time.

demand The frequency with which services/products need to be produced based on customer demand.

DFAD Design for access and delivery: providing the same support as DFMA but for the service sector.

DFM Related to DFMA but only focused on the design for manufacturing concepts.

DFMA Design for manufacture and assembly: a process used in 3P events and other design-related activities that seeks to explore how products (and services) can be designed so as to make them easier to make and assemble, as well as to buy. The latter is often achieved by reducing the component count or seeking to use different types of material or resources to produce the product or undertake the service.

eight wastes As the seven wastes with the addition of 'talent' as an eighth waste.

ELVSM Enterprise-level value stream mapping: a process that aims to produce a 10,000 foot view of an organization or process to enable high-level analysis to be undertaken of the strategic problems it faces.

Failure modes and effects analysis See FMEA.

FIFO First in, first out: the process of dealing with activities strictly in the sequence that they are presented at the 'front door'.

fishbone diagram   Also known as an *ishikawa diagram* or *cause and effect diagram*, these are used in problem-solving exercises to show the causes that are affecting or driving a particular issue.

flow   The process of arranging activities such that bottlenecks, delays between stages and other losses are minimized and the process is capable of continuous flow.

FMEA   Failure modes and effects analysis: used to assess the probability that something will happen, the potential damage that could occur if it happens and the likelihood that the failure would be detected before it came into effect so as to assign each risk in a process a 'risk priority number'.

future state   Also sometimes referred to as 'to be', this is a diagram that shows how a process or organization will be organized at some point in the future. Normally also accompanied by an implementation plan.

gemba   A Japanese term meaning 'the real place' and associated with places where work is done, for example the factory floor.

gemba square   A physical location in a work area from which you may undertake observations without interaction, with the aim of identifying improvements and sources of waste.

genchi genbutsu   A term meaning 'go and see for yourself' and referring to the need to visit the site of a problem and examine the facts to determine the precise cause of the problem rather than relying on reports and second-hand or third-hand accounts.

handoff chart   A diagrammatic representation of a process showing how information and people are 'handed off' from one person to another. Also called a *circle diagram*.

hansei   A term used to imply self-reflection. It is used by both individuals and groups to reflect on what has happened as part of a learning process.

heijunka   The process of levelling demand in variation and mix of product/activity over a fixed time period.

hoshin kanri   Also referred to as *policy deployment*, this is a structured way of creating a strategic plan.

ideal state   A creative process used in some value stream mapping activities to create an 'ideal solution' assuming there were no limitations on such things as funding etc. See also 'blue sky diagram'.

ishikawa diagram   See fishbone diagram.

JDI   Just do it: these are simple improvements and changes that do not need to be further debated and can just be implemented.

jidoka   Also known as *autonomation* and sometimes referred to as 'automation with a human touch', jidoka is the process of stopping whenever a problem is detected in order to understand why it has gone wrong and to put in place corrective actions.

jishu hozen   See autonomous maintenance.

jishuken   A Japanese word used to describe a 'hands-on knowledge workshop'.

JIT   Just in time: a strategic approach to reducing the level of work in progress and inventory with the aim of improving cashflow and flexibility within an organization.

kaikaku   A process of radical improvements, also called such things as 'step change' and 'breakthrough', and forming the basis of rapid improvement events.

kaizen   Meaning to improve yourself and your organization in small incremental steps. Often kaizen is associated with the term continuous improvement.

kaizen event   See rapid improvement event.

kamishibi   A term referring to boards (story books) used to audit the effectiveness and use of standard work.

kanban   Kanban means 'signal', 'signboard' or 'ticket'. A kanban is used to trigger demand for an activity, product or service.

kanban post   A storage container for kanban cards that are 'signalling' the need for a product/service to be delivered.

kobetsu kaizen   A focused kaizen activity that aims to tackle a very specific (and often quite small) task in contrast to a normal kaizen event (or rapid improvement event) that may tackle a much larger problem or area.

lead time   The total elapsed time taken from the start to the end of a process including all processing time as well as queuing and waiting time. Lead time is normally measured in hours or minutes of elapsed time.

leader standard work   The daily, weekly and monthly routines required to sustain Lean.

Lean   A business improvement strategy based on the Toyota Production System and designed to eliminate waste and improve effectiveness in processes.

machine cycle time   The work required to be undertaken by a machine during one 'cycle' of an activity.

manual cycle time   The work required to be undertaken by people during one 'cycle' of an activity.

MBWA   Management by walking about: the process of managers showing interest in processes and finding solutions by 'going to gemba' and interacting with staff and customers.

MDI   Managing for daily improvement: associated with the daily routines to be undertaken by teams to embed a culture of Lean within an organization.

mistake proofing   See poka yoke.

muda   A Japanese word associated with non-value-adding activity, or waste.

mura   A Japanese word meaning 'unevenness' and associated with variation or fluctuation in activity within a process.

muri   A Japanese work meaning 'overburden' or 'unreasonableness' and associated with putting unreasonable stress on a person, team or piece of equipment.

nemawashi   From a Japanese expression meaning 'going around the roots'. This is used to describe the practice of engaging people and gaining consensus for Lean.

non-value-adding activity (NVA)   Also known as *muda* or *waste*, this is an activity that uses up time, cost, resources or space but does not add value to the product/activity itself.

one piece flow   See continuous flow.

Overall Equipment Effectiveness (OEE)   Used to describe how effectively equipment is being used, and is calculated by multiplying the availability × productivity × quality to give a percentage.

pacemaker   A part of a process that is a bottleneck and needs to be scheduled to ensure the smooth flow of the rest of the process.

paper kaizen   A way of showing the cumulative work done by an individual or team in the form of a Yamazumi Chart. This can also show the cumulative work done before and after improvement to give a representation of the improvement achieved.

PDCA   Plan, do, check and act; also referred to as the *Deming cycle* for use in problem solving.

PDSA   A modified form of PDCA, in which the 'c' of 'check' has been replaced with the 's' of 'study'.

PID   Project initiation document: used in project management to define the requirements and plan for a project.

pitch   The amount of time required by an area to go through one cycle of work and produce one 'container' of products or outputs and calculated by multiplying takt time by the quantity of activity done in each 'container'. For example, if the container has 10 spaces and the takt time is 15 minutes then the pitch would be 150 minutes of work.

poka yoke   Also known as *mistake proofing* or error proofing. The process of designing out (or mitigating) the risk of problems arising in a process.

policy deployment   See hoshin kanri.

pull   See kanban, but also used as a term to mean 'to draw materials/equipment/people to me' in opposition to a push system.

push   The production of goods, or push of activity, irrespective of the ability of the downstream process to 'consume' the product or activity.

QFD   Quality function deployment: used to capture user/customer requirements and to convert them into tangible actions, changes and improvements to processes and products.

rapid improvement event (RIE)   A structured way of introducing Lean that brings a team of people together for a finite period of time at the end of which something has been changed.

rapid planning event (RPE)   An alternative name for a 2P or 3P event.

%RFT   The percentage of the time that a task is undertaken 'right first time' without problems being encountered.

runner, repeater, stranger   A runner is an activity undertaken 'regularly' (normally every day); a repeater is a common activity that occurs less frequently than runners (say weekly to monthly); a stranger is an activity that comes up rarely. In addition, sometimes the term 'alien' is added to runner, repeater or stranger to indicate completely unexpected activities.

safety stock   Material held to compensate for variations in the process and in supply.

scoping   The process of clarifying the purpose and objectives of a project prior to implementation. Scoping in Lean may involve an A3 or similar document.

sensei   Meaning 'teacher' in Japanese and normally applied to people with a deep understanding of Lean.

set-up time   The amount of time required to 'change over' a process and measured from the end of the last activity of type 'A' until the first good activity undertaken of type 'B'.

seven wastes   The seven main wastes (or non-value-adding activities) that are found in any organization. These are: waiting, over-production (or processing in service environments), rework, motion of people, transport of things, processing waste and inventory.

shadow board   A visual way of storing tools that have an outline or background that shows the shape of a tool that should be hung or placed at that point. Frequently used with both TPM and SMED.

Single Minute Exchange of Die (SMED)   A process designed to reduce set-up or changeover times and therefore the creation of a continuous flow system.

SIPOC   A mapping process that looks at the suppliers, inputs, processes, outputs and customers of an organization.

spaghetti diagram   Also known as a *string diagram*. A chart tracing a line showing the path taken by a physical item or person during an activity or process.

standard work   The process of formerly defining the work method, the tools, staff, quality, inventory and sequence of activities undertaken in a process.

supermarket   A stack of parts (or people) used to supply an area or process with raw material. For example, a queue of people waiting to see a doctor or a stack of material waiting to be processed.

takt time   From German and used to mean the 'beat rate of a process', takt time is the rate of demand by customers for activity or products and is calculated by dividing available time (ie the hours worked per day or shift) by the rate of customer orders or demand.

TIM WOOD   Another way of representing the seven wastes and standing for: transport, inventory, motion, waiting, overproduction, overprocessing and defects.

T-map   A *transformation map* is a visual way of displaying a strategic plan.

Total Productive Maintenance (TPM)   A process for improving efficiency by eliminating the downtime in a process through activities such as autonomous maintenance.

Toyota Production System (TPS)   The production system developed by the Toyota Motor Company that focuses on the elimination of waste throughout the value stream.

true north   The alignment of a team or entire organization so that they are all moving in the same direction towards a common goal.

value-added activity   Any activity that is done correctly the first time, wanted by the customer and for which they would normally be happy to pay for. Paying for a value-adding time usually means the exchange of money but could include the willingness of customers to invest time and other resources in the activity. In a public sector or non-customer-facing environment you can also determine whether something is value adding by asking: does the customer experience? Do they want it? Would they care significantly if you changed it? Is it done correctly 'first time'? If the answer is yes to all four questions then it is highly likely to be value adding.

value stream map (VSM)   A detailed process map showing all the steps involved in a process from end to end (E2E).

value stream mapping event   A Lean event involving an understanding of the current process (current state), the design of a future process (future state) and possibly the creation of a blue sky (or ideal state) diagram between the current and future state.

vertical value stream   A project planning tool that involves the creation of a vertical value stream map to plan out logical stage gates in a project.

visual workplace/management   The design of a work area using 5S to improve productivity and flow and to reduce the risk of accidents and the time lost 'hunting and gathering' materials and information. Also see 5S.

voice of the customer (VotC)   Listening to the actual words spoken by a customer to truly understand what they are looking to achieve.

VSM   See value stream mapping.

waste   See non-value-adding activity.

water spider   A material handler who has the job of checking kanbans and ensuring stock levels are kept at the correct level.

work-in-process (WIP)   Work that has started 'production' but is not yet completed.

WORMPIT   An acronym that summarizes the eight wastes and stands for: waiting, overproduction (or processing in a non-manufacturing environment), rework, motion and transport, processing waste, inventory and talent.

yamazumi   A chart used to visually depict the work done by staff in a 'stacked' format as you might find when undertaking a paper kaizen exercise.

REFERENCES

This section lists the specific reference texts that were consulted in the preparation of this book.

Baudin, M (2007) *Working With Machines*, Productivity Press, London

Bicheno, J and Holweg, M (2009) *The Lean Toolbox*, 4th edn, PICSIE Books, Buckingham

Ekvall, G (1995) Organizational Climate for Creativity and Innovation, *European Journal of Work and Organizational Psychology*, 5 (1), pp 105–23

Goldratt, E and Cox, J (2004) *The Goal: A process of ongoing improvement*, Gower Publishing, London

Goleman, D (1996) *Emotional Intelligence: Why it can matter more than IQ*, Bloomsbury Publishing, London

Goleman, D (2003) *The New Leaders: Transforming the Art of Leadership*, Sphere, London

Imai, M (1997) *Gemba Kaizen*, McGraw-Hill, New York

Jackson, T (2006) *Hoshin Kanri for the Lean Enterprise*, Productivity Press, London

Liker, J (2004) *The Toyota Way: 14 management principles from the world's greatest manufacturer*, McGraw-Hill, New York

Liker, J and Meier, D (2006) *The Toyota Way Fieldbook*, McGraw-Hill, New York

Mann, D (2005) *Creating a Lean Culture*, Productivity Press, London

Rother, M and Shook, J (1998) *Learning to See*, Lean Enterprise Institute, Cambridge, MA

Schein, E (1992) *Organizational Culture & Leadership*, 2nd edn, Jossey-Bass, San Francisco

Sobek, D and Smalley, A (2008) *Understanding A3 Thinking*, Productivity Press, London

Womack, J and Jones, D (2003) *Lean Thinking*, 2nd edn, Simon and Schuster, New York

In addition to the sources listed here, thanks is offered to the innumerable individuals, teams, companies, articles, books and other reference sources that have, over the last 20 years, contributed to the accumulation of knowledge that is encapsulated within this book.

INDEX